GOD AS MOTHER:

A FEMININE THEOLOGY IN INDIA

GOD AS MOTHER:

A FEMININE THEOLOGY IN INDIA

An Historical and Theological Study of the Brahmavaivarta Purāṇa

by

CHEEVER MACKENZIE BROWN

CLAUDE STARK & CO.
Hartford, Vermont 05047

 Published by Claude Stark & Co.,
Hartford, Vermont 05047.

Library of Congress Catalog Card Number: 74–76006

International Standard Book Number: 0–89007–004–0

First Printing

Printed in The United States of America

To my parents
True *aṃśas* of Rādhā and Kṛṣṇa

Contents

PART C

THE THEOLOGY OF RĀDHĀ AS PRAKṚTI

PART D

CONCLUSION

Acknowledgments

I wish to give thanks to Professor Daniel H. H. Ingalls, who initiated me into the study of Sanskrit and has provided much needed encouragement and advice on this project. I am also grateful to Professors Wilfred Cantwell Smith and John B. Carman for their constructive criticisms of various aspects of this study. I am indebted to the staff of Widener Library, especially to Mr. Edward J. Peterson, who has been most helpful in locating much needed material. I am thankful to Miss Alaka Hejib and Arvind Sharma for their assistance in obtaining and translating a Hindi article. I deeply appreciate the labors of Estelle Marr in typing the rough draft of this work, and the care of Maria Cedargren, who typed the final draft.

LIST OF ABBREVIATIONS

ABORI	*Annals of the Bhandarkar Oriental Research Institute*
ALB	*The Adyar Library Bulletin*
Ānand	Ānandāśrama Press edition
AV	*Atharva Veda*
BAP	*Brahmāṇḍa Purāṇa*
BhBhP	Adalbert Gail, *Bhakti im Bhāgavata Purāṇa*
BhG	*Bhagavad Gītā*
BhP	*Bhāgavata Purāṇa* (references to Veṅkaṭeśvara Press edition unless otherwise noted)
BKh	*Brahma Khaṇḍa,* Book I of the BVP
BrahmaP	*Brahma Purāṇa*
BS	*Brahma Sūtras*
BU	*Bṛhadāraṇyaka Upaniṣad*
BVP	*Brahmavaivarta Purāṇa* (references to Veṅaṭeśvara Press edition unless otherwise noted)
CHI	Haridas Bhattacharyya, ed., *The Cultural Heritage of India,* 4 vols. 2nd rev. ed. (Calcutta: Ramakrishna Mission Institute of Culture, 1953–1958)
CU	*Chāndogya Upaniṣad*
DBhP	*Devībhāgavata Purāṇa*
ERE	James Hastings, ed., *Encyclopaedia of Religion and Ethics* (New York: Charles Scribner's Sons, 1908–1927)
ESL	Horace Hayman Wilson, *Essays Analytical, Critical and Philological on Subjects Connected with Sanskrit Literature*

GKh	*Gaṇeśa Khaṇḍa*, Book III of the BVP
HPEW	Sarvepalli Radhakrishnan, ed., *History of Philosophy Eastern and Western*, vol. I (London: George Allen & Unwin Ltd., 1952)
HV	*Harivaṃśa*
IHQ	*The Indian Historical Quarterly*
JAOS	*Journal of the American Oriental Society*
JASB	*Journal of the Asiatic Society of Bengal*
JORM	*The Journal of Oriental Research, Madras*
JRAS	*The Journal of the Royal Asiatic Society of Great Britain and Ireland*
KālP	*Kālikā Purāṇa*
KJKh	*Kṛṣṇajanma Khaṇḍa*, Book IV of the BVP
KūrP	*Kūrma Purāṇa*
LiṅgP	*Linga Purāṇa*
MaitriU	*Maitrāyaṇīya Upaniṣad*
MārkP	*Mārkaṇḍeya Purāṇa*
MatP	*Matsya Purāṇa*
MBh	*Mahābhārata*
NārP	*Nāradīya Purāṇa*
NārPR	*Nārada Pañcarātra*
PadP	*Padma Purāṇa* (references to Ānandāśrama Press edition unless otherwise noted)
PKh	*Prakṛti Khaṇḍa*, Book II of the BVP
RV	*Ṛg Veda*
ŚB	*Śatapatha Brāhmaṇa*
SK	*Sāṃkhya Kārikā*
Vaṅg	Vaṅgavāsī Press edition
VarP	*Varāha Purāṇa*
VāyuP	*Vāyu Purāṇa*
Veṅk	Veṅkateśvara Press edition
ViP	*Viṣṇu Purāṇa* (references to Oriental Press edition unless otherwise noted)
VFM	Sushil Kumar De, *Early History of the Vaiṣṇava Faith and Movement in Bengal*
WZKSO	*Wiener Zeitschrift für die Kunde Süd- und Ostasiens*
ZDMG	*Zeitschrift der Deutschen Morgenländischen Gesellschaft*

FOREWORD

by Daniel H. H. Ingalls

For two years I watched this book grow. During that time I used to meet with C. Mackenzie Brown at irregular intervals. I would read what he had written and we would trade questions. What he wrote and what he talked of, the first always with accuracy, the latter with enthusiasm, won my interest in the theology of the Goddess, a subject of which I had previously had little knowledge, and gradually overcame a prejudice that at first I had held. I hope that this publishing of his book may have the same double effect on its readers.

The earliest literature of India tells us nothing of the Goddess. Such goddesses as we meet in ancient Sanskrit texts are decorative rather than essential. They are goddesses with a small 'g' rather than the singular embodiment that we might write with a capital. Uṣas, the goddess of dawn, receives twenty hymns in the *Rig Veda,* hymns of bright poetic imagery but lacking that intensity of religious concentration that characterizes the far more numerous hymns to male gods: to Indra, Agni, and Soma. In the *Mahābhārata* Viṣṇu's consort Lakṣmī, the goddess of wealth and beauty, does not yet share her husband's cosmogonic and metaphysical grandeur. The only evidence I can summon from Vedic literature of a sense of female ultimacy is the great Atharvan hymn to Earth (12.1). But the Earth in that hymn, while both female and divine, is not anthropomorphic, is not yet clearly distinguished as the Goddess. She is still the same earth that we walk on and that bears our crops. The *Mahā-*

bhārata knows the names of the Goddess; but its hymns in her honor are shown by the critical edition to be late insertions in the body of the text.

It is strange. The archeologists, who dig deeper than the written record, have piled up evidence of Goddess worship from the pre-Aryan sites of Harappa and Mohenjo Daro: hundreds of little terra-cotta figures dating back to the third millenium B.C. And anyone who has lived in modern India will remember the worship of Kālī, Dūrgā, Devī, for the Goddess goes by many names; will remember the shrines, the festivals, and the poetry by which the Goddess is again revered. But for a long period after the coming of the Aryans, say from about 1500 B.C. to the early centuries of the present era, the evidence for her worship is indirect or uncertain. It is after this silence of nearly two thousand years that the historical record resumes with the hymns of the *Harivaṃśa* and the *Viṣṇu Purāṇa,* with the descriptions of Kālidāsa, the "servant of Kālī," and with the rituals of the early Tantras.

What is strange about this Indian record is not so much the replacement of female by male hierophanies, a phenomenon that has occurred over most of the civilized world, as the fact that in India the Goddess reappears. In Mediterranean culture her embodiments disappeared for good. Diana and Berecynthia, Isis and Cybele, were exiled with the coming of Christianity. Somewhat later, Islam was to prove as severe. Ṭabarī tells us that the Prophet at first spoke of the principal goddesses of Mecca as "holy beings whose intercession is to be sought," but that these words were later expunged from the Qur'an. What we actually have in Qur'an 54.19–23 is an attribution of such statements to Satan. And the Prophet's followers continued to be intransigently masculine in outlook. In Christianity female hierophanies reappeared in the figures of Mary and the female saints. But here one cannot speak of a reappearance of the ancient Goddess. The figure of the virgin and its supporting theology are subordinate to those of her son and his father. Diana is as surely dead as are the *puellae et pueri integri* who sang her praise.

Why should the Indian record have differed? To such large questions there are no certain answers. One can only point to other peculiarities of Indian culture that seem to stand in a relation of affinity, to what Freud would have called a complemental series. India has shown a greater tolerance of religious diversity than Europe and the Middle East. Legend, it is true, speaks of the destruction of Buddhist stupas by Puṣyamitra, but the credibility of the legend is impaired by the many stupas that we know survived Puṣyamitra's reign. We hear of a southern king who executed Jains. D. D. Kosambi may have been correct in supposing that Buddhist monasteries of the Pala dynasty were raided and desecrated by land-hungry Hindus under the Senas. Some such events doubtless occurred, given the general predilection of humans to greed, obstinacy, and spite. But it is certain that they never occurred on an India-wide scale. There were no Hindu or Buddhist religious wars comparable to the jihads of early Islam or to the Protestant-Catholic wars of the 16th century. And for a very obvious reason: in India the political organization of religion was never as strong or as widely ramified as in the West. Indeed, the Indians were political atomists. Political organization was tight within a caste or a village. Within an empire, on the other hand, it was very weak. Castes and villages were allowed to follow their individual customs, in matters of religion as well as in matters of marriage and inheritance.

I suspect that within India's diversified culture the worship of the Goddess never ceased. The two-thousand-year silence of the record may be explained by the fact that all our texts from that period are either in Sanskrit or closely related languages, and there is no doubt that the Aryan-Sanskrit culture was strongly oriented toward masculine goals. The Aryans had come to India as warriors; they maintained their power by patriarchy; their bequeathal of property was patrilineal; and they worshipped male gods. The men and women who worshipped the Goddess are not likely in that period to have written at all; almost surely they did not write in Sanskrit.

Our earliest Sanskrit hymns to the Goddess, according to this view, are the continuation of an old religion, not an innovation. They first appear at the conjunction of two historical processes. On the one hand Sanskrit by the third century A.D. had become the nearly universal language of letters in India. On the other hand, the pre-Aryan worship of the Indians had spread by that time very widely among the Aryans. From the third or fourth century, at any rate, the religion of the Goddess becomes as much a part of the Hindu written record as the religion of God.

From this period onward the number of preserved Indian texts increases very rapidly. The diversity of religion revealed in these texts, the freedom that was allowed to local or sectarian groups to work out their own theology, makes classical Hinduism an ideal field for the researches of the historian and the analyst of religion. He may find in the Hindu record justification of the most various doctrines. In Europe, once a view had been judged by the central church to be heretical, all writings that supported the view were suppressed. We know nothing, for example, of Albigensianism except from the reports of the inquisitors who destroyed it. In India the writings of a comparable minority, say the sect of Madhva, are preserved as carefully as the works of its orthodox opponents. In India one can find texts to justify almost any imaginable theology; masculine monotheism, feminine monotheism, the dualism of God and Goddess, abstract monism, or the doctrine of the plenum or the doctrine of the void.

C. Mackenzie Brown is here concerned with the theology of the Goddess. He describes this theology chiefly as it appears in the *Brahmavaivarta Purāṇa,* a composite Sanskrit text that assumed its present shape perhaps as late as the 15th century A.D. The goal of this theology, the Goddess herself, is historically ancient. That is to say, the vision of the sacred as a woman may be in some respects the same vision that inspired the sculptors of Mohenjo Daro. But the theology of the *Brahmavaivarta* is far from primitive. Under the term theology I would include the reasoned exposition of the Goddess's nature, of her process of creation, of her relation to God, and of her relation to her worshippers. This body of doctrine draws on a long and sophisticated intellectual history. The old doctrines of the Sāṃkhya are put to use as well as the later doctrines of Tantrism. Sometimes we seem to have the view of male monotheism modified only sufficiently to admit of a dual godhead. Sometimes, though, the Goddess casts her partner into the shade. The Goddess may appear as mother, as beloved, as nature, as life, as the absolute. An eclectic scholar can make out of the *Brahmavaivarta Purāṇa* very nearly whatever he would like.

The excellence of Brown's exposition, in my judgment, is that it avoids eclecticism. He looks at the whole picture. He lets the text speak for itself and never forces it into a logical consistency that in fact it does not possess. The result is a picture of religious speculation of a higher order than I had been willing to admit.

At first I had been prejudiced against the subject of Brown's researches. What difference, I had asked myself, does it make if humans worship God as a woman instead of as a man? Are they not merely substituting one error for another? In reply to this prejudice it would not have been difficult for Brown to demonstrate that even an error may have a corrective value. We may postpone criticizing a religion for finding its ultimate truth in a being characterized by so human a limitation as sex. There is an immediate benefit, at any rate, in joining Rādhā to Krishna, in joining Pārvatī to Śiva, for the dogmatism of the purely masculine view is thereby corrected. This is to retreat a small step from my prejudice. Actually, Brown has brought me to retreat much farther. For the theology of the *Brahmavaivarta,* as it appears in his sympathetic but never careless account, is not the description of a female icon. It strives to express the possibilities of the Goddess rather than her iconic limitations. What it seeks is to construct a feminine theology that is free. I mean by this a theology that does not restrict feminine values in the world of the sacred by the strictures of subordination to which women were subject in the secular world of 15th-century India. Whether or not this effort succeeds, it is aimed surely at truth, not at error.

INTRODUCTION

Recently, it seems, theologians in the West have seriously begun to ponder whether the ultimate reality in the universe is male or female, or somehow includes or transcends both. What difference, we may ask ourselves, would it make to us personally if the Supreme Reality were a Woman, instead of a Man, or some union of the two? How would it affect our own faith, our attitudes and conduct towards men and women in our everyday lives, our ultimate fate? Would it alter our perception of the relationship of man and nature, spirit and matter, mind and body, intellect and feelings, subject and object? Such diverse concerns are more interrelated than they may at first appear. In any case, many Hindu thinkers, teachers, and writers from at least the early Christian centuries have deeply involved themselves with the problem of the feminine and masculine dimensions of ultimate reality and their ramifications within different aspects of life.

In the *Brahmavaivarta Purāṇa* (BVP), a late medieval work of Kṛṣṇaite Vaiṣṇavism, we see various attempts to come to terms with the bi-sexual nature of reality. This Purāṇa reveals to us something of the complexity of the issues involved. Viewed historically, the BVP seems to reflect a stage in transition from a basically masculine-oriented theology, centered upon Viṣṇu or Kṛṣṇa, to a feminine theology, centered upon Kṛṣṇa's consort Rādhā. One of the primary concerns of this study will be to illuminate the transition from a masculine to a feminine theology as it appears in our text. This will be the objective of the two main parts, B and C, dealing with the theologies of Kṛṣṇa and Rādhā respectively. Part A will treat of certain preliminary matters: the nature and role of Purāṇic literature in general within Hindu culture, the history and background of the BVP, and the theological strands found within our Purāṇa. Part D, the conclusion, will offer further remarks on the history of the BVP and its possible influence on later devotional movements.

The BVP is divided into four sections or *khaṇḍas*: the *Brahmakhaṇḍa* (BKh), *Prakṛtikhaṇḍa* (PKh), *Gaṇeśakhaṇḍa* (GKh), and *Kṛṣṇajanmakhaṇḍa* (KJKh). The first three constitute less than half of the whole Purāṇa. The BKh contains much cosmogonical material, as well as several legends revolving principally around a quarrel between Brahmā and his son Nārada. The PKh deals with the legends and worship of various goddesses, conceived as parts or fractions of the primordial goddess Prakṛti. It is this *khaṇḍa,* incidentally, that is of most significance for our study. The GKh tells the story of the birth of Gaṇeśa, and of Gaṇeśa's losing one tusk, cut off by Paraśurāma, whose story is also told. The long KJKh deals with the birth and deeds of Kṛṣṇa, along with his consort Rādhā. The Purāṇa as a whole consists of 20,000 to 25,000 *ślokas*.[1]

Relatively little research has been done on the BVP, undoubtedly due in part to its late date. Manuscripts of portions of the BVP were already available in Europe by the early nineteenth century. In Alexandre Hamilton and L. Langlès's *Catalogue,* published in Paris in 1807, an incomplete manuscript of the BVP is listed, with a description of the contents and a brief introductory comment on the nature of the Purāṇa as a whole.[2] Albrecht Weber, in the Vorrede to his *Handschriften-Verzeichnisse,* reports that his predecessor (Charles) Wilkens around the year 1827 purchased a few manuscripts that had earlier belonged to the Serampore College and had been obtained by (Georg Hein-

[1] A. S. Gupta, in his "The Extant BVP," says that the Ānand and Vaṅg editions each contain more than 22,000 *ślokas*, and the Veṅk about 25,000 (Purāṇa III, 101). But in his "Purāṇas and Their Referencing," Gupta says that the Ānand contains, by actual counting, 20,694 (*Purāṇa* VII, 349).

[2] *Catalogue des Manuscrits Samskrits de la Bibliothêque Impériale,* no. VIII (of Sanskrit manuscripts in Bengali characters), "Brahmâ Vaïvartikâ Pourâna." The manuscript was incomplete in the first and fourth *khaṇḍas*. The brief introductory comment referred to above is quoted in part below, p. 50, note 64. Note also in Hamilton's *Catalogue* no. XXXIV (of Sanskrit manuscripts in Devanāgarī characters), "Ganêsa Kavatcha" (extracts from the BVP).

rich) Bernstein in England. Among these manuscripts was one of the KJKh of the BVP.[3] This manuscript was utilized by A. F. Stenzler in his publication, in 1829, of *Brahma-Vaivarta-Puráni Specimen*, containing the text of two chapters or *adhyāyas* (KJKh 2–3), with a Latin translation, notes, and brief introduction. This work was reviewed by A. Langlois in *Journal des Savans*, Oct. 1832, pp. 612–621.

The first extended analysis of the entire BVP, as of many of the Purāṇas, was by Horace Hayman Wilson. In the years 1823–1832, he employed Indian pandits to draw up detailed indices of the Purāṇas.[4] He then had translated, or translated himself, passages that seemed of interest.[5] From these indices and translations, and with constant reference to the original texts, Wilson wrote up abstracts on some of the Purāṇas, showing "their purport, authenticity, and date."[6] The abstract on the BVP was first published in the *Journal of the Asiatic Society of Bengal* in 1832.[7] Wilson gives a description of each *khaṇḍa* of the BVP with translations of a few brief passages, and with occasional criticisms of the "contradictions" in the Purāṇa as well as of its philosophical views. The concluding paragraph of the abstract attempts to place the BVP in its historical context. Wilson earlier had already utilized the BVP in his "A Sketch of the Religious Sects of the Hindus." This was published in two parts, in *Asiatic Researches*, XVI (1828), 1–136, and XVII (1832), 169–313.[8] In the first part, dealing with the Vaiṣṇava sects, Wilson refers to and quotes from the BVP in his discussion of the Vallabhācārins and Rādhāvallabhins.[9] In the second, on the Śaiva and Śākta sects, he refers to

[3] *Die Handschriften-Verzeichnisse der Königlichen Bibliothek*, Vorrede, p. X. The manuscript is no. 463.

[4] See Wilson, "Analysis of the Puráńas," ESL, I, 5–6. Cf. Winternitz and Keith, *Catalogue of Sanskrit Manuscripts in the Bodleian Library*, II, 157–158.

[5] Manuscripts of the translations of selected chapters from the BVP are listed in Winternitz and Keith's *Catalogue*, II, 160, 161.

[6] "Analysis of the Puráńas," ESL, I, 7.

[7] The abstract appeared as "I.—Analysis of the Puráńas. 2. The Brahmá Vaivartta Purána" (JASB I [1832], 217–233). It was later published as section IV of "Analysis of the Puráńas," being part I of ESL, vol. I (vol. III of Wilson's *Works*).

[8] The two articles were later published together as vol. I of *Essays and Lectures Chiefly on the Religion of the Hindus* (vol. I of his *Works*). This volume will henceforth be referred to as *Sects*.

[9] *Sects*, pp. 122–124; 174–176.

the PKh in explaining Śākta doctrines.[10] Finally, in the Preface to his translation of the *Viṣṇu Purāṇa*, published in 1840, Wilson has a brief section on the BVP that supplements the historical research of his earlier articles.[11] The specific conclusions and contributions of Wilson will be considered in chapter 2, regarding the history of the text itself.

Further work in introducing the BVP to the West was carried on by Leloup de Cheray, who published in 1868 the text of selected passages from KJKh 2 and 3, with a French translation and commentary.[12] The first publication of the complete text of the BVP, so far as I know, was the Sarasvatī Press edition in 1888.[13] This was quickly followed by the Vaṅgavāsī edition in 1890. The Veṅkaṭeśvara edition was published in 1909–1910, and finally the Ānandāśrama edition in 1935. Rajendra Nath Sen published an English translation of the entire Purāṇa in 1920–1922 in the *Sacred Books of the Hindus* (vol. XXIV).

Meanwhile, the actual study of the Purāṇa was progressing rather slowly. Brief mention of the BVP has been made in some surveys of Sanskrit literature and Hindu religious movements by such writers as F. S. Growse,[14] M. Winternitz,[15] R. G. Bhandarkar,[16] and J. N. Farquhar.[17] For the most part, these relied upon Wilson. The BVP was not greeted with any great enthusiasm, even when it had been made available in published editions. It was regarded as "spurious,"[18] and as the product of a degenerate form of Vaiṣṇavism.[19] Winternitz referred to the BVP as "altogether a rather inferior production."[20]

[10] *Sects*, pp. 244–248.

[11] *The Vishńu Puráńa*, Preface, pp. LXV–LXVII (Wilson's translation of the ViP is now included as vols. VI–X of his *Works*).

[12] *Spécimen des Purâṇas: Texte, transcription, traduction et commentaire des principaux passages du Brahmâvaevarta Purâṇa.* Leloup published under the pseudonym, L. Leupol.

[13] Winternitz says that editions were published in 1887 and 1888 at Calcutta (*A History of Indian Literature,* I, 567, note 4). I assume this refers to only one edition, that of the Sarasvatī Press (Calcutta). See also A. Weber, *The History of Indian Literature,* p. 191, note 206.

[14] *Mathurá* (1883), pp. 75, 186–187, 314, 332.

[15] *A History of Indian Literature* (original German edition, 1908), vol. I, esp. pp. 567–569.

[16] *Vaiṣṇavism, Śaivism* (1913), p. 87 (1965 ed.).

[17] *Outline* (1920), esp. pp. 240, 271.

[18] Growse, *Mathurá,* p. 186. For my view of the term "spurious," see pp. 16 ff. below.

[19] Bhandarkar, *Vaiṣṇavism, Śaivism,* p. 87.

[20] *A History of Indian Literature,* I, 569.

Some writers, however, mostly Indians, were showing more interest in the Purāṇa. J. C. Roy published an article on the BVP and its dating in a Bengali journal.[21] Haraprasada Shastri, in the Preface of his *Catalogue*, vol. V (1928), has a brief historical analysis of the text of the BVP.[22] P. V. Kane and R. C. Hazra have seen in the BVP valuable source material for Hindu laws and customs of the medieval period.[23] We also find that the BVP has been used as a kind of reference book on Hindu attitudes towards women, as in M. W. Pinkham's *Woman in the Sacred Scriptures of Hinduism* (1942).[24] In this connection we may refer to B. Kakati's work on *Viṣṇuite Myths and Legends* (1952), one section of which is entitled "Female Initiative in Courtship (Episodes in the Brahmavaivarta Purāṇa)."[25]

Most use has been made of the BVP in connection with the Kṛṣṇaite literature and sectarian movements. W. Ruben, in his *Krishna, Konkordanz und Kommentar der Motive Seines Heldenlebens* (1944), gives a concordance of the Kṛṣṇa legend in the HV and the Purāṇas, including the BVP. In a study of the Bengal Vaiṣṇava movement, S. K. De deals with the BVP in its possible relation to the Caitanya school.[26] B. Majumdar, in a recent study on Kṛṣṇa, also discusses the BVP in connection with the Gosvāmins.[27] A. K. Majumdar, in an article on the Rādhā cult, utilizes the BVP, though he is rather disparaging, even contemptuous, of the work and of the Purāṇas in general.[28] Kakati, in his book already mentioned, also refers to the BVP in discussing "The Emergence of Rādhā."[29]

21 *Bhāratavarṣa*, 1337 B.S., Āṣādha, pp. 94–104. This reference is from Hazra, *Purāṇic Records*, p. 166. I was unable to obtain a copy of the article, but apparently Hazra has utilized its main conclusions regarding the history of the text. Cf. Sukumar Sen, *A History of Brajabuli Literature*, p. 475, where Roy's conclusions about the BVP are also mentioned.

22 *A Descriptive Catalogue of Sanskrit Manuscripts in the Government Collection under the Care of the Asiatic Society of Bengal*, V, Preface, pp. clvi–clxii.

23 Kane, *History of Dharmaśāstra*, I (1930), 160–167; and Hazra, *Purāṇic Records* (1936), pp. 166–167, 187–188. See also Hazra, "Studies in the Genuine Āgneya-Purāṇa," *Our Heritage*, I (1953), 209–210.

24 See her chapter on the Purāṇas, pp. 92–137.

25 Pp. 78–86.

26 VFM (1942), pp. 8–10.

27 *Kṛṣṇa in History and Legend* (1969), pp. 184–185.

28 "Rādhā Cult," ABORI XXXVI (1955), 247–249. Cf. S. K. Chatterji, "Purāṇa Legends and the Prakrit Tradition in New Indo-Aryan," *Bulletin of the School of Oriental Studies*, VIII (1936), 462.

29 *Viṣṇuite Myths and Legends*, pp. 71–77.

The BVP has been utilized in the study of other goddesses besides Rādhā. We may mention P. K. Maity's *Historical Studies in the Cult of the Goddess Manasā,*[30] and A. S. Gupta's "Conception of Sarasvatī in the Purāṇas."[31]

Various miscellaneous works that may be mentioned include Heinrich Zimmer's *Myths and Symbols in Indian Art and Civilization,* the first chapter of which, on "Eternity and Time," begins with the remarkable story of the "Parade of Ants" from KJKh 47.50–161.[32] In Joseph Campbell's *The Masks of God: Oriental Mythology,* passages from the BVP are quoted as examples of an extreme "amplitude of dionysiac madness."[33] An article in Hindi, entitled "Brahmavaivarta Mẽ Bhakti Kā Svarūp," by Ramniranjana Pandey, briefly deals with the nature of *bhakti* in the BVP, from a personal, devotionalistic point of view.[34]

One very important article is A. S. Gupta's "The Apocryphal Character of the Extant Brahmavaivarta Purāṇa."[35] Gupta brings together and summarizes much of the historical research on the BVP up to his time. Anantray J. Rawal also has considered various historical questions regarding the BVP, confining himself for the most part to a review of previous scholarly studies.[36] In chapter 2, the results of the past historical enquiries regarding the BVP will be presented along with some new facts and insights into the history of our text.

[30] See pp. 77, 129–130, 156, 216–217.

[31] *Purāṇa,* IV, 55–95.

[32] Pp. 3–11. This book was originally a series of lectures at Columbia University in the winter term of 1942. They were published in book form in 1946, after Zimmer's death.

[33] Pp. 361–364.

[34] The article appears in *Hindi Anusilana,* XIV. Through the kindness of Miss Alaka Hejib, I was able to obtain a typed copy of the article; and with the help of Mr. Arvind Sharma, I read through the Hindi text.

[35] *Purāṇa,* III (1961), 92–101. Cf. Gupta's article on "Purāṇas and Their Referencing," *Purāṇa,* VII (1965), 321–351, esp. pp. 336–349.

[36] "Some Problems Regarding the Brahmavaivartapurāṇa," *Purāṇa,* XIV (1972), 107–124.

PART A

CULTURAL, HISTORICAL AND THEOLOGICAL BACKGROUND

1

Purāṇa as Revealing Truth

The religious literature of India was not originally scripture, as it did not exist in written form. Rather, it consisted of an oral tradition that only later was committed to writing. The fact that the primary or original mode of transmission was oral rather than written by no means lessened the authoritativeness of this literature in the minds of Indians. We may distinguish two main types of this oral tradition, the *śruti* and the *smṛti.* The former may be called "revealed truth," the latter we shall refer to as "revealing truth." In what follows, we shall attempt to see the meaning and relationship of these two types of religious literature, and to consider in what sense the Purāṇas, which are classed as *smṛti,* may be regarded as revealing truth. We shall take into account not only the views of modern Western historical research and textual criticism, but also the traditional views and the standpoint of the pious Hindu.

Śruti is the truth that was heard by the ancient sages. This divine truth or knowledge (*veda*), for the sake of preservation, was gathered into various collections known as the Vedic *saṃhitās*. At first, there was some fluidity in the transmission of these collections, and accordingly, for each *saṃhitā,* there came to be established different text-traditions or *śākhās* (branches). These *śākhās* at an early age became frozen and were considered immutable. They were thus taught by the sages to their disciples with meticulous care, so that not the slightest alteration of this divine revelation should occur. Indeed, through a continuous chain of oral transmission, these *śākhās* have been preserved without change to the present day.

There are various traditional views regarding the ultimate source of this *śruti*. According to some schools, for instance the Nyāya and Vaiśeṣika, the authorship of the Veda is ascribed to God (Iśvara), while the Pūrvamīmāṃsā holds that it is authorless (*apauruṣeya*). In the latter case, the Veda is therefore uncomposed and self-determined, even regarding the very order of its words. The second-century B.C. grammarian Patañjali argued, however, that the Vedas, though not composed, were eternal in their meaning, rather than in the order of their syllables.[1] In any case, the Hindu tradition is in agreement that the Veda is not of human origin, and that it would be unthinkable for any human to attempt to change even one letter, or rather one sound, of this *śruti*.

Smṛti, literally "remembrance" or "recollection," is usually considered by Hindus themselves to be of human authorship, though as we shall see, in some instances a divine origin has also been attributed to it. Included in this literature are the epics and Purāṇas. These were originally transmitted orally by story-tellers (*aitihāsikas*, *paurāṇikas*) or bards (*sūtas*) and other reciters, usually non-Brahmans. Unlike the Vedic *śākhās*, which are communicated only to the initiates, the epics and Purāṇas were publicly sung or recited, and in the process underwent constant revision and recreation or elaboration. The fluid nature of this oral literature was by no means halted when it was committed to written form, so that several versions and recensions of these texts have arisen. Especially have the Purāṇas retained their fluidity, and in some instances, it even appears that whole new works were written and given the names of older Purāṇas.[2] Clearly the immutable sanctity of the Vedas was not seen as applying to the Purāṇas, and yet these works retain a strong, religiously authoritative value.

The question of authority directly concerns the origin or source of the Purāṇas. Hindu tradition has ascribed to the Purāṇas both divine and human authorship. In each case, there is considered to

[1] See Hiriyanna, *Outlines of Indian Philosophy*, pp. 312–313.

[2] Hazra lists three main ways in which the Purāṇic texts were revised: (1) by the addition of new chapters, (2) by the substitution of new chapters for old, and (3) by writing new Purāṇas preserving the old titles (*Purāṇic Records*, pp. 6–7).

be one original Purāṇa, later divided into a number of Purāṇas. Regarding the view of divine origination, several versions are found.[3] One version is that the original Purāṇa issued forth from the mouth of Brahmā in a hundred crore of *ślokas*, and was then abridged by Vyāsa into four lakhs, before he divided them into the present eighteen Purāṇas. In each *dvāpara yuga*, Vyāsa makes this division on earth, but in the worlds of the gods, the Purāṇa remains in its original, unabridged form.[4] We find that the BVP traces back its own origin to Kṛṣṇa. At the beginning of time, in Goloka, Kṛṣṇa gave it to Brahmā. The chain of transmission then was: Brahmā to Dharma, Dharma to Nārāyaṇa, Nārāyaṇa to Nārada, Nārada to Vyāsa, and Vyāsa, after bringing together the huge collection, to Sūta, the narrator of the BVP.[5]

As for the human origin of the Purāṇas, Vyāsa is said to have composed a *purāṇasaṃhitā,* which he then gave to his disciple, the bard Romaharṣaṇa. He in turn gave it to his six disciples, three of whom produced each his own *saṃhitā.* These three versions, with Romaharṣaṇa's, were considered as the four basic or early *purāṇasaṃhitās.*[6] The eighteen Purāṇas then were further versions or divisions of these.

In all the above traditions, Vyāsa is regarded as playing a crucial role, and in general, authorship of the Purāṇas is ascribed to him. But even according to the views of divine origin, the original Purāṇa is thought to have undergone extensive revision by Vyāsa, that is, by human agency. The principle of human revision of the Purāṇas, with qualifications of course, is thus a perfectly acceptable notion to the Hindu tradition. The authority of these works rests, then, on the character of Vyāsa and his disciples. Vyāsa is looked upon as the ideal sage, one who is thoroughly familiar with *śruti* and understands the true meaning of the Purāṇa.[7] He in fact is often called Veda-vyāsa, as he is considered to be the arranger of the Vedas in their present form.

[3] A. S. Gupta has gathered together many of the early Vedic, Brāhmaṇic, and Upaniṣadic, as well as Purāṇic references to the various views on the origin of the Purāṇas, in his article, "Purāṇas and Their Referencing" (*Purāṇa,* VII, 323–326). Our analysis above of the different views is greatly indebted to this article. See also Hazra, *Purāṇic Records,* pp. 1–2.

[4] For the Purāṇic references giving this view, see Gupta, "Purāṇas and Their Referencing," *Purāṇa,* VII, 323–324.

[5] BKh 1.59–63. Cf. KJKh 133.27–29, where Vyāsa is missing from the list of transmitters.

[6] Cf. Gupta, "Purāṇas and Their Referencing," *Purāṇa,* VII, 325.

[7] *purāṇārthaviśārada* (ViP III.6.15).

His disciples also are regarded as fully qualified transmitters and editors of the Purāṇas.

Modern scholars have rejected the notion of the divine origin of the Purāṇas and have also challenged the historic character of Vyāsa. The Purāṇas, as we have mentioned, were constantly revised and added to so that materials from very different ages have come to be included in any single Purāṇa. No one person, accordingly, could have been responsible for the Purāṇas, and therefore Vyāsa, whom tradition sometimes, but not always, regards as the author or compiler of the eighteen, is dismissed as "mythic." It is not only Western students who have recognized the fluid nature of the Purāṇic texts, but Indians themselves, trained in the methods of Western research.

A fundamental problem is raised here for the Indian student who, initiated into text-critical research methods, may still wish to look upon the Purāṇas as a sacred or truth-revealing literature. A Western student of the history of religion, also, cannot fully evade the issues involved, as they directly affect the basic problem of understanding another culture's world view. The French scholar, Madeleine Biardeau, has summarized the problem facing the Indian student as follows: "It cannot be concealed that the bards who narrated the [epic and Purāṇic] stories partly recreated them for each recitation. . . . To a modern brahmin's mind this means unauthoritativeness, sheer fancy and hopeless separation from the pure source of wisdom."[8] The response on the part of many Indian scholars has been to attempt to discover the most "authoritative" text, by which was meant the one most free of later additions and revisions. This of course implied that the oldest version, free of the "corruptions" introduced in the transmitting process, would be the most genuine. At the same time, these scholars have questioned whether there ever was an original, organic text that was the integral work of a single author, and if instead there was not merely a collection of disparate tales and legends.

This dilemma is well illustrated in the case of the great epic scholar V. S. Sukthankar, who began a critical edition of the MBh in the nineteen-twenties and thirties. Sylvain Lévi at the time noted that Sukthankar was caught midway between his own Indian tradition and that of the German philologists under whom

[8] "Textual Criticism," *Purāṇa*, X, 118.

he was trained. Lévi says of Sukthankar: "Il ne peut s'empêcher de tenir Vyāsa et Vaiçampāyana pour des personnages réels, authentiques; il admet un poème primitif, organique, à la base de tous les remaniements; mais il déclare aussi que 'pratiquement il n'a jamais existé un archétype' du poème."[9] Biardeau, a student of Lévi, has made several significant suggestions towards a reconciliation or synthesis of traditional views with a scientific approach. She has contrasted Sukthankar's critical edition of the MBh with Nilakantha's seventeenth-century vulgate edition. Nilakantha gathered together as many versions as possible, rather than eliminating and narrowing down to one "true version." Biardeau does not see this as "unscientific," for Nilakantha also was concerned with the genuineness of his text. His criterion for authoritativeness was simply very different from Sukthankar's. This criterion, Biardeau explains, rested in the Brahman community itself. Traditionally, Hindus were rather indifferent to the real or historical origins of different versions and did not attempt to account for textual differences in terms of historical change. Rather, they decided what was genuine by referring the matter to the local Brahman authorities. Biardeau writes:

> . . . any epic or purāṇic story is true if the local brahmins recognize it as part of their beliefs. These brahmins are the *śruta,* the people that warrant the authority of the local tradition because they are well-versed in the *śruti.* And if such a story is recognized by the brahmins, it is attributed to Vyāsa, the mythic author of epics and purāṇas, regardless of whether it is mentioned in any of the classical texts.[10]

It seems to this writer that Biardeau, in attempting to reconcile science and tradition, has in some ways widened the gap between an historical and a sympathetic understanding of the Hindu tradition. This split is made quite clear in such statements as the following: "The modern pandits are now in the name of science trying to . . . decide what is old enough to possibly date back to Vyāsa and use this as the basis for determining the authoritative version. They have introduced the historical dimension into the realm of myths where it cannot exist."[11] She asserts that the

[9] Lévi, book review of *The Mahā Bhārata* (Vishnu S. Sukthankar, ed.), *Journal Asiatique,* CCXXV, 282. This passage is quoted in English translation in Biardeau, "Textual Criticism," *Purāṇa,* X, 116.

[10] "Textual Criticism," *Purāṇa,* X, 121.

[11] *Ibid.,* p. 122.

approach of Western textual criticism and especially of historical philology is simply unsuited to the epic and Purāṇic tradition, in view of the diversity of its historical sources. Therefore, she adds, "It would just be wrong to make Vyāsa the historical origin of what has no single historical origin."[12] One may well agree with this last statement, but does this invalidate seeking answers to historical questions? Biardeau's feelings on this matter are apparently contained in her remarks concerning the problem of unity in the different text versions. She argues that their "unity is to be found in the meaning of the stories and not in their particular contents or historical bearing."[13] She similarly states that in these different versions, the "expression might slightly change, while the essential message has remained the same, that the meaning rather than the form is more important, a sign of a living tradition."[14] It is not at all evident, however, that the meaning has remained the same, or that there is one essential message. If we look carefully at any one legend or "myth" that appears in several versions in different Purāṇas, say the story of Prahlāda or the cosmogony of the golden egg, it seems that there is much more than just a "slight change" in expression. Rather, the myths or legends seem to have been understood in a variety of ways. One need not conclude that the various versions represent purely arbitrary and discordant interpretations, but instead that the stories or myths may contain within themselves many levels of meaning or different aspects of truth, and that no single interpretation can do justice to the complex of meaning. Hans Penner, in an article, "Cosmogony as Myth in the Vishnu Purāṇa," has pointed out the "multivalent significance" of mythic symbols, and his remarks may well be applied to most of the Purāṇic legends.[15] One might ask if the multivalent significance of the symbols does not derive from the multivalent nature of reality itself. It would seem, at least, that reality appeared to the epic and Purāṇic compilers in such a multi-faceted manner.

Despite Biardeau's rather extreme dismissal of historical textual research, she puts forth some guidelines that need to be seriously considered by the student of the history of religion. She states, for example, that the scientific study of the epics or Purāṇas "should

[12] *Ibid.*
[13] *Ibid.*, p. 123.
[14] *Ibid.*, p. 120.
[15] *History of Religions*, V, 290.

not begin by focusing our attention on the changes that took place in the process of transmitting the texts, but determine for any given time, whether a particular piece of oral literature had some relation to the actual beliefs of the people and how it was understood by them."[16] Yet in order to "determine for any given time" how a text was understood by a believer, it seems necessary to utilize historical and text-critical research methods.

An Indian writer, A. S. Gupta, supplies some answers to this problem. We may recall that Biardeau, though expressing much sympathy with the Hindu tradition, still refers to Vyāsa as "mythic." As Gupta points out, "We Indians however, are not used to regard all our ancient sages and heroes as mythical figures."[17] Gupta himself is wholly familiar with modern text-critical methods, their theoretical bases, and their rather destructive results in the past for the understanding or interpretation of the Purāṇas as significant religious literature. Yet he avoids the dilemma that confronted Sukthankar, for he sees no need to rediscover or reconstruct an original text of the MBh or the Purāṇas in their "pristine" form. On a practical level, he argues that if one does accept Vyāsa as an historical figure and author of the epics and Purāṇas, still the particular problems of oral and written transmission and the lack of complete manuscript material make it impossible to reconstruct the original text.[18] Gupta is not against all text reconstruction, however, as we shall see.

More importantly from a theological point of view, Gupta argues that the later revisions of the texts are not mere "corruptions." He asks:

> Are all these later additions the results of the tampering attempts of the interpolators beyond any justification, or are these additions the results of the desire on the part of the redactors to revise the texts of the Purāṇas from time to time and keep them in line with the current religious and social ideas of their times in order to preserve the encyclopaedic nature of the Purāṇas and keep them up to date?[19]

Gupta clearly feels the latter is the case. The later revisions of a Purāṇa, which he says would better be called additions or amplifi-

[16] "Textual Criticism," *Purāṇa,* X, 119–120.
[17] "Text-reconstruction," *Purāṇa,* XII, 305.
[18] *Ibid.,* pp. 305–309.
[19] *Ibid.,* pp. 306–307.

cations than interpolations, are as important as the original. The Purāṇas then are a living literature which Gupta likens to a living organism:

> The spontaneous growth in the form of additions and amplifications in the body of the Purāṇa-puruṣa is like the natural growth of a human organism. The grown-up form of a Purāṇa-text, therefore, is as important and valuable as its original or the pristine form, just as a grown-up human body is not less important than its early and undeveloped baby-form.[20]

Gupta then goes on to discuss various types of additions to the Purāṇas. The first he refers to as natural growth (*upabṛṃhaṇa*). He gives the following example from the KūrP. In I.51.14ab, there is reference to Śibi as an Indra, known also for his hundred sacrifices. This line is identical with ViP III.1.17ab.[21] The KūrP then follows with the half *śloka:* "He [Śibi] became a devotee of Śaṃkara [Śiva], delighting in his worship [*arcana*]." This is absent in the ViP. Gupta says of the extra line that the KūrP has added it to the body of its text, due to the predominantly Śaivite character of this Pūraṇa. As the line occurs in all manuscripts of the KūrP, it should be included in any reconstructed text.

There are other alterations, omissions, or additions, however, which are not "authentic or justifiable," according to Gupta. Aside from purely scribal errors, there are "spurious additions or interpolations . . . made with a desire on the part of the interpolator to amplify some description. . . . Some additions are tinged with sectarian zeal and motive. . . ."[22] Gupta then gives an example from the Nandi-nāgarī manuscript of the KūrP, which in I.4.65d reads: *sarvaṃ śivamayaṃ jagat* ("the whole world is constituted of Śiva"). No other manuscript of the KūrP has this reading. All others, Gupta says, have: *sarvaṃ brahmamayaṃ jagat.*[23] The Nandi-nāgarī manuscript therefore possesses a "Śaivite nature" due to "sectarian zeal" and its peculiar readings are to be excluded in any reconstruction of the text.[24]

20 *Ibid.*, p. 311.

21 The Oriental Press and Sarasvatī Press editions have slightly different readings, but this does not affect Gupta's main point.

22 "Text-reconstruction," *Purāṇa*, XII, 315.

23 The Veṅk, however, gives *viṣṇumayam* as a variant reading, as we shall mention later.

24 "Text-reconstruction," *Purāṇa,* XII, 316.

Several questions may be raised at this point, both practical and theological. First, Gupta apparently distinguishes between authentic and spurious revisions largely on the basis of the frequency of their occurrence in the available manuscripts of a text. Thus, the Śaivite addition in KūrP I.51.14, appearing in all the manuscripts, is acceptable as a natural growth. But the alteration in the Nandi-nāgarī manuscript is spurious, as it occurs only in this one instance. Why, though, this is any better grounds for spuriousness than in the former case is not clear. What in fact do we mean by "spurious"? Could not the revision of the Nandi-nāgarī manuscript represent part of the "natural growth" of the Purāṇa? Despite Gupta's likening this kind of revision to an "unnatural redundant growth of a limb in a human body,"[25] he does not set forth any convincing reasons for such an evaluation.

Let us look at some of the theological questions involved. In the case of the revision in the Nandi-nāgarī manuscript, we must first ask ourselves what this change meant to the redactor responsible for it. What is the difference between saying that the world is constituted of Brahman (or Brahmā) and that it is constituted of Śiva? We may note here that the Veṅk gives an alternate reading, *viṣṇumayam,* for *brahmamayam.* Did the redactor or redactors believe that *brahmamayam* was incorrect? Or did they wish to foist their own sectarian view upon the unsuspecting reader by taking unfair liberties with the text? Or rather was it an effort to interpret, to clarify, to make a commentary as it were in the text itself? Are Brahman, or Brahmā, Viṣṇu, and Śiva three different realities or deities, or three forms of one reality? Or identical? If, as many Hindus hold, Brahman/Brahmā, Viṣṇu, and Śiva are one reality, or different aspects of one reality, which version is spurious? The Nandi-nāgarī redactor apparently thought it worthwhile to make the change from *brahmamayam* to *śivamayam,* not because the former was incorrect, but because the latter was a clearer statement of the truth and more revealing of the nature of reality. If someone else perceives reality in the form of Viṣṇu, is the Nandi-nāgarī redactor wrong, or can reality reveal itself both as Viṣṇu and Śiva?

We do not mean to say by the above that there are no significant differences between the various versions. But we wish to emphasize that in attempting to explain away such differences

[25] *Ibid.,* p. 311.

in terms of purely historical factors, one is unlikely to understand the "spirit" that underlies the writing of such works. This "spirit" has been misunderstood by many Western text critics in the past. Among the historical factors by which they wish to explain the revisions of the text, "sectarian zeal" is one of the most popular, and carries with it the connotations of an underhanded or dishonest alteration of the text for selfish purposes. We do not wish to dismiss "sectarianism" altogether, but this term, as applied to the Purāṇas, must be used with considerable caution, as we shall see.[26] Let us simply point out now that if one of these text critics had redacted a text for the purposes he attributes to the actual redactors, he apparently would have been at pains to cover up his alterations, iron out "inconsistencies" and so forth. Yet the actual redactors felt no such need. Were they merely amateurish incompetents, or motivated by reasons other than those ascribed to them by the Western critics?

To understand the situation, we must consider the general role of the Purāṇas in Hindu culture. One must be aware that for the Hindus, truth is something to be discovered by each generation and by every individual. But it is a rediscovery, or recovery of truth, rather than the uncovering of something previously unknown. Truth was fully revealed in the past. The possibility of its rediscovery depends upon maintaining close links with that past. The word *purāṇa* itself means belonging to the past, or an ancient happening. The Purāṇic tradition preserves contact with the past, and is thus a primary means for rediscovering and reinterpreting truth. The Vedas are revealed truth, and even the perfect expression of that truth. But as we have indicated, they are reserved for the twice-born classes and are not to be recited in public. Śūdras and women are prohibited from even hearing the Vedas. The Purāṇas, on the other hand, may be heard by all, especially in the *kali yuga* when *dharma* is in universal decline.[27]

[26] See chapter 3, section 4, on Vaiṣṇavism and the problem of an open sectarianism.

[27] DBhP I.3.18–21 declares:

manvantareṣu sarveṣu dvāpare dvāpare yuge/
prāduḥ karoti dharmārthī purāṇāni yathā vidhi//
dvāpare dvāpare viṣṇur vyāsarūpeṇa sarvadā/
vedam ekaṃ sa bahudhā kurute hitakāmyayā//
alpāyuṣo 'lpabuddhīṃśca viprāñ jñātvā kalav atha/
purāṇasamhitāṃ puṇyāṃ kurute 'sau yuge yuge//
strīśūdradvijabandhūnāṃ na vedaśravaṇaṃ matam/
teṣām eva hitārthāya purāṇāni kṛtāni ca//

The Purāṇas are an "easier" form of truth, adapted to the conditions of class and world age. We may recall that, according to the view of the divine origin of the Purāṇas, Vyāsa in every *dvāpara yuga* divides them into eighteen, having already greatly abridged the "hundred crore celestial Purāṇa." Implicit in this is the notion that mankind can accept only a modified form of truth. It is assumed that the revisions are made in complete harmony with the truth contained in *śruti.* The Purāṇas represent, then, an interpretation or clarification of the *śruti,* revealing the eternal, immutable truth in a comprehensible form to all mankind in his changing, historical situation. This process of revealing truth by its very nature is never-ending. The truth, once revealed in *śruti,* must ever be newly interpreted or explained in *smṛti.* The truth may be constantly reinterpreted, but no past interpretation need be rejected if it is rooted in the Purāṇic tradition. This may help us to understand why the Purāṇas are inclusive rather than exclusive, preserving as many views as possible. From the standpoint of the Purāṇic compilers, dishonesty might well consist in the intentional rejection of a "myth" or legend or philosophical idea, even if it *apparently* does not accord with their version or interpretation. This is one aspect of the Purāṇic "spirit" spoken of above. An increasing number of Western scholars in the history of religion are beginning to realize that the primary task now in Purāṇic studies is precisely the sympathetic understanding of this "spirit."[28]

From the point of view of the role of *smṛti* just outlined, the Purāṇas may be considered as equal or even superior to the *śruti* as a religious authority. Very early, the Purāṇa (in the singular) was regarded as a fifth Veda. In CU VII.1.2, reference is made to *itihāsapurāṇa* as the fifth (Veda), and AV XI.7.24 says that the Purāṇa arises out of the *ucchiṣṭa* (remainder of the sacrifice) along with the hymns, chants, meters and sacred formulas.[29] The BhP refers to itself as the fruit fallen from the *kalpa* tree that is the Nigama (Veda).[30] And the BVP says that Vyāsa milked Sarasvatī, the goddess of knowledge, in the form of a wish-fulfilling cow, using the *śruti* as calves, and thereby attained the nectar-

[28] See, for instance, Kees W. Bolle, "Reflections on a Puranic Passage," *History of Religions,* II, 286.

[29] Cf. Gupta, "Purāṇas and Their Referencing," *Purāṇa,* VII, 323, and Hazra, *Purāṇic Records,* p. 1.

[30] BhP I.1.3.

like *Brahmavaivarta Purāṇa.*[31] Further, the BVP says that it dispels or destroys the delusions of the other Purāṇas, Upapurāṇas, and the Vedas.[32]

In this study, we shall be primarily concerned with understanding the views of the redactor or redactors who saw fit to put together the Purāṇa in its present form; or rather, with reality as perceived and interpreted by them. At the same time, historical and text-critical research will be utilized as a means to understand better their conception of reality, for this conception is rooted both in a living tradition and in the particular historical situation of the redactors. We do not mean to imply that the ultimate reality has changed or developed, but that the conception of it may have. We shall thus be concerned, to some degree, with the text-history of the BVP, to know its sources, its relationship to other Purāṇas and various schools of thought. We shall attempt thereby to identify what is of special importance to our Purāṇa, what is particularly emphasized or neglected, in order to discover how the BVP has utilized and reinterpreted and perhaps revitalized tradition.

We shall deal first with several problems regarding the history of the text, not because we consider such problems as the most important, but in order to provide some historical background to the theology of the BVP, and to avoid the necessity, later, of having to interrupt frequently the theological discussion with text-critical excursuses.

[31] BKh 1.1–2. The verse numbering at the beginning of the BKh is somewhat confused. In both Veṅk and Ānand, there is a short obeisance of four or five verses, and then a new numbering commences. Our reference is to the new numbering.

[32] *purāṇopapurāṇānāṃ vedānāṃ bhramabhañjanam*/ (BKh 1.43)

2

History of the Text

The BVP has long been considered to be one of the latest, if not the last, of the major Purāṇas. Wilson pointed out much internal evidence in support of the late date of the BVP: its knowledge of the MBh and Rāmāyana, of the other major and minor Purāṇas, and of the Pāñcarātra literature; its references to the philosophical systems, the Tarka (Nyāya), Vaiśeṣika, Sāṃkhya, Pātañjala, Mīmāṃsā, and Vedānta;[1] its claim to clear up the errors of the other Purāṇas; its frequent assertions that its own legends are often not to be found in other Purāṇas; its allusions to the supremacy of Mleccha rulers, probably referring to Muslim invaders.[2] Some legends in the BVP, Wilson admitted, might be of relatively ancient origin, but the Purāṇa as a whole, he felt,

[1] According to A. K. Majumdar, the *advaita* teacher Śaṃkara is mentioned in the BVP, but Majumdar does not give any references ("Rādhā Cult," ABORI, XXXVI, 248). S. K. De, in VFM (p. 9), says that there is explicit mention of Śaṃkara the teacher in KJKh 24.18:

kārāgāre ca saṃsāre durvahaṃ nigaḍaṃ param/
acchedyaṃ jñānakhaḍgaiś ca mahadbhiḥ śaṃkarādibhiḥ//

The translation in the SBH (vol. XXIV) takes Śaṃkara as a name of Śiva. I think De's interpretation is correct. In any case, in KJKh 129.71 and 74, there is unambiguous reference to Śaṃkara the teacher, as propounder of the *anirvacanīya* doctrine.

[2] "Analysis of the Puránas," ESL, I, 119–120. Much of Wilson's evidence given above, as he himself indicates, comes from supplementary chapters at the end of the BVP, and thus does not directly bear on the date of the main body of the Purāṇa. As we shall see, most of the Purāṇas, in fact, refer to all the other major Purāṇas, in what clearly must be late additions.

belongs to the modern sect of worshippers of the youthful Kṛṣṇa and Rādhā.[3] Wilson concludes that "the particular branch of the Hindu system which it [the BVP] advocates renders it likely to have emanated from a sect, which there is reason to imagine originated about four centuries ago with Vallabháchárya and the Gosáins of Gokula."[4]

F. S. Growse in part affirms Wilson's view, stating that "it is not improbable that they [Rūpa and Sanātana, two of the Gosāins or Gosvāmins] were the authors of the Brahma Vaivarta Purána. . . ."[5] J. N. Farquhar, however, suggests that "the kṛishṇa section [the KJKh] of the *Brahmavaivarta P.* seems to be a Nimbārka document interpolated into the Purāṇa."[6] Farquhar elsewhere adds that the GKh, which at times glorifies Kṛṣṇa, also is probably from the Nimbārka school.[7] Farquhar apparently regards these sections as being composed prior to A.D. 1350.[8] R. C. Hazra feels that the BVP was most probably first composed in the eighth century A.D., with various revisions and additions down to the sixteenth century.[9] Other scholars have pointed to the BVP's use of the name Rāyāṇa for Rādhā's husband[10] as evidence for dating the Purāṇa, in its final form, in the sixteenth century. Rāyāṇa is apparently derived from the sixteenth-century Bengali name Āyān.[11]

There is a general consensus, then, that the BVP in its final form is of relatively late date, and that the Purāṇa is not the work of a single author. The ascription of the Purāṇa to different schools might also suggest that it belongs to no one school exclusively. In fact, it is quite certain, as we shall see, that the BVP, in the course of its development, has incorporated the views of

3 *The Vishńu Puráńa,* Preface, p. LXVI.

4 "Analysis of the Puráńas," ESL, I, 120.

5 *Mathurá,* p. 75. Growse himself refers to Wilson's views.

6 *Outline,* p. 240.

7 *Ibid.,* p. 271.

8 Chapter VI of Farquhar's *Outline,* in which the BVP is mentioned, deals with the literature supposedly belonging to the period 900–1350.

9 *Purāṇic Records,* pp. 166–167.

10 In the BVP, Rāyāṇa is identified with an *aṃśa* of Kṛṣṇa. Rāyāṇa is also regarded as Kṛṣṇa's maternal uncle. An illusory form (*chāyā*) of Rādhā only is said to marry Rāyāṇa. See PKh 49.38–43.

11 See S. K. Chatterji, "Purāṇa Legends and the Prakrit Tradition in New Indo-Aryan," *Bulletin of the School of Oriental Studies,* VIII, 462; Sukumar Sen, *A History of Brajabuli Literature,* p. 478; cf. A. K. Majumdar, "Rādhā Cult," ABORI, XXXVI, 247, 249.

many schools and sects.[12] In what follows, we shall attempt to outline further aspects of the history and development of the text through a survey of references and parallels to the BVP in other literature.

1. References to the BVP in other literature

Most of the major Purāṇas and some of the minor give a list of the eighteen traditionally accepted major (*mahā-*) Purāṇas.[13] Though there are some variations in the lists, the BVP is included in almost all, as the tenth Purāṇa. The date of the original list is uncertain, but obviously was made up after the entire "canonical eighteen" had come into existence. It was then inserted into each Purāṇa. The list appearing in ViP III.6.19–21, probably the most original[14] and which includes the BVP, is at least older than the eleventh century A.D., as Alberuni copied it

[12] See especially chapter 3 below.

[13] For the references to these lists in the various Purāṇas, see A. S. Gupta, "Purāṇas and Their Referencing," *Purāṇa,* VII, 334–338.

We might also point out here the traditional definitions of Mahā- and Upa- Purāṇas. In the sixth-century A.D. lexicon of Amarakoṣa, *purāṇa* is defined as *pañcalakṣaṇa,* or having five characteristics (I.155 in the Calcutta 1911–1912 ed., or I.6.5 in the Bombay 1886 ed.). The commentator Maheśvara specifies the five characteristics as *sarga* (creation), *pratisarga* (secondary creation), *vaṃśa* (genealogies of gods, sages, kings, and so forth), *manvantara* (cosmic cycles, each ruled over by a Manu), and *vaṃśānucarita* (history of royal dynasties). Cf. ViP III.6.22–23. *Saura Purāṇa* 9.4–5 says these characteristics belong to both the Mahā- and Upa-Purāṇas (*Saura Purāṇa* 9.4–5 is quoted in Sanskrit by Gupta, "Purāṇas and Their Referencing," *Purāṇa,* VII, 332, and by Hazra, *Studies in the Upapurāṇas,* I, 24). In BhP XII.7.9–10, ten characteristics are named: *sarga, visarga, vṛitti, rakṣa, antara, vaṃśa, vaṃśānucarita, samsthā, hetu, apaśrāya.* The BhP adds, though, that some people distinguish between great and small Purāṇas, the latter having only five characteristics. (For a brief analysis of the ten characteristics, see Gail, BhBhP, pp. 16–17, where he compares BhP XII.7.9 with another list of the ten marks in BhP II.10.1, and with the list of five given in ViP III. 6.22–23.) In our own text, in KJKh 133.6–10, it is stated that *sarga, pratisarga, vaṃśa, manvantara,* and *vaṃśānucarita* are the five characteristics of an Upapurāṇa, while a Mahāpurāṇa has ten: *sṛṣṭi, visṛṣṭi, sthiti, pālana, karmavāsanā, manuvārtā, pralayavarṇana, mokṣanirupaṇa, harikīrtana,* and *devakīrtana.* Cf. Hazra, *Studies in the Upapurāṇas,* I, 25. This distinction of Upa- and Mahā- Purāṇas seems not to be particularly valid in view of the actual contents of both groups of Purāṇas. The Upapurāṇas, in fact, seem to be simply those Purāṇas excluded from the "canonical eighteen." In many cases, the Upapurāṇas may be later works, but not always. Cf. Gupta, "Purāṇas and Their Referencing," *Purāṇa,* VII, 332, and Hazra, *Studies in the Upapurāṇas,* I, 25–27.

[14] A. S. Gupta, "Purāṇas and Their Referencing," *Purāṇa,* VII, 336–340.

down as read to him from the ViP.[15] There is mention of eighteen Purāṇas in the MBh and HV, but Hazra has shown that the references are probably late additions. He asserts, however, that the canon of eighteen is at least as old as the first quarter of the seventh century A.D.[16] This would indicate that the BVP is at least as old as the sixth century A.D., but the extant BVP, for the most part, is a very different work from that referred to in the earliest Purāṇic lists.

Wilson already noticed the difference between the MatP description of the BVP and the extant version.[17] MatP 53.33–35 reads as follows:

> [That Purāṇa] which gives an account of the Rathantara Kalpa,[18]
> [As related] by Sāvarṇi to Nārada, joined with a glorification of Kṛṣṇa (*kṛṣṇamāhātmya*),
> [And] in which the history of Brahmavarāha is repeatedly told,
> Consisting of eighteen thousand [*ślokas*], is called the *Brahmavaivarta*.
> Whoever makes a gift of the *Brahmavaivarta Purāṇa* in the month of Māgha,
> On an auspicious day during the full moon is honored in Brahmaloka.[19]

The extant BVP, however, is narrated, not by Sāvarṇi, but by Sauti or Nārāyaṇa; it gives no account of the Rathantara Kalpa; and it contains at most only vague references to Brahmavarāha. We shall return to the term Brahmavarāha in a moment. Further, although the MatP passage refers to a *kṛṣṇamāhātmya*, this may not have been the principal topic of the earlier BVP, and certainly does not prove that Kṛṣṇa was its supreme deity.[20] In fact, it seems that the original BVP was the product of a Brahmā cult. This is already suggested by the final line of the MatP passage

15 *Alberuni's India* (Sachau, ed.), I, 131.

16 *Purāṇic Records,* pp. 2–4.

17 *The Vishṅu Puráṅa,* Preface, pp. LXV–LXVI.

18 According to MatP CCXC.2–11, the Rāthantara is the fourth of thirty *kalpas* constituting a month of Brahmā.

19 This is my translation of a combined Sanskrit text, based on a comparison of the one given by Wilson (and Hall) in *The Vishṅu Puráṅa,* Preface, pp. LXV and LXVI, and the Veṅk.

20 Cf. Gupta, "The Extant BVP," *Purāṇa,* III, 97.

just quoted, in which a gift of the BVP is said to lead to the world of Brahmā.[21] Gupta rightly points out that Brahmaloka, according to the extant BVP, is far inferior to Goloka, the supreme realm of Kṛṣṇa, and that the former is never aspired to by true Vaiṣṇavas.[22] Brahmaloka, of course, would be the supreme heaven for the worshippers of Brahmā.

Additional evidence for the Brahmāite nature of the original BVP is found in MatP LIII.67–68, in conjunction with PadP VI.263.81–85. In MatP LIII.67–68, a classification of the Mahāpurāṇas is given according to the *guṇas*, the three qualities of nature. The *sāttvika* Purāṇas are chiefly glorifications of Hari (Viṣṇu), the *rājasa* of Brahmā, the *tāmasa* of Agni and Śiva, and those of mixed *guṇas* of Sarasvatī and the Pitṛs. PadP VI.263.81–85 gives the names of the Purāṇas that belong to each class.[23] The BVP is included in the *rājasa,* and thus, according to the MatP, the earlier BVP must have been dedicated primarily to Brahmā.[24] In our next section, on parallels to the BKh, we shall find still further evidence in support of this view.

Gupta has noted, in connection with the MatP's classification of the Purāṇas, in which those dedicated to Śiva are *tāmasa,* that the extant BVP, contrary to the usually accepted view, regards Śiva, along with Viṣṇu, as *sāttvika,* only fools claiming that Śiva is *tāmasa.*[25] Gupta thus concludes that the present BVP "is clearly the work of the Bhāgavata-Vaishṇavas who joined hands with the Śaivas to overshadow the cult of Brahmā-worshippers, and they might have also modified or completely changed the genuine Brahmavaivarta to propagate their own views."[26] Although I

21 Similar statements are found in the *Skanda Purāṇa* and *Saura Purāṇa* (see Gupta, "The Extant BVP," *Purāṇa,* III, 98), and in the NārP, whose account we shall discuss shortly.

22 "The Extant BVP," *Purāṇa,* III, 98.

23 The PadP does not mention a mixed class.

24 Gupta refers to another classification of the Purāṇas in the *Bhaviṣya Purāṇa,* in which the BVP is not included. Gupta considers the PadP classification to be preferable ("Purāṇas and Their Referencing," *Purāṇa,* VII, 341–342). In the SkP, in the Śaṃkara Saṃhitā 2.30–35, the Purāṇas are named with reference to the chief deity of each. According to this list, the BVP is dedicated to Savitṛ (the Sun) (see Eggeling's *Catalogue,* part VI, p. 1363, for the Sanskrit text). In certain Tamil lexicons, the BVP is similarly said to belong to Sūrya (see Dikshitar, "The Purāṇas: A Study," IHQ, VIII, 766–767). It is unclear to me why the BVP was so characterized.

25 BKh 8.19–21. Cf. below, pp. 47–48.

26 "The Extant BVP," *Purāṇa,* III, 96.

would be more hesitant than Gupta to use the word "genuine" for the earlier BVP and "apocryphal" for the extant, his statement does point to an important aspect of the historical development of the text. As we shall see in the next chapter, there is indeed much cooperation and sympathy between the Śaivas and Vaiṣṇavas expressed in the extant BVP.

Not all of the other major Purāṇas are ignorant of the extant BVP. In NārP I.101.1 ff., we find a long description of the BVP. This description actually combines much of the old account, as found in MatP 53.33–35, with a detailed description of the contents of the four *khaṇḍas* of the extant BVP. It is possible that the NārP knew only the present BVP and took the old description from earlier Purāṇas. In any case, the NārP itself says that there was an older BVP, and explains the relation of the old version to the new in the following manner:

> The history of the Rathantara Kalpa, which has been related by me [Brahmā],
> In a Purāṇa of a hundred crores [of *ślokas*], was abridged and proclaimed by the Veda-knower,
> Vyāsa, putting it together in four parts, in what is called the *Brahmavaivarta;*
> This Purāṇa is known to have eighteen thousand [*ślokas*],
> Consisting of the Brahma-, Prakṛti-, Vighneśa- [Gaṇeśa-], and Kṛṣṇa- khaṇḍas.[27]

The NārP clearly has taken over the generally accepted Purāṇic theory of the origin of the Purāṇas from a single Purāṇa declared by Brahmā, consisting of a hundred crores of *ślokas*, which is then abridged by Vyāsa in every age into four lakhs of *ślokas*, and which is further divided into the eighteen Purāṇas in the human world.[28] The NārP then has ingeniously adapted the theory of Purāṇic origins in its explanation of the old and new BVPs.

The NārP has not kept the old MatP account separate from the description of the extant BVP, and has intertwined the two. Thus Sāvarṇi is mentioned as the narrator of the PKh, which is said to contain a *kṛṣṇamāhātmya*. And in NārP I.101.23–24, it is stated:

> Whoever, having copied this [Purāṇa], makes a gift of it during Māgha, along with a cow,

[27] NārP I.101.4–6ab.
[28] Cf. above, pp. 10–11.

He attains Brahmaloka, released from the bonds of ignorance.
And whoever reads or even listens to its list of contents,
Even he attains the desired fruit through the grace of Kṛṣṇa.

These verses implicitly testify to the Brahmāite nature of the first BVP, and the Kṛṣṇaite nature of the later. We may also note NārP I.101.3:

[The BVP] is the essence of *dharma, artha, kāma,* and *mokṣa* [the four ends of man], and is pleasing to Hari and Hara [Śiva].
The excellent *Brahmavaivarta* establishes the nondifference of these two.

The NārP, then, recognizes the Śaivite-Vaiṣṇavite character of the extant BVP.

As for the date of the NārP, Shastri assigns it to the eighth century A.D.[29] Hazra, however, has shown that the NārP is not of one date. NārP I.1–41 he dates as A.D. 875–1000 and I.42–125 (containing the description of the BVP) as "comparatively late," meaning at least after 1000.[30] A more precise dating for these latter chapters would, of course, be very helpful in determining the date of the extant BVP.

Another work that also makes reference to the extant BVP is the Nārada Pañcarātra (NārPR). According to this work:

Listening to the *Brahmavaivarta* is the supreme cause of *nirvāṇa*.
In this [Purāṇa] is explained the pure, *nirguṇa* Brahman, desired [by all].
The *Brahmavaivarta,* desired [by all], consists of four *khaṇḍas*,
Describing the manifestations of Brahma, Prakṛti, Gaṇeśa, and Kṛṣṇa.[31]

Bhandarkar asserts, regarding the date of the NārPR, that "The creed afterwards promulgated by Vallabhācārya is exactly similar to that set forth in this book. This Saṃhitā [NārPR], therefore,

29 *Catalogue,* Preface to vol. V, p. cxxxviii. Shastri elsewhere says that the BVP "must be as old as the Nārada-purāṇa, that is, between 800 to 900 A.D." (P. clix.)
30 *Purāṇic Records,* p. 132.
31 NārPR II.7.30–31.

must have been written a short time before Vallabha, that is, about the beginning of the sixteenth century."[32] Bhandarkar's statement that the NārPR doctrine is "exactly similar" to Vallabha's needs some qualification. In the NārPR, Rādhā occupies a significant position, while, as Gonda points out with reference to Vallabha's teachings: "In seinem System spielt Rādhā keine Rolle."[33] Among Vallabha's followers, however, Rādhā attained considerable importance. In any case, as we shall see, the NārPR shares many doctrines with the BVP, from which, it seems, the NārPR has borrowed them. Bhandarkar, in his statement quoted above, apparently merely assumed that the NārPR was written before Vallabha. It seems possible that the NārPR was somewhat later, but Bhandarkar is probably right in assigning it to the general period of the fifteenth-sixteenth century. The extant BVP would appear to be not much earlier than the NārPR.

Let us now turn to another type of literature that is familiar with a "BVP," namely the *smṛti*-commentaries or digests (*nibandhas*) from the twelfth century A.D. on.[34] Hazra has shown that of about 1500 lines quoted from the BVP in such works as Devanabhaṭṭa's *Smṛticandrikā* (twelfth or early thirteenth century[35]) and Gopālabhaṭṭa's *Haribhaktivilāsa* (sixteenth century), only thirty lines, except for repetitions, appear in the extant BVP.[36] All the verses that do appear in our text are from KJKh 8 and 26, dealing respectively with the *kṛṣṇajanmāṣṭamī* and *ekādaśī* rites. These facts further confirm the existence of an earlier BVP, but they also indicate that some portions of the earlier have been retained in the extant work.[37] Nonetheless, as

[32] *Vaiṣṇavism, Śaivism,* p. 41. Bhandarkar also notes here that the NārPR is not accepted as authoritative by the Rāmānuja school, and further, that the doctrine of the Vyūhas, peculiar to the Pāñcarātra school, is not found in it. The Vyūha doctrine is also absent from the BVP, despite its familiarity with Pāñcarātra literature (see below, p. 75).

[33] *Die Religionen Indiens,* II, 163. See also below, pp. 202–203.

[34] For a brief introduction to the Nibandha writers, see Kane, *History of Dharmaśāstra,* I, 246–247.

[35] This dating is according to Kane, *ibid.,* I, 344–346.

[36] *Purāṇic Records,* p. 166.

[37] At this point, it may be appropriate to note that the earlier BVP is perhaps not entirely lost. Shastri lists two fragmentary manuscripts of a BVP, called *Adi-Brahmavaivarta* in their own chapter colophons (these manuscripts are nos. 3820 and 3821, in Shastri's *Catalogue,* vol. V). Shastri says that this Adi-BVP seems to have nothing to do with Kṛṣṇa and the Prakṛtis or goddesses (*Catalogue,* vol. V, Preface, p. clix). Shastri, and

Hazra concludes, the BVP "with its present contents was not known to the writers of even the sixteenth century A.D. . . ."[38]

The evidence we have presented so far all suggests that the extant BVP in its final form dates from the fifteenth or sixteenth century.

2. Parallels to the BVP in other literature

Wilson has remarked that the BVP "records a great variety of legends of which no traces can be found in any of the other Puráńas, and it deals but sparingly in those which are common to all. It is of little value as a collateral authority, therefore, and most of the stories it contains are too insipid and absurd to deserve investigation. It contains, however, a few remarkable passages that bear an ancient character. . . ."[39] It is evident that Wilson, like so many Western scholars, was primarily interested in the earliest legends of Sanskrit literature. From such a point of view, the BVP is, indeed, of relatively little value as collateral material. However, if one is interested in the development of ancient legends, to see how a religious community has utilized, elaborated, and perhaps enriched tradition in its attempt to interpret that tradition in the light of the community's own evolv-

---

Gupta, who has briefly surveyed the chapter colophons of the Adi-BVP as given in Shastri's *Catalogue,* have emphasized the differences between the Adi-BVP and the extant BVP. (For Gupta's views, see "The Extant BVP," *Purāṇa,* III, 99–100.) But there may be significant similarities. For instance, the forty-third chapter of the Adi-BVP is called *"kalisvarūpanāmādhyāya,"* possibly corresponding to the seventh chapter of the PKh, containing a description of the Kali Yuga. The fifty-second chapter of the Adi-BVP is the *"narakahetunivedana,"* perhaps corresponding to PKh 30–31, describing the sins that lead to various hells. Of special interest is the fortieth chapter of the Adi-BVP entitled *"ekādaśīmāhātmya."* As noted above, the *ekādaśī* rite is dealt with in KJKh 26, and is one of two *smṛti* chapters that apparently belongs to both old and new BVPs. In any case, the study of the Adi-BVP manuscripts would seem to offer some hope for discovering more about the early text-history of the extant BVP. This interesting task lies beyond the scope of the present study.

38 *Purāṇic Records,* p. 166.

39 "Analysis of the Puráńas," ESL, I.91–92. Cf. Wilson's statement in *The Vishńu Puráńa,* Preface, p. LXVII: ". . . in the Prakŕiti and Gańeśa Khańḋas, are legends of these divinities, not wholly, perhaps, modern inventions, but of which the source has not been traced. In the life of Kŕishńa, the incidents recorded are the same as those narrated in the Vishńu and the Bhágavata; but the stories, absurd as they are, are much compressed to make room for original matter still more puerile and tiresome. The Brahma Vaivarta has not the slightest title to be regarded as a Puráńa."

ing historical situation, then the BVP takes on much more importance. This is especially true of the Rādhā-Kṛṣṇa materials, as Wilson himself admits, though often in a rather backhanded manner.[40] As for the statement that the BVP contains many legends not traced in other Purāṇas, this also reveals, indirectly, Wilson's "backward looking" approach to the Purāṇas. For Wilson really means, apparently, that there are no *earlier* traces of many BVP legends. As we shall see, there are significant *later* traces in various Purāṇic and other works. Wilson was very possibly unaware of, or simply disinterested in these latter, a matter of little surprise in view of his opinion that most of the BVP stories do not deserve investigation.

It turns out, in fact, that there are many too many stories and legends of the BVP occurring in either earlier or later Sanskrit literature to even begin a comprehensive study of such parallels in the scope of this work. In this section, then, I have selected a few key text-parallels for each of the four *khaṇḍas* of the BVP. They have been chosen with a view to the light they may throw on the historical and/or theological development of our text, both posterior to and prior to the compilation of the BVP itself. In some cases, a deeper analysis of the most significant parallels will be postponed to the chapters dealing directly with theological matters. The parallels selected, it should be noted, are sometimes parallel in content only, though often there is considerable identity in the literal wording as well.

a) *Parallels to the BKh*

It has been indicated above that the original BVP was the work of Brahmā worshippers. This is suggested by the title itself, which may be rendered as "The Metamorphoses of Brahmā." Although, as we have seen, the present BVP differs significantly from the earlier, the extant Purāṇa, I suggest, still bears traces of legends about these metamorphoses, principally in the BKh.[41] What, precisely, these metamorphoses are in our text is not en-

[40] See Wilson's statement quoted in the preceding note. And in his "Analysis of the Puráńas," ESL, I, 92, he says that the BVP "throws more light than any similar work upon the worship of the female principle or Prakŕiti, as well as of Kŕishńa and Rádhá."

[41] Cf. Gupta's statement: "Some meagre account of Brahmā is contained in the Brahma-Khaṇḍa only and there also he has been subordinated to Śrī-Krishṇa" ("The Extant BVP," *Purāṇa,* III, 96).

tirely clear, but clues as to what they once were are very possibly found in the ViP and BhP.

In ViP I.3.26–27, there is reference to two *mahākalpas*, constituting the first and second halves of Brahmā's life. The first is called the Pādma, the second the Vārāha. In the latter *kalpa*, according to ViP I.4.3 ff., Brahmā, identified with Nārāyaṇa, is said to have taken the form of a boar (*varāha*) in order to raise up the earth out of the primordial waters. This, incidentally, may explain the meaning of the term Brahmavarāha, as the boar incarnation of Brahmā. The history of Brahmavarāha, according to MatP 53.34, was one of the topics of the (original) BVP. This boar incarnation is usually associated with Viṣṇu or Hari, as we shall see. As for the Pādma Kalpa, it is sometimes also known as the Brāhma Kalpa,[42] but in BhP III.11.34–35, the two are distinguished. The Brāhma Kalpa is said to refer to an age at the very beginning of the first half of Brahmā's life, when he came into being. The Pādma Kalpa occurs at the end of the first half, when the world-lotus springs from the navel of Hari. Wilson says that according to a commentator, it was in the Pādma Kalpa that Brahmā was born from a lotus.[43] BhP III.11.36 then mentions the Vārāha Kalpa, of the second half of Brahmā's life, in which Hari becomes a boar (*sūkara*).

In BKh 5.4–15, there is reference to the Brāhma, Vārāha, and Pādma Kalpas. In the Brāhma Kalpa, it is said, Brahmā created the earth from the marrow of Madhu and Kaitabha, through the command of the Lord (Kṛṣṇa). In the Vārāha, Viṣṇu, in the form of a boar, raised up the earth from Rasātala. And in the Pādma, Brahmā, resting on the navel-lotus of Viṣṇu, created the three worlds. Although no definite conclusions can be made, at least until the recovery of the original BVP, there is a possibility that the original "Metamorphoses of Brahmā" referred to his creative activity in the three Kalpas. In the case of the Pādma Kalpa, the metamorphosis would refer to his birth from the world-lotus, perhaps already associated with Viṣṇu's navel-lotus. Brahmā's metamorphosis in the Vārāha Kalpa refers to his boar incarnation, as mentioned in the ViP, but which in the extant BVP has been shifted to Viṣṇu, in accord with the BhP. In the Brāhma Kalpa, Brahmā created the earth from the marrow of the two demons.

42 This is according to Wilson, *The Vishńu Puráńa*, I, 53, note 3.
43 *Ibid.*

This story is briefly mentioned at the end of BKh 4, where it appears in connection with the cosmic egg. Possibly, then, Brahmā's metamorphosis in the Brāhma Kalpa refers to his birth from the cosmic egg, a relatively ancient notion.[44]

Additional evidence favoring the above interpretation of the metamorphoses and the three Kalpas is the apparent fact that BKh 5.4–15, in which the three Kalpas are defined, does not fit properly into the text as it now stands. Both *adhyāyas* 5 and 6 seem out of place, for they interrupt the account of Brahmā's creation of the earth from the marrow of Madhu and Kaitabha, beginning in BKh 4 and continued in BKh 7. Further, BKh 5.4 states that the history of the Brahma (*sic*) Kalpa has already been narrated, and that the remaining two Kalpas will next be described. But the history of the Brāhma Kalpa, in which Brahmā creates the earth from the marrow of the demons, has been only briefly mentioned, the main account being in BKh 7.1 ff. Moreover, there does not seem to be in the extant BKh any description of the Pādma and Vārāha Kalpas. Rather, there is merely the brief definition of each of the three Kalpas in BKh 5.13–15. The fact that all three Kalpas are defined suggests that BKh 5.13–15 is not the account of the remaining two (Pādma and Vārāha) indicated in BKh 5.4. It seems at least plausible, then, that BKh 5.4–15 is based on an old fragment from the original BVP.

The above suggestions are admittedly somewhat speculative, but more in their specific details than in their general purport. For if the BVP was originally the work of a Brahmā cult, one would suppose it to have contained many legends about Brahmā, especially in his creative roles. And when the earlier BVP was revised or almost wholly rewritten by Kṛṣṇaite Vaiṣṇavas, Brahmā's functions in many cases would naturally have been taken over by Kṛṣṇa. One apparent example of this is found in the account of the emanation of various gods and goddesses from Kṛṣṇa's body in BKh 3–4. Included among the emanations is Dharma from Kṛṣṇa's breast (*vakṣas*),[45] and Kāma from his heart (*mānasa*).[46] In BhP III.12, various gods and sages are described as arising from Brahmā's body, including Dharma from his breast

[44] See below, pp. 172–174.
[45] BKh 3.41–43.
[46] BKh 4.6–7.

(*stana*),[47] and Kāma from, or in, his heart (*hṛd*).[48] We shall study later another example where Brahmā's role has apparently been taken over by Kṛṣṇa.[49] In any case, in the BKh as it now stands, Brahmā clearly is subordinated to Kṛṣṇa. Our text thus represents a rather late phase in the long decline of Brahmā beginning at least in late epic times.

b) *Parallels to the PKh*

The PKh is mainly concerned with the description of several goddesses, their deeds and worship. These goddesses are conceived as parts or fractions of Prakṛti. Several of the legends about individual goddesses may be traced back to earlier Purāṇas and the Epics. For instance, the story of Sāvitrī and Satyavat, in PKh 24 ff., goes back to the Sāvitryupākhyāna of MBh 277–283. And many of the legends connected with Durgā, in PKh 57 ff., go back at least to the famous *Devīmāhātmya* of the MārkP, to which we shall have occasion to refer later.[50] Yet the PKh also contains many legends of relatively late origin, some of which occur in other late literature. These legends, in some cases, may have been original with the BVP and then were taken over by other works. The legends of later origin concern especially Rādhā and her relations with other goddesses. Hazra states, for instance, that the *Mahābhāgavata Purāṇa*, the *Bṛhaddharma Purāṇa*, and the DBhP all contain the story of Gaṅgā's origin from the liquefied bodies of Rādhā and Kṛṣṇa, who had "melted" upon hearing Śiva's praise of Kṛṣṇa.[51] This story is also found in PKh 10.114 ff. As we shall see shortly, the DBhP has almost certainly borrowed from the PKh. Hazra does not venture to say what historical relationships may exist between the various accounts, but I would suspect that the BVP's is the most original.[52] Both the NārP and the NārPR contain brief accounts of legends about Rādhā as Prakṛti. These accounts are of great importance for the theological development of the doctrine of Prakṛti, and we shall postpone consideration of them.[53] Another late work, the *Śiva Purāṇa*, has utilized a part of the PKh account concerning

[47] BhP III.12.25.
[48] BhP III.12.26. Cf. ViP I.5.28 ff.
[49] See below, pp. 175–176.
[50] See pp. 187, 190, below.
[51] "The Devī-bhāgavata," JORM, XXI, 75.
[52] We shall see below, pp. 165–166, that there are certain reasons for thinking that the *Mahābhāgavata Purāṇa* is later than the BVP.
[53] See pp. 158–162, 164–165, below.

Tulsi and her husband Śankhacūḍa.[54] These various parallels help to establish a relative chronology of the BVP with other works, but too little research has been done on the late materials to be able as yet to say much about an absolute chronology of the texts.

One of the most interesting and significant parallels to the PKh is found in the ninth *skandha* of the DBhP. The first forty-nine *adhyāyas* (out of fifty) of DBhP IX are in large part literally identical with PKh 1–47.[55] The DBhP has sometimes altered the PKh reading, in order to show the superiority of Devī over Kṛṣṇa. Often the DBhP has merely substituted the name of Devī for Kṛṣṇa.[56] That the DBhP has borrowed from the PKh and not vice versa is made evident by the many instances in the DBhP in which verses proclaming the superiority of the Devī occur in passages still retaining the view of Kṛṣṇa as supreme. A few parallel passages from the PKh and the DBhP, illustrating the manner in which the latter has utilized and reinterpreted the former, have been gathered together in Appendix A. Hazra dates the DBhP as no later than A.D. 1200, on the basis of its being mentioned, explicitly or implicitly, in the commentaries of Śrīdhara (on the BhP) and others.[57] But it seems hardly possible for the ninth *skandha* of the DBhP to have belonged to the Purāṇa at this time.

The parallels mentioned above indicate that the PKh has played a significant role in the transmission, elaboration, and interpretation of goddess mythologies. The PKh, in gathering together many ancient materials into a sort of encyclopaedia of goddesses, also developed a comprehensive theology of the Divine in its feminine manifestations. The PKh, in addition, served as a point of departure for further developments in feminine theology, the clearest example being found in the DBhP.

c) *Parallels to the GKh*

This *khaṇḍa*, dealing with the birth of Gaṇeśa and other legends regarding the elephant-headed god, is perhaps the least

[54] Cf. Hazra, "The Problems Relating to the Śiva-Purāṇa," *Our Heritage*, I, 65. *Śiva Purāṇa* II.5.28–41 roughly follows PKh 16–21. The relatively marked subordination of Śiva to Kṛṣṇa in the PKh account is considerably softened in the *Śiva Purāṇa*.

[55] Cf. Hazra, "The Devī-bhāgavata," JORM, XXI, 68, note 66.

[56] Hazra gives a few examples in *ibid.*

[57] "The Devī-bhāgavata," JORM, XXI, 70. Cf. Sharma, "Verbal Similarities between the Durgā-Sapta-Śati and the Devī-Bhāgavata-Purāṇa and Other Considerations Bearing on Their Date," *Purāṇa*, V, 110.

paralleled of all the *khaṇḍas* of the BVP.[58] However, one significant parallel occurs in the BAP. The BAP, and the VāyuP, according to Pargiter, are two of the oldest Purāṇas and were originally one.[59] After the original Purāṇa was split into two text-versions, new sections came to be added to either one or the other. These additions are easily detected, as they appear in only one version, the BAP or VāyuP, but not in both. Kirfel has made a chapter-concordance of the two Purāṇas, in order to show what special sections appear in each.[60] The BAP contains two special sections, the major one being III.21–58 (in the Veṅk). This section tells the story of Rāma Jāmadagnya, including his encounter with Gaṇeśa, in which the latter lost one of his tusks. S. N. Roy has pointed out that Rādhā appears in the BAP legend in a rather exalted position. Roy concludes that the description of Rādhā in the BAP is close to the views of the KJKh of the BVP.[61] Roy is certainly correct in sensing the similarity between the BAP and the BVP, but he was apparently unaware that the BAP section contains direct parallels, not with the KJKh, but with the last several chapters of the GKh, both in general content, and occasionally in actual wording.[62] It seems more likely that the BAP has borrowed from the GKh and not vice versa, for the role of Rādhā in the BAP legend is more developed. In both the GKh and BAP, it is related how Paraśurāma, a devotee of Śiva, cuts off one of the tusks of Gaṇeśa, the son of Pārvatī or Durgā. She becomes incensed at Paraśurāma. In the GKh version, she is appeased by Viṣṇu. In the BAP, first Kṛṣṇa tries to overcome Pārvatī's anger, but only Rādhā is finally able to calm the irate goddess. In the GKh account, Rādhā appears only in a eulogy by Paraśurāma of Durgā, identified with Rādhā. It seems unlikely that the compiler of the BVP, had he been borrowing from the BAP, would have reduced Rādhā's role in this way. Later, we shall see that various notions relating to Rādhā in her cosmogonic role and which almost certainly were first developed in the BVP, appear also in the BAP. Accordingly, Roy's dating of the insertion

[58] See Wilson, "Analysis of the Puráńas," ESL, I, 103, 120. Cf. Farquhar, *Outline,* p. 271.

[59] *Ancient Indian Historical Tradition,* pp. 23, 77–78.

[60] *Das Purāṇa Pañcalakṣaṇa,* Einleitung, pp. XII–XIII.

[61] "On the Date of the Brahmāṇḍapurāṇa," *Purāṇa,* V, 318.

[62] For examples of literal parallels, cf. BAP III.39.1 ff. and GKh 36.1 ff.; BAP III.40.60cd–63 and GKh 40.18cd–21; BAP III.41.47–50 and GKh 42.16–19ab, and so forth.

of the Paraśurāma legend into the BAP around A.D. 1000 is a few centuries too early.[63]

d) *Parallels to the KJKh*

Extended accounts of the Kṛṣṇa legend occur in HV II.1 ff., ViP V.1 ff., BhP X.1 ff., BrahmaP 181.5 ff., PadP VI.245 ff. (Veṅk) or 272 ff. (Ānand), as well as in BVP IV (KJKh).1 ff.[64] The oldest of these accounts is the HV, upon which the others are modelled. In the Vaiṣṇava tradition, it is the BhP that has been especially cherished. Ingalls has pointed out that the HV is the least brahmanical-orthodox of the accounts. The ViP "pietizes" the adventures of Kṛṣṇa, while the BhP "transforms them through its doctrine of mystical love."[65] Ingalls compares the HV to the root of the tree of the Kṛṣṇaite tradition, the BhP to its trunk, and such works as Jayadeva's *Gīta Govinda* and the poems of Sūr Dās to its branches.[66] The BVP may be considered as one of these branches. It has eroticized the Kṛṣṇa legend, largely by the introduction of Rādhā, and goes far beyond the mystical-erotic tendencies of the BhP. Rādhā appears neither in the ViP nor the BhP, though already in the former, there is mention of a favorite *gopī* of Kṛṣṇa, who later becomes identified with Rādhā.

The love of Rādhā and Kṛṣṇa was immortalized by the *Gīta Govinda* of Jayadeva (twelfth century A.D.). The opening stanza of this poem may possibly refer to an incident described in KJKh 15.[67] In the latter, it is related how Nanda (Kṛṣṇa's foster father), caught in a rainstorm in the forest, entrusted the babe Kṛṣṇa to Rādhā who happened by. Rādhā then carried Kṛṣṇa away, when suddenly he disappeared from her lap, to reappear as a young man in a magically constructed Rāsamaṇḍala, where they were married by Brahmā. They then indulged in amorous sports. In the first verse of the *Gīta Govinda,* Nanda apparently asks Rādhā to take Kṛṣṇa home, as the sky is dark and cloudy. Rādhā and

[63] "On the Date of the Brahmāṇḍapurāṇa," *Purāṇa,* V, 319.

[64] See Ruben's concordance of these accounts in his *Krishna, Konkordanz und Kommentar,* pp. 297–318. See also Kirfel's "Kṛṣṇa's Jugendgeschichte in den Purāṇa," *Beiträge zur Literaturwissenschaft und Geistesgeschichte Indiens,* pp. 299–300. Kirfel mentions that a long account of Kṛṣṇa occurs in the Purāṇic *Gargasaṃhitā,* 1 ff. He also gives references to several short accounts of the Kṛṣṇa legend.

[65] "The *Harivaṃśa* as a *Mahākāvya,*" *Mélanges D'Indianisme,* p. 384.

[66] *Ibid.,* pp. 384–385.

[67] Cf. De, VFM, pp. 8–9; A. K. Majumdar, "Rādhā Cult," ABORI, XXXVI, 248–249; B. Majumdar, *Kṛṣṇa in History and Legend,* p. 195.

Kṛṣṇa then go off to a jungle bower, on the banks of the Yamunā, where they engage in their love-making.[68] Despite the parallels, there is little evidence for supposing that Jayadeva knew of the BVP. Both probably relied on older, unknown sources.[69] The BVP differs markedly from Jayadeva on two points: Rādhā in the BVP is a goddess, but in the *Gīta Govinda* she appears in her human aspect, and she is married to Kṛṣṇa in the BVP, but not in the *Gīta Govinda,* at least not explicitly. In this respect, we may note, the BVP is opposed to the *parakīyā* doctrine (that Rādhā is the mistress of Kṛṣṇa) that prevailed in late Bengal Vaiṣṇavism.

Our preliminary survey shows that the extant BVP belongs to the late medieval Kṛṣṇaite movement of North India. It seems closely related to both the Vallabha and Caitanya schools. Though it is doubtful that the BVP could have been the work of Nimbārka's immediate followers, as Farquhar suggests, Nimbārkite influence can hardly be ruled out in a work that attempts to embrace several points of view.[70] More definite historical conclusions, and the possible influence of the BVP on later religious developments, must await consideration of the theological doctrines of the BVP.[71]

[68] *meghair meduram ambaraṃ vanabhuvaḥ śyāmāstamāladrumair naktaṃ*
bhīrur ayaṃ tvam eva tad imaṃ rādhe gṛhaṃ prāpaya/
itthaṃ nandanideśataś calitatayoḥ pratyadhvakuñjadrumaṃ
rādhāmādhavayor jayanti yamunākūle rahaḥkelayaḥ//

For various traditional interpretations of this stanza, see B. Majumdar, *Kṛṣṇa in History and Legend,* p. 195.

[69] Cf. De, VFM, p. 10.

[70] De writes: "The suggestion that the whole of the Uttara-khaṇḍa of the Purāṇa [the KJKh] is a Nimbārkite interpolation is hardly convincing . . . the exaltation of Rādhā is a distinctive feature of the Purāṇa as well as of Jayadeva and of Nimbārka sect. It is possible that Jayadeva derived and developed his erotic mysticism from the same source as Nimbārka himself; and to the same obscure source probably the writer of the latter portion of the Purāṇa was indebted for his extremely sensuous treatment of the Rādhā-legend" (VFM, pp. 9–10).

[71] See chapter 11 below.

3

Theological Strands in the *Brahmavaivarta Purāṇa*

In some respects it is misleading to speak of a theology of the BVP. First, there is not one theology in our Purāṇa, but rather a number of theological strands: popular, Tāntric, Śaivite, Vaiṣṇavite and others. Further, each of these has undergone a long process of development, with older notions and ideas being preserved side by side with the new. Each main theological strand, therefore, is made up of a number of threads. Finally, the various strands or threads have been interwoven or synthesized in a variety of ways in different parts of the BVP.

It must be emphasized that the diverse theological views and viewpoints were not considered as discordant by the Purāṇic compilers. Yet, as we have seen, the extant BVP is a product of a Vaiṣṇavite-Kṛṣṇaite school. Kṛṣṇaism forms the basic theological framework, within which the other viewpoints are accommodated. In the process of adaptation and synthesis, a new structure was created: the emerging feminine theology associated with Rādhā as Prakṛti. We shall deal then with the theology of the BVP in two parts. In the first, we shall outline the main features of the Kṛṣṇaism that appear in our text and attempt to place it within the general development of Vaiṣṇava theology. Accordingly, chapters four to six below (Part B) will analyze the BVP's conception of Kṛṣṇa, of his devotees, and of the nature of salvation. This will be done with minimal reference to the theological ideas relating to Rādhā and Prakṛti. Some distortion as a result will be unavoidable, but this approach will hopefully allow for a clearer understanding and appreciation of the evolving "Rādhāism." This latter will be outlined in chapters seven to ten (Part C), on the relation of Rādhā or Prakṛti to Kṛṣṇa, her cosmogonic and her redemptive roles.

Before treating of the special topics in the Kṛṣṇaite theology, it will be helpful to discuss the relationship of the Kṛṣṇaite to some of the other theological strands. The rest of this chapter will briefly consider the popular, Tāntric, and Śaivite strands, and the Vaiṣṇavite-Kṛṣṇaite evaluation and synthesis of them.

1. The popular strand

For the most part, there is little explicitly articulated "popular theology" in the BVP, in the sense of abstract philosophizing and formulation of doctrines. Rather, such theology is found attached to the tales and legends taken over from popular folklore and embedded in many of the ritual observances. These legends and rites form a large part of the materials upon which the more intellectually structured doctrines are based, so it would be wrong in this sense to make a rigid distinction between popular and scholastic or intellectual. What is meant by "popular theology" in the present context is the common or worldly understanding of, and approach to, the legends and rituals, in contrast to the higher understanding of the Vaiṣṇavas. Let us give some examples.

Underlying such popular theology seems to be the notion of a multitude of powers in the cosmos. In the PKh, for instance, we find several goddesses charged with a variety of tasks and responsibilities. Sarasvatī oversees all knowledge and by her grace a fool may become wise.[1] Ṣaṣṭhī is the presiding deity of children, guarding them from misfortune.[2] Manasā protects men from snake-bite.[3] Rādhā is the presiding deity of love (*preman*) and life, and through reciting or hearing her eulogies, a man or woman may attain a good spouse, as well as wealth and other benefits.[4] It is especially Lakṣmī, though, who is associated with wealth and fortune.[5] And there are many others. The BVP by no

1 PKh 4.11.
2 PKh 43.4–6.
3 PKh 45.10. Cf. PKh 46.145–147.
4 PKh 1.45; 55.92–101.
5 PKh 35.34.

means denies the powers residing in the various deities, but it is generally understood that they all derive ultimately from Kṛṣṇa or Hari. This is made quite explicit in the story of Ṣaṣṭhī, related in PKh 43. A king, whose son was still-born, beseeches the goddess to restore the infant to life. Ṣaṣṭhī replies:

> I [am able to] give sons to those without sons . . .
>
> . . . .
>
> Through *karma* a man is endowed with many sons or is without descendants.
>
> . . . .
>
> Through *karma* a man's son is born dead; through *karma* [his sons] are long-lived;
> Through *karma* they are endowed with virtues or lacking in limbs.
> Therefore, O King, *karma* is supreme over all, according to *śruti*.
> It is the Bhagavat, Hari, who bears the form of *karma*, and by its means he bestows the fruits [of action].[6]

Ṣaṣṭhī then easily revives the king's dead child by means of her divine knowledge.

The true Vaiṣṇava already understands that Kṛṣṇa is the ultimate source of all favors and the author of *karma*. The difference in understanding between the Vaiṣṇava and the common man, however, is not primarily a matter of intellectual awareness, according to the BVP, but a question of a person's whole inner orientation, the proper conditioning of his heart. The common devotee performs worship for a variety of purposes, including both mundane and otherworldly goals such as *mokṣa*.[7] The highest devotee, though, has no personal desires, even for *mokṣa*.[8] The worship of the common man represents a valid but initial stage of devotion below that of disinterested *bhakti*.

2. Śāktism (Tāntrism)

Tāntric doctrines and practices have thoroughly pervaded the BVP. Regarding doctrinal aspects, it is especially the view of the Absolute as a union of the male and female principles of the

[6] PKh 43.27a, 29ab, 30–31.
[7] PKh 23.82.
[8] See pp. 93 ff., below.

universe that has deeply influenced our Purāṇa. Among the Śāktas, these two principles are identified with Śiva and Durgā respectively. Every existing masculine and feminine entity is but a manifestation of these two. Śāktism further has raised the female above the male. Durgā is the Śakti, the energy of the cosmos. Without her, the world is lifeless, and even Śiva is merely a corpse (*śava*).[9]

In the BVP it is said that the world without Durgā, "though living, is dead as it were."[10] And Śiva says to Durgā, "I, the Lord of all, am as a corpse without you."[11] Such notions also occur in the Vaiṣṇava strand of our text. Thus the gods say to Padmā (Lakṣmī) that "the world is as though dead without you."[12] Kṛṣṇa himself confesses to Rādhā, "Without you I am lifeless in all actions."[13] The interaction between the Śākta and Vaiṣṇava views, especially concerning the relation of Rādhā and Durgā, is complex, and we shall postpone further consideration of these doctrinal aspects to the chapters dealing with Prakṛti. The few examples above should be sufficient to show the openness of our text to Tāntric theological ideas.

As for Tāntric practices in our Purāṇa, among the standard topics relating to the various goddesses described in the PKh are included *pūjāvidhi* (rules of ritual worship), *kavaca* (amulets) and *mantra* (sacred formulas or prayers).[14] In addition, throughout the BVP, there are frequent references to *bhūtaśuddhi* (purification of the bodily elements), *prāṇāyāma* (breath control), *nyāsa* (placing the fingers or palms of the hands on various parts of the body), *mudrā* (mystical gesture), *bīja* (root or seed syllable of a *mantra*), *maṇḍala* (geometric diagram) and other meditative aids.[15] Some of these are general yogic practices,

[9] We may note here a play on the words *śiva* and *śava*. In the Devanāgarī, these are and The letter ("i") is said to represent the Śakti, without whom, then, becomes . See Zimmer, *Myths and Symbols in Indian Art and Civilization*, p. 206. Cf. Avalon, *Principles of Tantra*, I, 366.

[10] PKh 2.76.

[11] KJKh 43.8. Cf. GKh 2.11.

[12] KJKh 56.76. Cf. PKh 1.29.

[13] PKh 55.81.

[14] Gupta has cited the prevalence of these, especially in the PKh and the GKh, as further proof of the late origin of the extant BVP ("The Extant BVP," *Purāṇa* III, 98).

[15] In our text, *bhūtaśuddhi, prāṇāyāma,* and *nyāsa,* along with *kavaca, stotra, dhyāna,* and *pūjā,* often occur as successive steps of meditation and/or worship of a god or goddess. See, for example, BKh 26.94 ff.; PKh

such as *prāṇāyāma*, but others are more specifically Tāntric, such as *nyāsa* and *maṇḍala*, though these also are not confined to Tāntric circles. In any case, these clearly appear in specifically Tāntric forms in the BVP.[16]

Our Purāṇa is also thoroughly familiar with the Tāntric theory of the six *cakras* (vital centers of the body). In KJKh 110.6 ff., knowledge is said to be of five kinds. The first concerns the purification of the *nāḍīs* (energy paths), piercing of the *cakras*, and the worship of the Lord united with the *kuṇḍalinī* (the serpent power). The *cakraṣaṭka* (sixfold centers) are specifically named.[17] In BKh 13.12, the *gandharva* Upavarhana leaves his body by passing through or piercing the six *cakras*, blocking the sixteen *nāḍīs* such as *iḍā* and *suṣumnā*, then leading his vital wind to the *brahmarandhra* (aperture at the crown of the head), where he unites himself with the Ātman. In GKh 35.3 ff., Manoramā dies in a similar manner, confining her breath in the *brahmarandhra* conjoined with the thousand-petalled lotus (*sa-*

55.7 ff.; and 64.2 ff. (Cf. Avalon, *Principles of Tantra*, II, Introduction, pp. lxxxvii f.) *Nyāsas* are of various kinds. BKh 26.94–95 refers to *aṅgāṅgayor nyāsa, mantranyāsa*, and *varṇanyāsa*. PKh 55.7 refers to *mantranyāsa* and *karāṅganyāsa*. PKh 64.2 refers to a threefold *nyāsa* (*nyāsatraya*): *svakara, aṅgāṅga*, and *mantra*. PKh 64.33 refers to *jīvanyāsa*. For a discussion of the general meaning and various types of *nyāsas*, see Avalon, *Principles of Tantra* II, 365, 373–380. See also Avalon, *The Great Liberation*, pp. 41–42 (on *kara-* and *aṅga- nyāsa*); and Woodroffe, *Shakti and Shâkta*, pp. 517–521. For *mudrā* in our text, see GKh 29.31, where Śiva is instructing on the mystery of Brahman by *tattvamudrā*. For *bīja*, see KJKh 123.55 (Ānand).

Regarding the *maṇḍalas*, these are geometric patterns incorporating squares, circles, triangles, often in lotus-shaped designs. Various goddesses or *śaktis* are then represented in the corners of the triangles, or on the petals of the lotuses. The lotuses may be of six, eight, twelve, sixteen, or thirty-two petals. (See Avalon, *Tantrik Texts*, VIII [*Tantrarāja Tantra*, Part I], Introduction, pp. 17–18; XII [*Tantrarāja Tantra*, Part II], Introduction, p. 37.) In PKh 64.56 and BKh 26.95, there are references to a triangular *maṇḍala* (*trikoṇamaṇḍala*), and in 64.81–87, to an eight-petalled lotus (*aṣṭadala*), on which the eight *nāyikās* are to be worshipped. (On the *nāyikās*, see Monier-Williams, *Brāhmanism and Hindūism*, p. 188.) In the center, nine *śaktis* are also to be worshipped. These nine are: Brahmāṇī, Vaiṣṇavī, Raudrī, Maheśvarī, Narasiṃhī, Vārāhī, Indrāṇī, Kārttikī, and Sarvamaṅgalā. These are the *mātrikās*, or mothers of the universe and manifestations of the supreme Śakti. They are usually eight, though sometimes nine, sixteen, or more. (See Monier-Williams, *Brāhmanism and Hindūism*, p. 188. Cf. Avalon, *Tantrik Texts*, VIII, Introduction, p. 8.)

[16] See preceding footnote.

[17] The six are: *mūlādhāra, svādhiṣṭhāna, maṇipūra, anāhata, viśuddha*, and *ājñā*. For a rather lengthy discussion of these *cakras*, see Avalon, *The Serpent Power*, pp. 102–180.

hasradala). Brahmā commits suicide in this way in KJKh 35.68 ff. Of special interest is the description of Brahmā's meditation in KJKh 20. This chapter deals with Brahmā's theft of Kṛṣṇa's companions and their cows. Kṛṣṇa recreated all that was stolen by his *māyā,* maintaining the illusion for a year. Brahmā himself became deluded, seeing Kṛṣṇa everywhere. Brahmā then,

> Assuming the posture of meditation, folded his hands together,
> His hair standing erect, tears in his eyes, like one distressed.
> Iḍā, Suṣumnā, Madhyā, Piṅgalā, Nalinī, Dhurā
> These six *nāḍīs*, by yoga, obstructing with effort,
> Mūlādhāra, Svādhiṣṭhāna, Maṇipūra, Manohara,[18]
> Viśuddha, and Paramājñā, these six *cakras* also obstructing,
> Brahmā caused the vital wind to ascend the six *cakras* in order,
> Leading it to the Brahmarandhra and confining it there.
> Then he brought the Madhyā into his lotus-heart,
> And caused the vital wind, turning it about, to unite with the Madhyā.
> ....
> Uttering the supreme *mantra* of Hari, having ten syllables . . .
> Meditating on his lotus-feet . . .
> He [Brahmā] beheld in his lotus-heart a mass of light.
> In the midst of the light was a beautiful form,
> Two-armed, flute in hand, adorned in yellow dress [i.e. Kṛṣṇa],
> ....
> Who was observed in his Brahmarandhra, in his heart, and in the external world.[19]

This passage shows the synthesis of the emotionalistic Vaiṣṇavite devotionalism (hair standing erect, tears in the eyes[20]) with Tāntric meditation. It may be noted that the parallel account of Brahmā's theft and becoming deluded in the BhP (X.13) has no reference to this Tāntric meditation. The BhP, though, considered Viṣṇu to reside in the lotus-heart of his devotees,[21] while in

18 Manohara is an unusual name for Anāhata.
19 KJKh 20.26–30, 31cd–33, 35ab.
20 For these emotional marks of *bhakti,* see below, pp. 91–92.
21 *tvaṃ* [Viṣṇu] *bhāvayogaparibhāvitahṛtsaroja āsse* . . ./ (BhP III.9.11)

Tāntrism, the lotus-heart is the place where the *iṣṭadevatā* is to be meditated upon.[22] The synthesis of Tāntric meditation theory with Kṛṣṇaite *bhakti* was thus easily accomplished.

It is evident that our text readily accepts the Tāntric meditative practices and theory, but certain Tāntric rites or customs are much less enthusiastically embraced. Let us consider first the practice of animal sacrifice. In KJKh 91.21 ff., there is reference to animal sacrifices to the goddess Bhavānī, the presiding deity of Vṛndāvana, the sacred home of Kṛṣṇa. In PKh 42.84, and 54.47, human sacrifice (*naramedhaka*) appears as an accepted rite. And in PKh 64.92 ff., we find the following rules for sacrifice:

> O best of saints [Nārada], hear the rules for sacrifice.
> An auspicious man,[23] buffalo, goat, sheep, and so forth may be offered.
> Durgā is pleased for a thousand years by the offering of a man,
> A hundred years by a buffalo, ten years by a goat.
> . . . .
> O best of saints, hear the way of human sacrifice.
> I shall tell of it as it is stated in the *Atharva Veda*. Transgression of these rules will destroy the fruit.
> [The victim should be] without father or mother, young, free of disease,
> Married, initiated, leaving alone the wives of others,
> Of legitimate birth, pure, of virtuous Śūdra parents.
> Having purchased him from his relatives for a good price,
> The sacrificer should bathe him and then perform *pūjā* with cloth and sandal.
> The victim should then be made to wander for a year . . .
> At the end of which he should be presented and given over to Durgā.
> . . . .
> A wise man, having praised and offered up the victim, should grasp his amulet,
> And bowing prostrate on the ground, give the priest his fee.

22 See Avalon, *The Serpent Power*, p. 120.

23 The word is *māyāti*. According to Monier-Williams' Dictionary, there is some question about the meaning of the word, but it apparently refers to *narabali*. His reference is the BVP. Monier-Williams has relied on Böthlingk, who took his information from the *Śabdakalpadruma*, which quotes *māyāti* from the PKh.

Interestingly, the KālP, dated by Payne as probably from the fourteenth century,[24] says in its Rudhirādhyāya (Blood Chapter) that Devī is satisfied by the sacrifice of a man for a thousand years, and by three men for a hundred thousand.[25] The KālP also gives the following *mantra,* to be said to the victim just before the slaughter:

> O victim, excellent in form, you have been obtained by my good fortune.
> Therefore I bow [to you], having the form of all, and the form of the victim.
> Through an offering pleasing to Caṇḍikā, you destroy the misfortune of the sacrificer;
> Honor to thee, O victim, fit as a sacrifice to Vaiṣṇavī.
> Beasts were created for the sake of sacrifice by Svayaṃbhū himself.
> Thus I shall kill you today, since in a sacrifice, slaughter is no slaughter.[26]

Let us note the mention of Vaiṣṇavī, which apparently refers to the name of a goddess.[27] The sacrifice of a victim to Vaiṣṇavī, according to this passage, entails no sin, as sacrificial killing is not murder. It is possible that Vaiṣṇavī here is another name of

24 *The Śāktas,* p. 9.

25 *nareṇa balinā devī sahasraṃ parivatsarān/*
vidhidattena cāpnoti tṛptiṃ lakṣaṃ tribhir naraiḥ//
(KālP 71.18)

This passage is quoted in English translation by Payne, *The Śāktas,* p. 10. An English translation of the whole of the Blood Chapter (*adhyāya* 71 in the Veṅk) appears in *Asiatic Researches,* V (1799), 371–391.

26 *varas tvaṃ bale* [text has *bāle*] *rūpeṇa mama bhāgyād upasthitaḥ//*
praṇanāmi tataḥ sarvarūpiṇaṃ balirūpiṇam/
caṇḍikāprītidānena dātur āpadvināśana//
vaiṣṇavībalirūpāya bale tubhyaṃ namo namaḥ/
yajñārthe paśavaḥ sṛṣṭāḥ svayam eva svayaṃbhuvā//
atas tvāṃ ghātayāmy adya tasmād yajñe vadho 'vadhaḥ/
(KālP 57.8–11)

This appears in English translation in Karmarkar, *The Vrātya or Dravidian Systems,* p. 212, but no reference is given in the KālP. This passage is not from the "Blood Chapter" (*adhyāya* 71), but the two *adhyāyas,* 57 and 71, share many verses. Thus, 57.10cd–11ab has the following parallel in 71.39:
yajñarthe paśavaḥ sṛṣṭāḥ svayam eva svayaṃbhuvā/
atas tvāṃ ghātayiṣyāmi tasmād yajñe vadho 'vadhaḥ//

27 The KālP says that the rules of sacrifice are given in the Vaiṣṇavī Tantra (KālP 71.2) and thus Vaiṣṇavī may refer to the sacrifices as prescribed by this text.

Caṇḍikā, though this is not certain. We may compare the above with PKh 65.10–12:

> By the offering of a victim, O Brahman [Nārada], Durgā is pleased with men,
> But the sin of slaughter is incurred, there is no doubt.
> The dedicator, donor, slaughterer, nourisher, protector,
> And the two binders [of the victim], these seven share in the murder.
> "Whoever kills another is slain by him in turn," thus the Vedas proclaim.
> For this reason, Vaiṣṇavas perform Vaiṣṇavī-*pūjā*.[28]

Here, Vaiṣṇavī may refer to the mode of worship belonging to the Vaiṣṇavas, but also to the goddess Vaiṣṇavī. At times, in the BVP, Vaiṣṇavī appears as a name of Durgā.[29] But Vaiṣṇavī and Durgā also are seen as two different forms of Bhagavatī, with important differences in their respective worship. Thus in PKh 64.45–49:

> *Sāttvikī*, *rājasī*, and *tāmasī*, these are the three kinds of worship
> Of Bhagavatī, declared in the Vedas. They are the best, intermediate, and worst.
> That of the Vaiṣṇavas is *sāttvikī;* of the Śāktas and so forth, *rājasī;*
> Of the uninitiated, the unvirtuous and the forest tribes, *tāmasī*.
> The best, which is void of slaughter, is Vaiṣṇavī *pūjā*.
> Vaiṣṇavas go to Goloka through the favor of Vaiṣṇavī.
> The worship of Maheśvarī [Durgā] is *rājasī* and involves the offering of victims.
> Śāktas and others, of *rājasa* nature, go thereby to Kailāsa.
> The mountain tribes go to hell through *tāmasī pūjā*.[30]

Payne asserts that animal sacrifice, at one time, was probably performed in all Hindu temples. It was first abandoned by the Vaiṣṇavas, and then by the Śaivas, till only Śāktas today practice it. Payne further says that animal sacrifice may never have been

[28] This is a translation of the Vaṅg. The Veṅk and Ānand are seriously altered and make little sense.

[29] E.g., PKh 57.3.

[30] Again, the Vaṅg has the best reading.

permitted in *pañcāyatana* temples.[31] As we shall soon see, the BVP accepted the idea of *pañcāyatanapūjā*, with some modifications.[32]

Blood sacrifice is common to both the so-called Right-hand and Left-hand Śāktas. The latter are famous for their *cakrapūjā*, the worship involving the *pañcatattva*, or five *makāras*: *madya, māṃsa, matsya, mudrā,* and *maithuna.*[33] The BVP, as far as I know, makes no specific reference to the *pañcatattva.* It does, however, mildly censure the eating of fish (*matsya*) and meat (*māṃsa*).[34] Yet our Purāṇa does not seem overly concerned with meat-eating or with the other *makāras*, with the exception of *maithuna* (sexual intercourse). Our text repeatedly condemns intercourse with any woman except one's own wife, all others being of prohibited degree.[35] It is uncertain, though, how prevalent among the Vāmācārins (left-handed Tāntrics) was the practice of intercourse with women not one's wife.[36] In any case, in PKh 7.16, it is stated that among the evils of the *kali* age, "All men, lying and deceitful, will delight in the Vāmācāra path."[37]

It seems, then, that the BVP generally accepts the theological and philosophical tenets of Tāntrism, and many of its practices. Certain rites or customs, however, are regarded with considerable reserve, and the Vāmācāra is specifically condemned.

3. Śaivism

Earlier we referred to the cooperation of Śaivites and Vaiṣṇavites in producing the extant BVP.[38] It was pointed out that Śiva, with Viṣṇu, is considered as *sāttvika.* Brahmā is regarded as *rājasa* and Kālāgnirudra as *tāmasa.* Kṛṣṇa, though, is *nirguṇa* (beyond the

[31] Payne, *op. cit.*, p. 11.

[32] See below, pp. 51 ff.

[33] For a brief and clear account of the *cakrapūjā* and the five *tattvas*, see "Chakrapūjā" in Walker, *The Hindu World.*

[34] In PKh 23.37, a Brahman who eats fish is said to lose his privileges or prerogatives. In PKh 30.58, a Brahman who eats fish or meat for his own sake goes to hell. A similar stricture is given in PKh 58.92.

[35] See, for instance, PKh 58.30; 58.66; KJKh 30.86 ff.

[36] See Woodroffe, *Shakti and Shâkta*, pp. 553–580, esp. pp. 556, 560, 566–567, 578–80. Woodroffe's approach, as is well known, is highly apologetic, but he does at least show the many restraints on the sexual-yogic practices of the Tāntrics.

[37] *vāmācāraratāḥ sarve mithyākāpaṭyasaṃyutāḥ/*

[38] See pp. 25–26 above.

three qualities of *sattva, rajas,* and *tamas*).[39] There is thus a general subordination of Śiva to Kṛṣṇa. This is seen in many other ways. There are, for instance, three eternal worlds according to our text, Śivaloka, Vaikuṇṭha, and Goloka.[40] This indicates the high favor in which Śiva is held, but Śivaloka, with Vaikuṇṭha, is found to be far below Goloka, the world of Kṛṣṇa, above which there is no other world. In addition, Śiva is said to be a portion of Kṛṣṇa[41] and to arise out of the left side of Kṛṣṇa's body.[42] Also there are said to exist numberless universes, each containing a Brahmā, Viṣṇu, and Śiva.[43] And in the KJKh, we have two accounts of the humbling of Śiva by Kṛṣṇa.[44]

Despite Śiva's humiliation, he is still dearly beloved by Kṛṣṇa. The BVP says it is a sin to slander Śiva, who is dearer to Kṛṣṇa than his own life.[45] Kṛṣṇa himself declares:

> Among my favorites, a Brahman is dear to me.
> Lakṣmī, ever residing on my breast, is dearer than a Brahman.
> Rādhā is yet dearer, and my devotees are dearer still.
> Dearest of all is Śaṃkara [Śiva]; no one is dearer than he.
>
> . . . .
>
> My heart resides with my devotees, my life with Rādhā,
> My Self with Śaṃkara, who is dearer than my life.[46]

It is a doctrine of our Purāṇa that "those who are the excellent portions of Kṛṣṇa are intensely devoted to him."[47] It is not surprising then that Śiva, a portion of Kṛṣṇa, is his devotee. We find

[39] BKh 8.19–21. Cf. LiṅgP I.1.22, where Kālarudra is *tāmasa,* Brahmā is *rājasa,* Viṣṇu is *sāttvika,* and Maheśvara (Śiva) is *nirguṇa.* See Agrawala, "The Pāśupata Yoga," *Purāṇa,* I, 237. See also Schrader's *Introduction to the Pāñcarātra,* p. 95, for Ahirbudhnya as a *sāttvika* form of Śiva, and Avalon, *The Great Liberation,* p. 3, on Sadāśiva as a *sāttvika* aspect.

[40] This notion of the three eternal worlds appears in the BKh (e.g. 7.20; cf. 5.15; 2.6–12). In the PKh, only two worlds are eternal, Śivaloka not being mentioned (see PKh 2.5–6; 3.9–10; 7.79).

[41] GKh 6.68; 40.99; KJKh 36.15.

[42] BKh 3.18; PKh 2.84.

[43] PKh 3.8; 8.16–17; 10.56.

[44] Both accounts are in KJKh 36.

[45] PKh 30.158–159. Cf. PKh 13.26, where Sudarśana and Śiva are said to be dearer to Kṛṣṇa than his life. In PKh 20.16, only Śiva and Kṛṣṇa are said to be able to bear Sudarśana, and in KJKh 36.116, Sudarśana, Śiva, and Kṛṣṇa are said to be equal in valor.

[46] KJKh 75.89cd–91ab, 92cd–93ab.

[47] PKh 60.79ab. Cf. KJKh 19.63.

frequent references to Śiva as the best of Vaiṣṇavas.[48] Accordingly, Śiva seeks to become the servant of Kṛṣṇa[49] and confesses his own dependence upon the latter.[50] Śiva is often portrayed as in constant meditation on Kṛṣṇa, weeping with ecstasy of devotion and so forth.[51] Of all those who know Kṛṣṇa, it is Śiva, the best of Vaiṣṇavas, who knows him best.[52] Thus, by Śiva's grace a votary may attain faith in Kṛṣṇa.[53] Śiva in fact states that those who oppress Vaiṣṇavas will be punished by Kṛṣṇa, and that the hearts of non-Vaiṣṇavas are impure.[54] He further exclaims that Vaiṣṇavas are dearer to him than his own followers.[55]

Kṛṣṇa, who is filled with love for his devotees, has made Śiva equal to himself on account of Śiva's long devotion (*tapas*).[56] Kṛṣṇa asserts that Śiva is fully his equal in splendour, knowledge and virtue.[57] Further, the forms or bodies (*vigrahas*) of Śiva and Kṛṣṇa alone are eternal, not those of other beings.[58] It is through Śiva's devotion to Kṛṣṇa, finally, that not mere equality, but actual identity is apparently attained:

> Sleeping or awake, Śiva is constantly absorbed in meditation of Kṛṣṇa.
> As is Kṛṣṇa, so is Śaṃbhu; there is no difference between Mādhava and Īśa.[59]

Here we find, incidentally, full justification for the statement in the NārP concerning the BVP as teaching the non-difference between Hari and Hara.[60]

It is not just in theory or doctrine that our text manifests a

[48] BKh 3.22; 9.86; 11.16; PKh 27.132; 56.62; GKh 3.5; KJKh 26.5; 67.30.
[49] BKh 6.10 ff.
[50] BKh 17.33 ff.
[51] PKh 56.57 ff.
[52] PKh 34.18–19.
[53] PKh 36.109, 111.
[54] PKh 60.37–39.
[55] KJKh 16.64.
[56] KJKh 65.24–26.
[57] KJKh 36.15. Cf. BKh 6.29–30.
[58] KJKh 43.64.
[59] *svapne jāgaraṇe śaśvat kṛṣṇadhyānarataḥ śivaḥ/*
yathā kṛṣṇas tathā śaṃbhur na bhedo mādhaveśayoḥ// (PKh 56.61)
Cf. DBhP III.6.55:
yo hariḥ sa śivaḥ sākṣād yaḥ śivaḥ sa svayaṃ hariḥ/
etayor bhedam ātiṣṭhan narakāya bhaven naraḥ//
[60] See p. 27 above. Cf. ViP V.33.46–48, where Viṣṇu declares his non-difference from Śiva.

sympathy towards Śiva or Śaivism in general. Among Śaivite practices, *liṅga*-worship is perhaps most characteristic, and it is this rite that is especially noted with favor in the BVP. Often we are told that whoever does not worship the *liṅga* of Śiva commits a great sin and goes to hell.[61] It is also said that whoever worships Śiva, having constructed his *liṅga* from clay, dwells in Śiva's world as many years as the number of grains in the clay.[62] Upon returning to India, the worshipper becomes a king. And Kṛṣṇa says to Śiva:

> Who, having constructed your *liṅga* of clay, joined with the
> *yoni* of Prakṛti,
> At a place of pilgrimage, worships it a thousand times with
> devotion . . .
> He shall rejoice with me in Goloka for a crore of *kalpas*.
> And who worships at that place a lakh [of *liṅgas*], with
> proper gifts,
> Shall not fall from Goloka; he shall be equal to us.[63]

Śaivite devotional practices lead, then, to the ultimate goal of the Vaiṣṇavas.

4. Vaiṣṇavism and the problem of an open sectarianism

Our study above has affirmed the ultimately Vaiṣṇava character of our text, but a Vaiṣṇavism that exhibits considerable toleration towards other sects. Wilson has commented that the BVP "is perhaps the most decidedly sectarian work of the whole collection [of Purāṇas], and has no other object than to recommend faith in Kṛishṅa and Rádhá. . . ."[64] In view of what has already been said, this would seem to be a misleading statement. Certainly our

---

[61] PKh 30.167; 31.16.
[62] PKh 27.112–113.
[63] BKh 6.42–45. Cf. KJKh 85.151 ff.
[64] Wilson, "Analysis of the Puráñas," ESL, I, 91. Cf. the comment of Hamilton and Langlès: "Ce Pourâna [the BVP] est très-remarquable, en ce qu'il présente un système de théisme singulièrement pur, sans mélange de polythéisme. Krichna y paroît comme l'être éternel, incorporel, incréé, d'où tous les autres tirent leur origine. Les trois personnes de la Trinité indienne ne sont pas seulement créés, mais elles sont même mortelles; ainsi elles n'y figurent même pas comme les anges de Mohammed" (*Catalogue des Manuscrits Samskrits*, pp. 36–37). Hamilton and Langlès agree with Wilson on the Kṛṣṇaite nature of the text, but give it a very different interpretation!

text "recommends faith in Kríshńa and Rádhá," but the other gods and goddesses are highly respected and the performance of their worship readily accepted. In this connection, we may note the frequent mention of offerings to a group of six deities, referred to as the *devaṣaṭka:* Gaṇeśa, Dineśa (Sūrya), Vahni, Viṣṇu, Śiva and Śivā (Durgā).[65] Sometimes only five are mentioned.[66] Often the worship of these six or five is to be performed before offering *pūjā* to one's chosen deity (*iṣṭa* or *abhīṣṭa* [*deva*]).[67] All these rituals, in turn, form part of the preliminary worship of yet other deities, such as Sarasvatī or Sāvitrī.[68]

The above manner of worship is clearly related to the *pañcāyatanapūjā* of the Smārta Brahmans.[69] This form of worship is traditionally traced back to Śaṃkara and his reorganization of religious schools in line with his *advaita* philosophy.[70] According to this view, although Brahman is One, it manifests itself in different forms to different individuals.[71] Five of these forms (Gaṇeśa, Sūrya, Viṣṇu, Śiva, and Durgā), representing the chief deities of the five principal orthodox cults, were the special objects of worship in the household *pūjā* of the Smārtas. The devotee's own or chosen deity, one of the five, was placed in the center of the other four. In this way, a ritual synthesis of religious tolerance and cult affiliation was achieved.

The underlying principle of the *pañcāyatanapūjā* allowed for considerable elaboration or innovation, so that other manifestations might easily replace one of the above mentioned, as seems to have happened with the evolution of Kṛṣṇa- and Rāma-*pañcāyatanas.*[72] In the BVP, however, even though Kṛṣṇa is the chosen deity, as it were, he is not included in the list of five or six deities. Possibly Kṛṣṇa-*pañcāyatana* had not been developed by the time of our text, but it also seems reasonable that the absence

65 See, for instance, PKh 4.35–36. Variations in this list occur. PKh 64.61 mentions Vahni, Sūrya, Candra, Viṣṇu, Varuṇa, and Śiva.

66 KJKh 8.15 and 16.80 both refer to *pañca devatāḥ.*

67 PKh 4.36; 23.45.

68 PKh 4.35 ff; 23.42 ff.

69 See Monier-Williams, *Brāhmanism and Hindūism,* pp. 410–416; cf. Banerjea, "Cult Syncretism," CHI, IV, 331–332.

70 See Gonda, *Die Religionen Indiens,* I, 332; II, 83; Venkateswaran, "Rādhā-Krishna *Bhajanas* of South India," *Krishna: Myths, Rites, and Attitudes* (Singer, ed.), p. 146.

71 The roots of such a view go far back beyond Śaṃkara, to RV I.164.46, where the One is said to be known by various names: *ekaṃ sad viprā bahudhā vadanty agniṃ yamaṃ mātariśvānam āhuḥ//*

72 See Venkateswaran, *op. cit.,* p. 146.

of Kṛṣṇa in the *devaṣaṭka* may implicitly point to his transcendency, beyond the other gods. This would illustrate what in any case appears to be the dominant attitude of our Purāṇa, an attitude that may be described as "open sectarianism."

To understand better the nature of an open sectarianism and some of the theological problems it faces, let us look more closely at the tolerance of the *pañcāyatanapūjā*. Theoretically, the *pañcāyatana* ideal would seem to make sectarian affiliation a matter of relative indifference. We find this conclusion echoed in such statements as the following (in reference to a hymn to Durgā):

> Whoever recites [the hymn] at morning, noon, and evening, filled with devotion,
> Whether Śaiva, Vaiṣṇava, or Śākta, is freed from misfortune.[73]

At the same time, Vaiṣṇavas are often distinguished from others, as in PKh 60.46 ff., where Vaiṣṇavas are regarded as *sāttvika*, Śaivas and Śāktas as *rājasika*. And in PKh 29.25–26, it is said that Śaivas, Śāktas, Sauras, and Gāṇapas never see the envoys of Yama, god of death, while Vaiṣṇavas do not see them even in dream.[74]

The choosing of one's *devatā* is by no means a trifling matter. It is seen as involving not only man's choice, but also God's encountering man in one of these forms.[75] This "choice" seems to be based in part, then, on the existential response to the "call of God." At the same time, some devotees wish to provide a more philosophical and metaphysical explanation or justification of "their choice" as the best or highest. One such explanation is that their *iṣṭadevatā* is in reality not a form of the Supreme, but the Supreme himself. The other deities are then forms of this one God. In the BVP, of course, all "other deities" are seen as forms or parts of Kṛṣṇa.[76] This approach provides a firmer foundation for the Kṛṣṇaite devotee in his beliefs and ritual observances. The worship of other gods can then be seen as a step or stage to the supreme devotion, to Viṣṇu or Kṛṣṇa. For instance, it is said:

73 KJKh 27.45.

74 Vaṅg.

75 See Venkateswaran, *op. cit.*, pp. 159–161.

76 See, for instance, BKh 3–5, where all the major gods and goddesses emanate from Kṛṣṇa.

Whoever worships a deity with devotion attains him at first,
And in time attains the supreme abode of Viṣṇu with the god.[77]

This recalls the statement made about the worship of Śiva's *liṅga* leading to Goloka. A more detailed step theory is found in the following:

After worshipping for seven births deities that are portions of Hari,
Men come to worship Prakṛti, through her compassion.
Worshipping Viṣṇumāyā [Prakṛti], full of compassion, for seven births,
They attain devotion to Śiva . . .
Worshipping Śaṃkara . . .
In a short time they attain Viṣṇu-*bhakti* from Maheśvara.
They worship *saguṇa* (quality-endowed) Viṣṇu, who is *sattva*.

. . . .

The *sāttvika* Vaiṣṇavas, worshipping *saguṇa* Viṣṇu,
Attain *bhakti* to *nirguṇa* Śrī Kṛṣṇa.[78]

And finally, we find that, among three forms of slandering God (Viṣṇu), the third is to consider him equal to other gods.[79] For such an offense, a man dwells in hell for the life of Brahmā.

The BVP, in summary, not only presents a variety of theological strands, but also a variety of attitudes, more and less tolerant, towards the various strands. Our text was aware of sectarian differences and the theological problems involved in an open sectarianism. Its approach was to include as many different theological viewpoints as possible, to show that none was incompatible with Kṛṣṇaism, while at the same time demonstrating that Kṛṣṇaism was capable of embracing them all. The resulting Kṛṣṇaite theology of our Purāna is thus consciously, and perhaps unconsciously, influenced by the various viewpoints it has brought together. In the following chapters, we shall be concerned immediately only with the Kṛṣṇaite strand, keeping in mind, however, that it is an open Kṛṣṇaism, in intent as well as in results.

[77] BKh 14. 47cd–48ab.
[78] PKh 62.23–26ab, 27.
[79] BKh 17.49.

PART B

THE KṚṢṆAITE THEOLOGICAL FRAMEWORK

4

The Conception of God in the *Brahmavaivarta Purāṇa*

1. Kṛṣṇa, Hari, Nārāyaṇa, Viṣṇu

In the beginning of the KJKh, in *adhyāyas* 4 to 6, an account is given of the gods on their way to the Supreme Lord of the universe, to enlist his aid in relieving the earth of her burden. This account is based on much older works such as the ViP and BhP.[1] In these earlier versions, the Supreme Lord (*bhagavān parameśvaraḥ*), referred to as Viṣṇu or Hari, consents to become incarnate on earth as Kṛṣṇa to destroy the demons oppressing the world. In BhP X.1.2, there is reference to Viṣṇu's descent through a portion of himself (*aṃśenāvatīrṇasya viṣṇoḥ*), and in other places of the BhP, Kṛṣṇa is referred to as a fraction or part (*kalā, aṃśa*) of Hari or Viṣṇu.[2] It would appear, then, that Kṛṣṇa is

[1] See ViP V.1 and BhP X.1.

[2] See, for instance, BhP IV.1.58; X.2.18; X.2.41; X.20.48; X.43.23. These references have been collected by De in VFM, p. 244 (my citations are to the Veṅk).

The terms *aṃśa* and *kalā* have long been associated with the *avatāra* doctrine. Thus in the MBh we find *aṃśenāvatara* (Bombay: I.64.54 = Critical: I.58.51) and *aṃśāvataraṇa* (Bombay: I.67.161 = Critical: I.61.99). In Kālidāsa's *Raghuvaṃśa* the gods follow Rāma to earth by parts (*aṃśair,* X.49). (See Hacker, "Zur Entwicklung der Avatāralehre," WZKSO, IV, 50–53.) In HV II.49.32, there is reference to Viṣṇu's *aṃśāvataraṇa,* though in the Critical Ed., this passage is shown to be a later addition. In the ViP, there are several references to *kalās, aṃśas,* and *aṃśāṃśas* in connection with the *avatāra* notion. For instance, in ViP V.1.61, the gods are to descend to earth by *kalās* and *aṃśas.* See also ViP V.1.1–4, which contains several

subordinated to the Supreme Lord or Bhagavat, as a partial aspect of him. Yet we also find, in BhP I.3.28, this statement concerning the *avatāras* of the Lord: "These are the portions and fractions of the Puṃs, but Kṛṣṇa is Bhagavat himself."[3]

The great apologist of the Caitanya school, Jīva Gosvāmin, wished to prove that Kṛṣṇa indeed is the Bhagavat, and not just an aspect of him. He considered the verse just quoted (BhP I.3.28) to be the authoritative statement of the BhP on God, in light of which all other statements are to be interpreted. In various ways, he reconciled those verses which seem to speak of Kṛṣṇa as an *aṃśa* of the Supreme with this basic "*mahāvākya*" (great saying).[4] De summarizes Jīva's method of interpretation as follows:

> Partly by the direct testimony, and partly by a reconciliation, of various texts culled from the *Mahābhārata, Viṣṇu-purāṇa, Hari-vaṃśa, Padma-purāṇa* and *Bhāgavata,* as well as by an unceremonious rejection of texts which celebrate other sectarian deities like Śiva, he [Jīva] gradually builds up a series of favourable texts round the central Mahāvākya, which is elaborately shown to declare emphatically the supreme godhead of Kṛṣṇa.[5]

It is noteworthy that Jīva did not call upon the BVP to support his views. This is all the more significant in that the BVP, with relatively little ambiguity, asserts the full lordship and supremacy of Kṛṣṇa. Let us refer again to the account of the gods on their way to the Supreme Lord, in KJKh 4–6.

The gods, having arrived in Hari's celestial realm, Vaikuṇṭha, offer praise to him, who is endowed with four arms. Hari responds:

---

references to *aṃśāvatāra, aṃśāṃśena, et cetera.* The *Viṣṇudharma* refers to Vāsudeva's incarnations as *kalayāvatīrṇaḥ, aṃśāvatīrṇena,* and *aṃśāṃśakas.* These are quoted by Hazra in *Studies in the Upapurāṇas,* I, 132–133, note 58. Hazra dates the *Viṣṇudharma* between 200 and 300 A.D. (*ibid.,* pp. 137–143). He further points out, "Like the Narasiṃha-p., Viṣṇu-p. and other early works, the Viṣṇudharma names both Kṛṣṇa and 'Lāṅgalī Rāma' as partial incarnations of Viṣṇu. . . ." (*Ibid.,* p. 145.) Hermann Jacobi also comments, briefly, on the *aṃśas* and *aṃśāṃśas* of Viṣṇu in "Incarnation (Indian)," ERE VII, 197.

[3] Cf. De, VFM, pp. 240–241.

[4] For Jīva's arguments in detail, see De, VFM, pp. 244–245.

[5] VFM, p. 245.

Go [O Gods] to Goloka; I shall follow with Śrī.

. . . .

There I am the two-armed Kṛṣṇa, with the *gopīs* and Rādhā.
Here [in Vaikuṇṭha] I am united with Kamalā . . .
I am Kṛṣṇa and Nārāyaṇa, dwelling in Śvetadvīpa.[6]

The gods then proceed to Goloka, fifty crores of *yojanas* above Vaikuṇṭha. There, in the midst of a blazing effulgence, they discern the form of Kṛṣṇa, the color of a raincloud, lavishly ornamented, and holding a flute. Kṛṣṇa, realizing the intention of the gods to enlist his aid, agrees to descend to the world.

According to this account, Hari is considered as the Supreme, and at the same time, Kṛṣṇa is seen to be the highest or essential form of Hari. In most cases, our text does not distinguish between Hari and Kṛṣṇa, using the two names synonymously.[7] Occasionally, as we have just seen, Hari is associated with Vaikuṇṭha, and in a four-armed form, in contrast to the two-armed form of Kṛṣṇa. Most often, however, it is Nārāyaṇa who is that aspect of Kṛṣṇa which is four-armed and dwells in Vaikuṇṭha,[8] even though Nārāyaṇa is also associated with Śvetadvīpa.[9] Nārāyaṇa, usually considered as subordinate to Kṛṣṇa, arising from the latter's left side,[10] may still at times be identified with the Supreme. For example, in GKh 7.76, it is Nārāyaṇa who is said to be the two-armed Lord of Goloka and the four-armed ruler of Vaikuṇṭha. But even in this case, it is evident that the two-armed form is superior, for the following verse (7.77) mentions that Goloka is fifty crores of *yojanas* above Vaikuṇṭha. The general view of our text regarding the supremacy of the two-armed Kṛṣṇa-form to the four-armed Nārāyaṇa-form is similar, of course, to that of the Caitanya school, where it was argued that the best form of God is that which most resembles man.[11]

In KJKh 4.67 ff., quoted above, Hari declares that he himself

[6] KJKh 4.67ab, 69–70ab.

[7] It seems that in the Kṛṣṇaite schools of Vaiṣṇavism, there was a tendency to accept Hari as a name for the Supreme, identified with Kṛṣṇa, but to neglect or lower Viṣṇu. This at least appears to be the case in the schools of Nimbārka and Caitanya (cf. Chaudhuri, "Nimbārka," HPEW, I, 338, and Maitra, "Caitanya," HPEW, I, 361.) Our text clearly is similar in this respect.

[8] E.g., PKh 2.57–59.

[9] See note 12 below.

[10] See PKh 2.57–59.

[11] Cf. De, VFM, pp. 248–250.

dwells in Vaikuṇṭha, while as Kṛṣṇa he resides in Goloka, and as Nārāyaṇa in Śvetadvīpa.[12] The relationship of these various manifestations or forms is one of nondifference. Śiva declares, for instance:

> He who is in Goloka is in Vaikuṇṭha, and precisely he is in Śvetadvīpa.
> There is no difference between the whole (*aṃśin*) and the parts (*aṃśa*) . . . like fire and sparks.[13]

In the succeeding verses, Śiva refers to the Supreme as Paramātman, identified both with Viṣṇu and Kṛṣṇa.[14] Viṣṇu, however, is usually the name of an aspect of Kṛṣṇa. In BKh 18.21–27, it is said that Kṛṣṇa, as two-armed, resides in Goloka; as four-armed, in Vaikuṇṭha; and as bearing the form of Viṣṇu, in Śvetadvīpa. Viṣṇu is frequently associated with this lesser realm.[15] Further, as we have already mentioned, Viṣṇu is included in the *trimūrti,* as one of the *saguṇa* forms of the Godhead, while Kṛṣṇa is *nirguṇa.*[16] And finally, the source of all *avatāras* is identified with Kṛṣṇa, who therefore is not to be regarded as an *avatāra* of Viṣṇu. Śiva, in praising Kṛṣṇa, states:

> With ease (*līlayā*), by his own *aṃśas* and *kalās,* for the protection of the worlds (*jagatām*),
> He [Kṛṣṇa] maintains many *avatāras,* as their eternal seed (*bīja*).[17]

And in KJKh 22.36 ff., the demon Dhenuka says that Kṛṣṇa, by various portions or fractions (*aṃśa, kalā*), is Vāmana, Varāha, Nṛsiṃha,[18] Mīna, Kūrma, Sahasradhṛk (Śeṣa), Rāma Dāśarathi,[19] Paraśurāma, Kapila, the two sages Nara and Nārāyaṇa, and Dharmasūta. Dhenuka concludes his enumeration by saying to Kṛṣṇa:

[12] KJKh 4.70ab is ambiguous as to whether Kṛṣṇa, Nārāyaṇa, or Hari dwells in Śvetadvīpa, but the passage as a whole makes the best sense if Nārāyaṇa is the Śvetadvīpa resident. Also, in 67cd, Nara and Nārāyaṇa are said to be *śvetadvīpanivāsinau.*

[13] BKh 17.37.

[14] BKh 17.39, 40.

[15] E.g., PKh 3.59; 60.96; 61.51.

[16] BKh 8.19–21.

[17] BKh 18.29cd–30ab.

[18] This *avatāra* is not connected with a portion, but is said to be fully Kṛṣṇa himself (*svayaṃ pūrṇa*).

[19] This *avatāra* is not connected with a portion, nor is it said to be *pūrṇa.*

Now you yourself, most complete and perfect (*paripūrṇa-tama*), have the form of Kṛṣṇa,
The eternal seed of all *avatāras*.[20]

Again comparing the views of the BVP with those of the Caitanya school, we find that, according to Jīva Gosvāmin, Kṛṣṇa is the source of the *guṇāvatāras* (Brahmā, Viṣṇu, and Śiva), as well as of the *puruṣāvatāra* and *līlāvatāras*.[21] These *avatāras* are considered as perfect (*pūrṇa*), since they are manifestations of Kṛṣṇa, but Kṛṣṇa himself is most perfect (*pūrṇa-tama*).[22] The BVP, though not elaborating and systematizing its *avatāra* doctrine to the same extent, seems in basic agreement with the Caitanya school.

Kṛṣṇa appears in our Purāṇa, then, as the *aṃśin* rather than merely as an *aṃśa*. Unlike the BhP, there is little need for reconciliation of apparently contradictory statements. Hari, and at times Viṣṇu and Nārāyaṇa, may be used to refer to the Supreme. Kṛṣṇa, however, appears not only as the greatest name of the Supreme,[23] but also as the Supreme himself.

2. Kṛṣṇa in himself

The conception of God in the BVP is an attempt to synthesize several diverse, and at times seemingly contradictory, theological and philosophical strands. We have referred already to several of the theological strands, such as the Tāntric, and Vaiṣṇavite, and also to the fact that each of the strands is made up of several

20 *adhunā kṛṣṇarūpas tvaṃ paripūrṇatamaḥ svayam/*
sarveṣām avatārāṇāṃ bījarūpaḥ sanātanaḥ//
(KJKh 22.49)

Cf. KJKh 1.8:
kena vā prārthitaḥ kṛṣṇa ājagāma mahītalam/
sarvāṃśair eka eveśaḥ paripūrṇatamaḥ svayam//

And KJKh 9.12–14:
sūkaro vāmanaḥ kalkir bauddhaḥ kapilamīnakau/
ete cāṃśāḥ kalāś cānye santy eva katidhā mune//
kūrmo nṛsimho rāmaś ca śvetadvīpavirāḍ vibhuḥ/
paripūrṇatamaḥ kṛṣṇo vaikuṇṭhe gokule svayam//
vaikuṇṭhe kamalākānto rūpabhedāc caturbhujaḥ/
goloke gokule rādhākānto 'yaṃ dvibhujaḥ svayam//

Cf. also NārPR I.15.20, where there is reference to *kalāvatīrṇa, aṃśa, paripūrṇatama, pūrṇa,* and *kalāṃśa.*

21 See De, VFM, pp. 184–5; 246.

22 *Ibid.*, p. 246.

23 See below, p. 86.

threads. The Kṛṣṇaite theology of our text brings together monistic and dualistic, acosmic and theopanistic,[24] illusionistic and realistic notions of all kinds. These views in part reflect different ways of looking at ultimate reality, or represent various aspects of that reality itself. Accordingly, the BVP is able to accept many different views, for each is appropriate in its own way. This tolerance of the text is reflected in the following passage:

> The Lord has nine forms. . . .
> The six schools each assign to him a form,
> The Vaiṣṇavas and Vedas one each,
> And the Purāṇas one also. In this way he has nine forms.
> The Nyāya and Śaṃkara call him indescribable,[25]
> The Vaiśeṣikas call him eternal,
> The Sāṃkhya calls him the eternal god in the form of light,
> The Mīmāṃsā [calls him] the form of all; the Vedānta, the cause of all;
> The Pātañjala, the infinite; the Vedas, the essence of truth;
> The Purāṇas, self-willed; and the *bhaktas*, having an external body or form.[26]

Although the characterization of the views of the various schools is rather imprecise, the inclusive rather than exclusive attitude of the Purāṇic compilers is evident.

Some views, according to our text, are more limited than others, or from a lower standpoint. The different levels of insight, then, must be distinguished. We shall attempt to do this in part by comparing the BVP with other Purāṇas, especially the BhP, where the same general openness and tolerance is found.[27] Further, the BhP already contains many of the diverse theological-philosophical doctrines of the BVP. These two Purāṇas differ, however, in their manner of structuring or bringing together the various elements. This is especially clear in regard to God's transcendent aspect.

In the passage quoted above, one of Kṛṣṇa's forms or epithets

[24] Rudolph Otto has made the important distinction between pantheism (all is God) and theopanism (God is all). The pantheistic notion, raising the world to the Absolute, Otto argues, does not exist in India (*Viṣnu-Nārāyana*, pp. 59–60). Cf. Gail, BhBhP, pp. 26–27.

[25] Veṅk and Ānand have "describable," surely a mistake.

[26] KJKh 129.72–76. Regarding the nine forms of God, cf. Gonda, *Aspects of Early Viṣṇuism*, p. 95.

[27] Cf. Gail, BhBhP, pp. 20–21.

was "indescribable" or "indefinable" (*anirvacanīya*).[28] This term is not uncommonly applied to Kṛṣṇa elsewhere in our text.[29] *Anirvacanīya,* of course, indicates that the human intellect is insufficient to comprehend God. Thus, Kṛṣṇa is said to be beyond speech and mind.[30] In the BhP, as Gail points out, Viṣṇu in himself is also incomprehensible to the human intellect.[31] Nevertheless, in both Purāṇas, the supreme or transcendent nature of God is indicated in several ways: by the identification of Viṣṇu or Kṛṣṇa with the Supreme (*para* or *parama*) Brahman, the Supreme Ātman, and the Supreme Puruṣa; by the ascription of certain negative and positive attributes; and finally by paradox.

The identification of Kṛṣṇa with Brahman or Para(ma) Brahman is of constant occurrence throughout the BVP. The nature of Brahman in the Hindu tradition has been variously conceived, especially regarding its two main forms or aspects, as *saguṇa* (with qualities or attributes) and *nirguṇa* (without attributes). In *advaita* (non-dualist) circles, the latter was regarded as the higher, or Paraṃ Brahman. In the more theistic schools such as Rāmānuja's, Brahman is regarded as ultimately *saguṇa.*[32] Rāmānuja interprets the scriptural statements asserting that Brahman is *nirguṇa* as denying only evil qualities and the defiling *guṇa*s of material nature.[33] Brahman is *saguṇa,* then, in the sense of being endowed with auspicious qualities. Included in these are the well-known *ṣaḍguṇa*s, *jñāna, bala, aiśvarya, vīrya, śakti,* and *tejas.*[34] These six *guṇa*s formed an important part of Pāñcarātrika doctrines. In the *Ahirbudhnya Saṃhitā,* these six attributes are considered as *aprākṛta,* and distinguished from the *triguṇa*s of *prakṛti.*[35]

In the BVP, these two aspects of Brahman, *nirguṇa* and *saguṇa,* are applied to *Kṛṣṇa.*[36] More often, Kṛṣṇa is referred to simply as

[28] This term was used by Śaṃkara not for God but for the unmanifest chaos out of which creation, or manifest names and forms, proceed. Among the later followers of Śaṃkara, the term became applied to *avidyā* and *māyā.* See Hacker, "Eigentümlichkeiten," ZDMG, C, 261–264.

[29] GKh 32.59; 32.61; KJKh 5.97; 18.40; 19.26; 20.37; 25.102; 94.39; 94.69.

[30] *vāṅmanasoḥ param* (BKh 18.32).

[31] BhBhP, p. 22.

[32] Cf. Hiriyanna, *Outlines,* p. 387.

[33] *Vedārthasaṃgraha,* pars. 83 and 84. Cf. Carman, "Rāmānuja's Conception," *Ānvīkṣikī,* I, 104.

[34] See Carman, "Rāmānuja's Conception," *Ānvīkṣikī,* I, 97.

[35] See Schrader, *Introduction,* pp. 31–34.

[36] E.g. PKh 54.109.

nirguṇa, which in turn is identified with Paraṃ Brahman.[37] Seemingly, then, the BVP is in basic conformity with *advaita* views. But let us look more carefully at the general usage and sense of *nirguṇa* and *saguṇa* in our text. The relation of these two forms of Kṛṣṇa is often explained in cosmogonical terms. In GKh 42.36, it is said of Kṛṣṇa:

> He who is *nirguṇa* is unstained, as he is not conjoined with the *śakti*s.
> Desiring to create, depending upon *śakti,* he who is *nirguṇa* becomes *saguṇa.*

In PKh 54.109:

> He [Kṛṣṇa], as *puṃs,* is *nirguṇa;* with time, he is *saguṇa.*

Time, of course, is associated with the notion of creation.[38] And in GKh 7.113a, cf:

> [You Kṛṣṇa] are *nirguṇa.* . . .
> You are *saguṇa* when associated with nature (*prākṛtika*) through a portion, for the sake of creation.

These examples indicate that Kṛṣṇa, in his creative aspect, is considered as *saguṇa,* while in his supreme aspect, he is *nirguṇa.* Our text, therefore, often uses *nirguṇa* in the sense of *triguṇāt para,* or beyond the three *guṇa*s involved in material nature, that is, *sattva, rajas* and *tamas.* We find, in fact, that *nirguṇa* frequently occurs together with the phrase *prakṛteḥ para,* as epithets of Kṛṣṇa.[39] *Triguṇāt para* also appears in close association with *prakṛteḥ para,* as in PKh 48.48–49.

At times, *nirguṇa* also seems to have the sense of denying evil or limiting qualities. This may well be the case when *nirguṇa* appears in a series of negative attributes, such as *nirlipta* or *nirañjana* (unstained).[40] That *nirguṇa* does not necessarily mean the negation of all qualities seems evident by the numerous positive attributes assigned to Kṛṣṇa, apparently in his supreme aspect. These attributes will be considered below. Further, though Kṛṣṇa is spoken of as *triguṇāt para,* it is said that the wise

[37] E.g., PKh 42.80; 46.75.

[38] Cf. Hacker, *Prahlāda,* pp. 645–646.

[39] See, for instance, PKh 10.19; 10.57; 27.144; 40.28; 42.80; 46.54; 54.84; 54.160; 56.5; 63.34.

[40] PKh 11.89; cf. PKh 7.87; 34.27–28; 63.34–36.

describe him as having a form endowed with six qualities (*ṣaḍguṇarūpa*).[41] Although these six are not specified, these probably refer to the *aprākṛtaguṇas* of the Pāñcarātrikas.

Finally, in one passage, Kṛṣṇa himself expounds on the nature of Brahman.[42] He explains that (the neuter) Brahman has two forms, *nirguṇa* and *saguṇa.* Then, shifting from the neuter Brahman to the masculine Bhagavat, Kṛṣṇa says that he (the Bhagavat) is *saguṇa* when resting on or resorting to *māyā* (*māyāśrita*)[43] and *nirguṇa* when beyond *māyā.* Kṛṣṇa next discusses various views people hold on the relation of *māyā* or *prakṛti* to Brahman.[44] He finally says:

> My form also, in this manner, is twofold: two-armed and four-armed.
> I am four-armed in Vaikuṇṭha, with Padmā and my attendants;
> In Goloka I am two-armed, with the *gopīs* and Rādhā.[45]

The parallel between the two forms of Brahman and those of Kṛṣṇa may suggest an identity between *nirguṇa* Brahman and the two-armed aspect of Kṛṣṇa, and between *saguṇa* Brahman and the four-armed aspect. From the *advaita* viewpoint, this would seemingly involve a contradiction, for *nirguṇa,* in the sense of no attributes at all, and "two-armed," are mutually exclusive. If *nirguṇa* merely means the absence of negative attributes, there is no such problem. *Nirguṇa* in the BVP often seems to have this last meaning, as we have seen. Yet, this term appears so frequently in our text, one wonders if it did not convey to the compilers of the Purāṇa something beyond the mere negation of negative qualities, expressing to them the paradoxical transcendence of Kṛṣṇa, who is both *nirguṇa* in the Advaitic sense and somehow also endowed with auspicious qualities. We shall return to this point in discussing Kṛṣṇa's *nirākāra* and *sākāra* nature.

Equally as frequent as Kṛṣṇa's identification with Brahman is his identification with Ātman or Paramātman. This doctrine, though, involves not only Kṛṣṇa's transcendent aspect, but also

41 KJKh 5.100.
42 KJKh 43.57 ff.
43 Cf. BhG IX.8, where Kṛṣṇa says that he sends forth creation after taking as his base *prakṛti* (*prakṛtim . . . avaṣṭamya*). Śaṃkara glosses *avaṣṭamya* with *āśritya.*
44 We shall discuss these views below in chapter 8.
45 KJKh 43.66–67ab.

his immanence, especially in relation to man, and thus shall be dealt with later.

Of special importance for our text is the conception of Kṛṣṇa as *puruṣa, puṃs, paramapuruṣa* and *puruṣottama.*[46] The significance of this identification lies in the fact that *puruṣa* is frequently paired or contrasted with *prakṛti.* In the classical Sāṃkhya of the SK, *puruṣa* and *prakṛti* are the spiritual (conscious) and material principles of the universe. It is the apparent involvement of *puruṣa* with *prakṛti* that initiates material evolution. There is actually a plurality of *puruṣas*, existing as the individual souls or spirits in every body.[47] Liberation is the discrimination of the spirit from *prakṛti. Puruṣa,* then, is ultimately entirely distinct from *prakṛti. Puruṣa* in this sense is closely related to the Upaniṣadic conception of the universal *puruṣa* identified with Brahman-Ātman.[48]

These various conceptions of *puruṣa* may help us to understand the BVP's views on Kṛṣṇa and *puruṣa.* Kṛṣṇa, in his transcendent aspect, as already noted, is referred to as *prakṛteḥ para.* This indicates that he, as Puruṣa, is pure spirit, unstained by material nature. In his aspect as creator, he becomes joined with *prakṛti.* Yet if Kṛṣṇa is the one reality, *prakṛti* cannot be a separate ontological principle. Accordingly we find Kṛṣṇa identified with both *puruṣa* and *prakṛti.*[49] There are many variations of these themes. Thus Kṛṣṇa is regarded as "Himself *puṃs,* himself *prakṛti,* and beyond *prakṛti.*"[50] And he is said to be *prakṛti, puṃs,* and beyond both, and through *māyā,* to bear the forms of a man, woman, and eunuch.[51] Kṛṣṇa, then, comprises all that is masculine, feminine, and neuter.[52] The above formulations of the divine nature point to a transcendency that transcends any dichotomy between the transcendent and the mundane.

Such notions are by no means original with the BVP. In ViP

[46] For *paramapuruṣa,* see PKh 3.21; for *puruṣottama,* PKh 10.175; 38.23.

[47] See SK 18.

[48] *Puruṣa* has yet another aspect as the cosmic Puruṣa, deriving from the *puruṣasukta* of RV X.90. Gail has pointed out these three conceptions of *puruṣa* in relation to the BhP. See BhBhP, pp. 22–23.

[49] PKh 18.60; KJKh 36.67.

[50] PKh 34.29ab.

[51] GKh 32.33–34. Cf. KJKh 113.31, where Kṛṣṇa himself is *puṃs,* himself *strī,* and himself *napuṃsaka.*

[52] Cf. GKh 29.46, where Siva is said to bear the form of a woman, eunuch, and man. Cf. also MaitriU VI.5, and *Śvetāśvatara Upaniṣad* IV.5; V.10.

I.2.23–24, Viṣṇu is identified, apparently, with Brahman, *puṃs* or *puruṣa,* and *pradhāna* (material nature). In the BhP, Viṣṇu is identified with *puruṣa* and *prakṛti,*[53] and is also said to be beyond or behind both.[54] Our text differs from earlier works not so much in its views of *puruṣa,* but in its views of *prakṛti,* and therefore, of course, in its conception of the relation of *puruṣa* and *prakṛti.* It is not only *puruṣa* that is conceived on different levels, but *prakṛti* as well, as we shall see in part C below.

Let us now turn to the attributes of Kṛṣṇa. Regarding negative attributes, reference has already been made to *anirvacanīya,* as well as *nirlipta* and *nirañjana.* Others include: without a second; formless, without limitations or obstructions; without beginning, middle, or end; uncontrolled; uncreated; without support; fearless; without desire; without parts; inactive; without modification; and imperishable.[55] These negative attributes reflect for the most part an Advaitic viewpoint. *Nirguṇa* may perhaps also be included among the negative attributes, though if taken in the Advaitic sense it is no attribute at all. Particularly significant is the juxtaposition of various negative attributes with their positive counterparts in intentional paradoxes, to be dealt with later.

Many of the positive attributes ascribed to Kṛṣṇa in himself are also Advaitic in flavor. To be sure, from the Advaitic standpoint, these are not actually attributes (*guṇas*) but are identical with Brahman and thus constitute its essence (*svarūpa*).[56] This "positive essence," in the BVP, is described by the following terms: the one, the true or real, eternal, beyond the beyond, the whole or complete, self-ruling, self-willed, omniscient, eternal or supreme bliss, consisting of light or illumination, having the nature of knowledge.[57] For the most part, these terms occur also in

[53] BhP X.10.31.

[54] BhP V.3.5.

[55] *advitīya, nirākṛti, nirākāra, nirupādhi, nirvirodha, anādimadhyānta, niraṅkuśa, anirmita, nirāśraya, nirmūla, niḥśaṅka* (Vaṅg, PKh 34.27), *nirīha, niṣkāma, nirvyūha, nirutsāha, nirvikāra,* and *akṣara.*

These have been gathered from several passages, and many appear several times in similar series of attributes. Each of the above can be found at least once in the following places: BKh 15.49; PKh 7.87–88; 11.89; 20.17; 34.27–28; 38.21; 46.75; 63.35; KJKh 16.51.

[56] Cf. Hacker, "Eigentümlichkeiten," ZDMG, C, 286.

[57] *eka, satya, satyasvarūpa, nitya, sanātana, parātpara, paripūrṇatama, svatantra, svecchāmaya, sarvajña, sarvavit, nityānanda, paramānandarūpaka, paramāhlādaka, tejorūpa, jyotis, svayaṃjyotis, jyotirmaya, jñānarūpa.*

See BKh 2.26–27; PKh 2.5; 2.12; 2.30; 2.88; 3.30; 4.13; 7.77; 11.93; 11.104; 34.26–27; 49.48; 54.168; GKh 32.59; KJKh 6.2; 102.6.

the BhP.[58] Some of them, we may recall, correspond to the nine forms of Kṛṣṇa referred to at the beginning of this chapter. But the view of the *bhaktas* has not yet been mentioned, namely, that Kṛṣṇa is endowed with an eternal form or body (*nityavigraha*). Elsewhere in our text, the positive attributes *sākāra, nityarūpa, nityarūpin, nityadehin,* are also ascribed to Kṛṣṇa.[59] Regarding Kṛṣṇa's eternal body, we may note the following conversation between Sanatkumāra and Kṛṣṇa, before a throng of *munis*:

Sanatkumāra:
It is useless to inquire into the welfare of Kṛṣṇa, [for he is] the seed of welfare.

....

Śrī Kṛṣṇa:
It is appropriate to inquire into the welfare of one who bears a body (*śarīradhāriṇaḥ*).
Why then, O Brahman, do you not inquire into my welfare?
Sanatkumāra:
O Lord, welfare and misfortune always attend a body derived from nature (*śarīre prākṛte*),
But concerning an eternal body that is the source of welfare, an inquiry into welfare is useless.
Śrī Kṛṣṇa:
Whoever bears a body is derived from nature (*prākṛtika*), according to tradition.
There is no body, O Brahman, without that eternal nature.
Sanatkumāra:
Those bodies sprung from blood and semen are derived from nature, according to tradition.
How is the body of the [cosmic] seed, the Lord of nature, derived from nature?[60]

Kṛṣṇa continues to argue that, as the son of Vasudeva in his present incarnation, his body is derived from blood and semen, but Sanatkumāra does not give in, and finally asks, "Where in the Veda is your body described as dependent on blood and

[58] Cf. BhP V.12.11; X.14.23; X.14.32; X.28.15. These passages contain the following:
eka, satya, nitya, sanātana, pūrṇa, paramānanda, ajasrasukha, jyotis, svayaṃjyotis.

[59] E.g. PKh 20.17; 34.27; GKh 32.29.

[60] KJKh 87.19cd, 22–25 (Ānand has a better reading than Veṅk).

semen?"[61] Despite Kṛṣṇa's protestations, there is little doubt that he wields an eternal body not derived from material nature. In Rāmānuja's school, God also is thought to have a body distinct from nature and constituted of *nityavibhūti,* a kind of "matter without its mutability."[62]

What, then, does Kṛṣṇa's eternal form or body look like? In the BVP there is hardly an extended passage describing the nature of Kṛṣṇa that does not go into some detail regarding his physical appearance. Frequently we find intermingled with the abstract or philosophical epithets, consisting of negative and positive attributes as given above, long descriptions of Kṛṣṇa's figure as dark blue, seated on a throne, two-armed, flute in hand, dressed in yellow cloth, his bright face charming and lovely with its red lotus-eyes, his neck adorned with wreaths, his limbs burdened with gems and anointed with sandal and other unguents, and so on.[63]

In the BhP, Viṣṇu's form is also described, and in terms similar to the BVP's portrayal of Kṛṣṇa, though usually less elaborated and less repetitious. Such a description of Viṣṇu's form is found, for instance, in BhP VI.4.36–40. But in the context, it becomes clear that this form is not the highest aspect of God. The description of Viṣṇu's figure follows a hymn of praise by Prajāpati, in which God's supreme nature or essence is described in abstract terminology of a decidedly Advaitic flavor. Prajāpati asserts that Viṣṇu's essential nature cannot be described in words or represented in imagination, and then near the end of his eulogy he declares:

> The Infinite Lord, without name or form, for the sake of favoring his devotees worshipping his feet,
> Assumes names and forms through his births and deeds; may he, the Supreme, be gracious to me.[64]

[61] KJKh 87.32ab.

[62] Hiriyanna, *Outlines,* p. 405. Cf. Carman, "Rāmānuja's Conception," *Ānvīkṣikī,* I, 104. As we shall see, in the BVP, not only Kṛṣṇa has an eternal body, but also his devotees residing in the eternal Goloka. Goloka and its inhabitants are all considered as distinct from or above nature. Similarly in Rāmānuja's school, the bodies of God and of liberated souls, as well as Vaikuṇṭha, are said to be made up of *nityavibhūti* (Hiriyanna, *Outlines,* p. 405). For similar views in Nimbārka's school, see Chaudhuri, "The Nimbārka School of Vedānta," CHI, III, 339.

[63] See, for instance, BKh 2.13–26. Cf. De, VFM, p. 250.

[64] BhP VI.4.33.

The BVP also contains the notion that Kṛṣṇa takes on a form to favor his devotees,[65] and thus seems implicitly to subordinate Kṛṣṇa's *sākāra* (endowed with form) aspect to his *nirākāra* aspect. This view is also reflected in statements asserting the impossibility of worship or meditation without a form or image.[66] Closely related to the above explanation of Kṛṣṇa's *sākāra* aspect is the notion that he takes on a form in order to incarnate himself and relieve the earth of her burden.[67]

We find that the attributes *nirākāra* and *sākāra* are sometimes placed in parallel with *nirguṇa* and *saguṇa*.[68] This also would suggest that Kṛṣṇa's *sākāra* form is inferior to his *nirākāra* aspect, for *nirguṇa* and *saguṇa*, when paired, usually refer to his transcendent and creative aspects respectively.

So far, all the explanations of Kṛṣṇa's *nirākāra* and *sākāra* aspects suggest a subordination of the latter. But there is another explanation not yet mentioned:

> Kṛṣṇa, the self-willed, is both with form and without form.
> Yogins always meditate upon him as formless, as a mass of light.
> They call the Lord the Supreme Brahman, the Supreme Ātman.
>
> . . . .
>
> Vaiṣṇavas, who are his devotees and possess penetrating vision, do not agree.
> They say, "How can there be light without someone possessing the light!?"
> That Supreme Brahman, endowed with light, abides in the midst of a sphere of light.[69]

Following this passage is a description of the Supreme Brahman: it is two-armed, dark blue, flute in hand, and so forth. The formless aspect is clearly subordinate! What appears formless is merely Kṛṣṇa obscured by blinding light. The real or essential Kṛṣṇa, the beautiful, dark blue form that is the source of the light, is perceptible only to his devotees. This explanation of Kṛṣṇa's *sākāra* and *nirākāra* aspects is repeated several times

[65] E.g., PKh 7.88.
[66] E.g., BKh 18.17.
[67] E.g., KJKh 94.37–39.
[68] E.g., GKh 32.29; KJKh 5.96.
[69] PKh 2.12cd–13, 15–16ab.

throughout the BVP and seems to represent the fundamental attitude of our text.[70]

We should be careful, though, not to see this as necessarily a rejection of the Advaitic viewpoint. We may illustrate this by reference to the great sixteenth-century Advaitic scholar, Madhusūdana Sarasvatī. In his work, *Advaitasiddhi,* there is an important section or argument (*vāda*), called the *nirākāravāda,* in which he establishes the formless nature of the Supreme Brahman. At the end of this *vāda,* there appears a short stanza which breaks forth from the logical prose style of the *vāda* proper. In the verse, Madhusūdana proclaims:

> I know no reality higher than Kṛṣṇa, whose face is charming like the full moon, with eyes like lotuses.
> His hand is adorned with a flute; his complexion is the color of a new rain-cloud; he is dressed in yellow silk; and his upper and lower lips are ruddy like the *bimba* fruit.[71]

In another work, Madhusūdana writes:

> There are those who have controlled their *minds* by constant and intense meditation. By such *minds* they see the unique supreme Light. Let such *yogins* do so. As for *me,* let that Thing alone be for the delight of my eyes, That which is somewhat dark-bluish in Effulgence, and which runs and plays on the banks of the river Yamunā.[72]

T. K. Venkateswaran asserts that Madhusūdana's writings reveal "the dialectical and paradoxical tension in which his mind lived, between the qualityless, transcendent impersonal Brahman, on the one hand, and the particular, concrete, quality-flooded Person Krishna, on the other."[73] The paradox involved was not resolved by logic, but rather "by the existential living of an individual life."[74]

[70] See BKh 2.14–27; 17.66–68; 21.32–33; 28.37–39; GKh 7.115–118; 42.38–40; KJKh 9.15; 102.9; 107.89–91; 119.46–47; 129.68–69. Cf. NārPR II.8.29–37.

[71] *vaṃśīvibhūṣitakarān navanīradābhāt pitāmbarād*
aruṇabimbaphalādharoṣṭhāt/
pūrṇendusundaramukhād aravindanetrāt kṛṣṇāt paraṃ
kim api tattvam ahaṃ na jāne//
(*Advaitasiddhiḥ,* p. 234)

[72] Quoted in Venkateswaran, "Rādhā-Krishna *Bhajanas* of South India," *Krishna: Myths, Rites and Attitudes,* p. 149.

[73] *Ibid.,* p. 150.

[74] *Ibid.*

The parallels between Madhusūdana and the BVP are clear. In both there is a dialectical movement between an impersonalistic monism and theistic devotionalism, or, as Venkateswaran calls it, a move "from '*bhakti* to *jñāna* and back.'"[75] Yet in the BVP there is perhaps less of an impulse towards *jñāna*, and a quicker return to *bhakti*. This becomes clearer when the BVP speaks from a soteriological rather than a primarily ontological point of view, as we shall see.

The ascription to Kṛṣṇa of pairs of attributes such as *nirākāra* and *sākāra*, *nirguṇa* and *saguṇa*, is in part an attempt to express his incomprehensible, transcendent nature through paradox, even though the philosophical explanations of the contrasting attributes tend to deprive them of their paradoxical quality. For instance, in PKh 11.108 (Vaṅg), Brahmā beholds Kṛṣṇa as *nirākāra* and *sākāra* at the same time. And in a eulogy offered by Brahmā to Kṛṣṇa in KJKh 5.93–118, we find the following statements: Kṛṣṇa is *saguṇa* and *nirguṇa*, *sākāra* and *nirākāra*, manifest and unmanifest,[76] bodiless and possessing a body;[77] he is the senses and beyond all senses,[78] not witnessing and the witness of all,[79] able to walk but having no feet,[80] seeing all but without an eye,[81] having no hands or mouth but able to eat.[82] It is clear that these assertions are intentional paradoxes, showing the incomprehensible nature of God, for the passage itself refers to Kṛṣṇa as *avitarkya* (not to be inferred by reason) and *anirvacanīya*.[83] Other paradoxes in the BVP are: stained and unstained,[84] independent and dependent,[85] denser than the dense yet more subtle than the subtle,[86] visible in (or by) all yet invisible,[87] pervading the world and beyond the world,[88] eternal and transient,[89] and

[75] *Ibid.*
[76] *vyakta, avyakta.*
[77] *aśarīra, vigrahavad.*
[78] *indriya, atīndriya.*
[79] *asākṣin, sarvasākṣin.*
[80] *gamanārha, apāda.*
[81] *acakṣus, sarvadarśana.*
[82] *hastāsyahīna, bhoktṛ.*
[83] KJKh 5.95, 97.
[84] *lipta, nirlipta* (KJKh 20.43).
[85] *svatantra, asvatantra* (KJKh 20.47).
[86] *sthūlāt sthūlatama, sūkṣmāt sukṣmatama* (GKh 32.28).
[87] *sarvadṛśya, adṛśya* (GKh 32.38).
[88] *jagadvyāpi, jagatpara* (KJKh 20.39).
[89] *nitya, anitya* (KJKh 71.15; Ānand has the correct reading).

free of desire yet the form of desire.[90] Regarding this last, we may note that in KJKh 15, after the wedding ceremony of Kṛṣṇa and Rādhā, for the satisfaction of his new bride, Kṛṣṇa submits to his servant Kāma, who is normally subdued by the servants of the servants of the Lord.[91] Kṛṣṇa's sexual desires are strongly emphasized in our Purāṇa, so that although he is *nirīha* and *niṣkāma,* he is also called *mahākāmin* and *sakāma.*[92]

The BVP often is content to let such paradoxes stand by themselves, but even when the text attempts to give rational explanations, the paradoxical nature of the Supreme is not completely abolished. Let us consider the explanation of Brahman's or Kṛṣṇa's *nirguṇa* and *saguṇa* nature already mentioned. Our Purāṇa stated that when Brahman is dependent upon *māyā,* it is *saguṇa;* when independent, *nirguṇa.* These two forms or states are then related to each other in terms of creation and pre-creation, through the principle of *māyā.* Many of the other paradoxes may also be explained in this way, such as dense and subtle,[93] or visible and invisible. In PKh 30.155, it is said that Kṛṣṇa, through *māyā,* takes on many forms, even though he is one. But what, then, is this *māyā,* and its relation to Kṛṣṇa?

Gail has pointed out that many paradoxes in the BhP are also explained through *māyā.* Thus, Viṣṇu is eternally inactive, but through *māyā* he appears active in the world.[94] In the same way, the paradox of Viṣṇu's being beyond the world and yet being its material cause is resolved. Gail goes on to say, however, that paradox is not completely interpreted out of Viṣṇu's nature, for this *māyā* still belongs to him (as *nijamāyā*), and remains an es-

90 *niṣkāma, kāmarūpa* (BKh 3.12).

91 KJKh 15.146–147.

92 PKh 2.30; 11.41.

93 In BhP II.10.33–36, there is a discussion of the *sthūla* (dense) and *sūkṣma* (subtle) forms of the Lord. The dense or gross form is the physical universe. Higher than this is the subtle form, unmanifest, without attributes (*nirviśeṣaṇa*), eternal, and beyond mind and speech. Both these forms, however, are creations of *māyā!* Gail, commenting on this passage, remarks that the subtle-dense paradox falls entirely within the realm of *māyā,* and may be understood in terms of a potency-act-relationship, thereby losing its paradoxical nature. The real paradox that remains is Viṣṇu's inactivity as Brahman, and activity as creator (Gail, BhBhP, p. 28). In the BVP, the *sthūla-sūkṣma* paradox is not placed within *māyā* but is ascribed directly to Kṛṣṇa. (See GKh 32.28; KJKh 100.25–27.) We do find, though, that the universe emanating from Kṛṣṇa is described as consisting of the subtle and gross (GKh 42.67), but this in itself is not a paradox.

94 Gail, BhBhP, p. 33. See BhP VI.9.35–36.

sential aspect of his being. *Māyā* points to the irrational in the idea of the Divine and preserves its mystery.[95] These remarks of Gail apply equally well to the BVP, for *māyā* is part of Kṛṣṇa's essential being. In fact, whereas in the BhP *māyā* is not actually identified with Viṣṇu,[96] in the BVP Kṛṣṇa is called both *māyin* (possessing *māyā*) and *māyā* itself.[97] Therefore, all attempts to rationalize the paradoxes will ultimately stop short before this double aspect of Kṛṣṇa.

3. Kṛṣṇa and the world

We have seen above that Kṛṣṇa's *saguṇa* nature is associated with his role as creator. In BKh 8.19–21, Kṛṣṇa is equated with *nirguṇa,* while the three gods of creation, preservation, and destruction, Brahmā, Viṣṇu and Kālāgnirudra, are equated with the three *guṇas*. Yet these three gods are none other than portions of Kṛṣṇa himself: "Dividing his form, by his parts, [Kṛṣṇa] becomes the creator, preserver, and destroyer [of the universe]."[98] The association of Kṛṣṇa or Viṣṇu with the three functions of creation, preservation, and destruction is by no means new. In ViP I.1.2 and I.2.59–61, the notion of Hari or Viṣṇu assuming different roles through the three *guṇas* is already found.

In the BVP, Kṛṣṇa in his creative role is called the first of all, the cause of all causes, the seed of all.[99] He is not only cause, though, for he is both cause (*kāraṇa*) and effect (*kārya*).[100] In creation, everything receives its birth from Kṛṣṇa.[101] Yet he is also the offspring (*janya*) as well as the father (*janaka*).[102] Further, he is present everywhere[103] and all-pervading,[104] for he is the form of all (or is all forms).[105] Kṛṣṇa, then, is clearly both the efficient and the material cause of the universe. This is also indicated by the identification of Kṛṣṇa with both *puruṣa* and *prakṛti.*

95 Gail, BBhP, p. 33.
96 Hacker, *Prahlāda,* p. 647.
97 GKh 32.34.
98 GKh 32.32.
99 *sarvādya* (PKh 3.39), *sarvakāraṇakāraṇa* (PKh 2.16; 11.93), *sarvabīja* (PKh 2.26).
100 KJKh 113.32.
101 PKh 8.5.
102 KJKh 113.32.
103 *vidyamānam . . . sarvatra* (BKh 18.10).
104 *sarvavyāpi* (BKh 28.35).
105 *sarvarūpa* (PKh 2.16); *viśvarūpin* (PKh 3.52).

But as we shall see later, *puruṣa* and *prakṛti* express the cosmogonic process not only in terms of an efficient and material cause, but also in terms of a procreator and procreatrix.[106]

The relation of God to the world as its material cause implies a realistic view of the world. But our Purāṇa often seems to adopt a more illusionistic attitude. This is seen in the various contrasts of Kṛṣṇa with the universe, frequently referred to as *ābrahmastamba* (everything from Brahmā to a blade of grass).[107] Although the *ābrahmastamba* derives entirely from Kṛṣṇa,[108] it is ontologically very different from its source. Thus, while Kṛṣṇa is eternal, uncreated, unchanging, the *ābrahmastamba* is ephemeral, created or artificial, and changing. The universe is frequently likened to a bubble or a ripple in water.[109] And finally, Kṛṣṇa is *satya,* while the universe is false (*mithyā*) or like a day dream.[110]

Before leaving Kṛṣṇa's creative aspect, it is worth mentioning one cosmogonic notion that plays little role in our Purāṇa. This concerns the doctrine of the four *vyūhas*, or cosmic manifestations of God. This doctrine, going back to the Nārāyaṇīya and developed by the Pāñcarātrikas, appears in a modified form in the school of Caitanya.[111] Yet despite the similarity of doctrines of the BVP to the Caitanya school and the familiarity of the BVP with Pāñcarātra ideas and literature,[112] the *vyūha* theory is almost wholly neglected in our text. To be sure, there are occasional references to Pradyumna, Aniruddha, and Baladeva, as in KJKh 117.18, where these three appear with Kṛṣṇa as the fourth.[113] But they have no significant cosmogonic role. The reason for the lack of interest in the *vyūha* theory on the part of our text may be due to the emphasis given to *prakṛti*'s creative functions.

106 See pp. 131, 167 ff., below.
107 Cf. SK 54.
108 PKh 10.55.
109 BKh 24.32–33.
110 PKh 36.83; 48.48; 53.27; KJKh 78.17.
111 Among the various kinds of *avatāras* of the Supreme, according to the Caitanya school, the first is as the Puruṣa, for the purpose of creation. This Puruṣa has three aspects: Saṃkarṣaṇa, Pradyumna, and Aniruddha, who have various cosmogonic roles. See De, VFM, p. 184. For the Vyūha theory and the cosmogonic notions of the Pāñcarātrikas, and their relative neglect by Rāmānuja, see Van Buitenen's introduction to *Rāmānuja's Vedārthasaṃgraha,* pp. 36–39.
112 See, for instance, KJKh 133.5; 133.23–24, where five Pañcarātras are mentioned: Vāsiṣṭha, Nāradīya, Kāpila, Gautamīyaka, and Sanatkumārīya.
113 Cf. KJKh 129.39.

Kṛṣṇa as the preserver is the ruler or Lord of all.[114] Frequently it is said that by his command, the wind blows, the sun gives heat, the rain falls, fire burns, Ananta supports the worlds, and Kūrma holds Ananta.[115] Thus Kṛṣṇa is the real support of all (*sarvādhāra*),[116] and has no support himself. In this connection, we may note that one of the main reasons for Kṛṣṇa's *avatāras* is to support the earth, or relieve her of her burdens.[117]

As for Kṛṣṇa's destructive role, at the end of time, all the worlds dissolve back into him, just as they emerged from him at the beginning of time.[118] Kṛṣṇa is Lord of Time both as creator and as destroyer.[119] He controls not only Time but also Death, as he is the time of Time and death of Death.[120]

4. Kṛṣṇa and man

In KJKh 73.94ab, Kṛṣṇa declares: "I am in all beings, and all are in me always."[121] The idea of all beings dwelling in Kṛṣṇa is less

114 PKh 2.79.

115 Cf. PKh 17.65–66; 34.40–52; 53.30–32. Ananta is the world-supporting serpent, Kūrma the cosmic tortoise.

116 PKh 2.21.

117 *bhārāvataraṇāya* (KJKh 87.21). Regarding the protection-motif of the *avatāra* doctrine, in KJKh 27.155–156, Viṣṇu is said to incarnate as Rāma, in order to relieve the earth and subdue demons. Similarly, it is said that Kṛṣṇa incarnates for the preservation or protection of beings (BKh 18.29–30). These reasons are all closely related to the famous passage in BhG IV.7–8. Another kind of reason is related to the play or sport (*līlā*, *krīḍā*) of the Lord. The *līlā*-motif suggests not only the Lord's enjoyment, but also the effortlessness of his incarnation. (See, for instance, BKh 18.29–30). The *līlā*-motif was already considerably developed in the BhP (e.g. BhP VII.9.13. Cf. Gail, BhBhP, pp. 35–38). One aspect of the *līlā* is Kṛṣṇa's amorous diversions with the *gopīs*. The BVP, as might be expected, has elaborated on this particular aspect, specifically in connection with Rādhā. Our text declares, in fact, that Kṛṣṇa incarnated only for Rādhā's sake (KJKh 2.13–16; 6.229; 13.100–102). *Adhyāyas* 2 and 3 of the KJKh explain the circumstances under which Kṛṣṇa promised to Rādhā to descend to earth. Briefly, as the result of a love quarrel in Goloka between Rādhā and Kṛṣṇa, she had been cursed by Kṛṣṇa's guardian, Śrīdāman, to descend to earth. Kṛṣṇa then agreed to follow her. In *adhyāyas* 4–6, the more usual account, concerning the relief of the earth's burden, is given.

118 GKh 42.67.

119 Cf. PKh 53.45–46.

120 BKh 15.54.

121 *ahaṃ ca sarvabhūteṣu mayi sarve ca santatam/*

Cf. BhP III.24.46:

ātmānaṃ sarvabhūteṣu bhagavantam avasthitam/
apaśyat sarvabhūtāni bhagavaty api cātmani//

emphasized in our Purāṇa than Kṛṣṇa's dwelling in all beings.[122] The significance of the latter for our text is indicated by the frequently repeated epithets of Kṛṣṇa as *sarvātman* (Self of all)[123] and *sarvāntarātman* (inner Self of all).[124] Kṛṣṇa, as Paramātman is one, but by *aṃśas* and *kalās*, he resides in separate individuals. For this reason, it is said, when one person eats, another is not thereby satisfied.[125] Kṛṣṇa is regarded as non-different from his parts, like fire and its sparks,[126] so the relationship of Kṛṣṇa, the Supreme Self, to embodied beings, appears to be a type of *bhedābheda* (non-difference in difference).

Does Kṛṣṇa indwell in beings *as* their soul, or merely abide *next to* the individual soul (*jīva*)? On the relationship of Ātman to *jīva*, the BVP sometimes asserts that Kṛṣṇa, as Ātman, is *sākṣin* and *bhojayitṛ* (witness and "feeder"), whereas the *jīva* is *bhoktṛ* (enjoyer). The *jīva* alone is associated with *karma* as *bhoktṛ* and is *saguṇa,* while the *bhojayitṛ* is *nirguṇa*.[127] Thus, even though Kṛṣṇa enters into bodies, he is unmingled with *karma*.[128] The *jīva,* however, is nothing but the reflection of the Ātman. Kṛṣṇa himself declares:

> The jīva is my reflection in all beings everywhere.
> It is the enjoyer and agent of good and bad acts.[129]
> As the image of the moon or sun is reflected in many jars of water,
> And when the jars are broken, the image is reunited (*saṃśliṣṭa*) with its source, so in me
> The *jīva* is reunited in time, when creatures die, my dear.[130]

This monisticizing tendency is carried even further by the iden-

[122] In the BhP, the idea of all existing in God is illustrated by Kṛṣṇa's two revelations to his mother of the universe within his mouth (X.7.35 ff.; 8.36 ff.). These theophanies are absent in the BVP. Cf. Gail, BhBhP, pp. 30–32.

[123] E.g., PKh 3.39.

[124] E.g., PKh 12.9.

[125] KJKh 112.54 ff. Cf. KJKh 126.83 ff. By his *aṃśas* and *kalās*, Kṛṣṇa resides not only in all embodied beings, but in all images (*pratimāsu*) as well (KJKh 112.59).

[126] BKh 17.37.

[127] PKh 60.30. Cf. Pkh 25.13–16.

[128] KJKh 78.30.

[129] Cf. NārPR II.1.27–28:
paramātmasvarūpaś ca bhagavān rādhikeśvaraḥ/
nirliptaḥ sākṣirūpaś ca sa ca karmasu karmiṇām//
jīvas tatpratibimbaś ca bhoktā ca sukhaduḥkhayoḥ/

[130] KJKh 67.46–48ab.

tification of Kṛṣṇa with the *jīva* itself: "He [Kṛṣṇa] is the Ātman and the *jīva* of all. . . ."[131] And: "You [Kṛṣṇa] are the *jīva,* enjoying and suffering (*bhogin*); you are the reflection of yourself, the witness."[132] The BVP here teaches a monism of God and the human soul, but of a somewhat different tone from Śaṃkara's *advaita.* For Śaṃkara, the *jīva* is identified with Ātman and Brahman, but not the reverse. Nor is Brahman-Ātman spoken of as *bhogin.*

It is perhaps in order, here, to point out again that the monisticizing tendencies of the BVP are strongest when the point of view is primarily ontological. The emphasis in such cases is on Kṛṣṇa as the one true reality, upon whom all else does and must depend. Such knowledge will turn a man towards Kṛṣṇa. But the ontological approach is subordinated in our text to the devotional and soteriological. These latter, to be dealt with in our next two chapters, presuppose for the most part a dualistic ontology that at times is quite explicit.

Our analysis above has shown that the BVP has taken over many traditional Vaiṣṇavite conceptions of God, synthesizing them in its own particular way. Yet it is in its doctrine of Kṛṣṇa in relation to *prakṛti* that the BVP is most original and creative, hints of which we have already seen. Let us then keep in mind the main features of the BVP's conception of Kṛṣṇa for our discussion later of *prakṛti.*

[131] PKh 18.60c.
[132] GKh 7.114cd.

5

The True Vaiṣṇava and Supreme Devotion

In chapter 3 above we discussed Vaiṣṇavas in relation to other sects, principally Śaivas and Śāktas. Here we shall examine the BVP's view of the Vaiṣṇava in himself, or rather, in his relation to God. This relationship is conceived in the BVP primarily in terms of *bhakti,* so we shall also be looking closely into the nature of devotion.

The followers of Hari or Kṛṣṇa are most often referred to simply as *bhaktas* (devotees). Kṛṣṇa himself frequently refers to his votaries as *madbhaktas.*[1] Another common name used by Kṛṣṇa for his devotees is *manmantropāsakas* (worshippers or followers of my *mantra*).[2] This epithet points to the external definition of a Vaiṣṇava, repeated many times in our text:

> Into whose ear, from the mouth of his *guru,* has entered the *mantra* of Viṣṇu,
> He is a Vaiṣṇava, greatly purified, according to the wise.[3]

By taking the *mantra,* it is said, a man saves not only himself, but his family and relatives, ancestors, servants and others. It is further declared that by the mere acceptance of the *mantra,* a

[1] E.g., PKh 6.94; 10.72; 10.86.

[2] E.g., PKh 6.93: *manmantropāsakā bhaktā.*

[3] PKh 60.55. See also BKh 11.41; PKh 6.114; 10.43; GKh 8.70. Cf. NārPR II.2.15:

gurumantrāt [?] *kṛṣṇamantro yasya karṇe viśed aho/*
taṃ vaiṣṇavaṃ mahāpūtaṃ pravadanti purāvidaḥ//

man becomes a *jīvanmukta* (liberated while still living),[4] and even becomes Nārāyaṇa.[5]

The receiving of the *mantra,* in itself an external act, implies a radical reorientation of the devotee to God. This becomes clear from examining the other features of the true Vaiṣṇava. These are described in some detail in PKh 6.112–122. In response to Lakṣmī's inquiry about the nature of his devotees, Hari first refers to the receiving of his *mantra,* and then continues:

> He loves and honors me and is possessed of my virtues;
> He is praiseworthy because of my virtues and is constantly intent on me.
> Merely remembering my virtues, he is filled with joy, his hair erect.
> His voice faltering, tears in his eyes, forgetful of himself.
> He does not desire happiness, nor the fourfold *mukti, sālokya* and so forth,[6]
> Nor the position of Brahmā, nor immortality; his desire is to serve me.[7]

This passage touches upon three basic motifs: the devotional acts of worship, the emotional ecstasy of the votary, and his complete lack of selfish desire. Let us deal with these in order.

1. The nine acts of devotion: *navadhā bhaktilakṣaṇa*

Such acts as *pūjā,* concentration upon God, and remembering his virtues, mentioned in the quotation above, form part of a group referred to by our Purāṇa as *navadhā bhaktilakṣaṇa* (the nine characteristics of *bhakti*). A complete list of these characteristics is given in our text at least five times, with some variations in each.[8] The following list appears in KJKh 1.33–34: *arcana* (homage), *vandana* (obeisance), *mantrajapa* (*mantra*-recita-

[4] PKh 10.47; 36.96.

[5] PKh 65.36.

[6] See below, chapter 6, section 3.

[7] PKh 6.117–119. The idea of the true Vaiṣṇava's not desiring the various forms of *mukti* as void of *sevana* is found also in the BhP, in III.29.13. Below, under *dāsya,* we shall give special attention to this notion in the BVP and its relation to the BhP.

[8] These lists occur in BKh 6.15–16; PKh 27.141–143; 36.73–74; 63.19–20; and KJKh 1.33–34. The first, fourth, and fifth of these specifically refer to themselves as *navadhā bhaktilakṣaṇa.*

tion), *sevana* (service), *smaraṇa* (remembrance), *kīrtana* (praise), *guṇaśravaṇa* (hearing the virtues), *nivedana* (surrender), and *dāsya* (servitude). We shall deal with these in greater detail after a consideration of certain aspects of their historical development within the Vaiṣṇava movement.

The list of nine marks from the KJKh is almost the same as that given by Prahlāda in BhP VII.5.23–24: *śravaṇa, kīrtana, viṣṇoḥ smaraṇa, pādasevana, arcana, vandana, dāsya, sakhya,* and *ātmanivedana.* The KJKh list has replaced *sakhya* (friendship) with *mantrajapa.* The notion of nine *bhakti* marks, then, is not original with the BVP. In the history of Vaiṣṇavism, however, the number of defining characteristics has varied considerably. In the BhP itself, thirty marks of the supreme *dharma* are given, the last nine of which correspond to Prahlāda's list in VII.5.23–24.[9] Prahlāda himself elsewhere refers to a six-limbed service to Viṣṇu.[10] Sixfold worship also appears in the NārPR.[11] Among the Caitanya Gosvāmins, Jīva lists eleven acts; Gopālabhaṭṭa says there may be eight, nine or sixteen; and Rūpa refers to sixty-four.[12] The Gosvāmins are known for their love of exhaustive classification and analysis, so this kind of elaboration is not surprising. The extension of the number of characteristics was facilitated by the fact that the nine basic marks in the BhP are not narrowly defined terms but broad notions, each covering a variety of activities. Gail states that *smaraṇa, śravaṇa,* and *kīrtana* serve as "Dachbegriffe" for such activities as *gai* (to sing), *gṛ* (to invoke), *brū* (to explain), *paṭh* (to recite), *smṛ* (to remember), *dhyai* (to meditate upon), *kṛ* (to compose), and *varṇ* (to describe).[13] We find, then, that Jīva Gosvāmin includes *stotra* (hymn of praise) under *kīrtana, dhyāna* (meditation) under *smaraṇa,* and such ritual acts as *nirmālyadhāraṇa* (eating the remains of food offered to God), and *caraṇāmṛtapāna* (drinking the water used to bathe the feet of the image) under *arcana.*[14] In

[9] The thirty marks or characteristics appear in BhP VII.11.8–11.

[10] *Namas, stuti, karma, pūjākarma, smṛtiścaraṇayoḥ,* and *śravaṇaṃ kathāyām* (VII.9.50).

[11] *kurvanti vaiṣṇavāḥ śaśvat ṣaḍvidhaṃ bhajanaṃ hareḥ//*
smaraṇaṃ [or *śravaṇaṃ* in one reading] *kīrtanaṃ*
caiva vandanaṃ pādasevanam/
pūjanaṃ satataṃ bhaktyā paraṃ svātmanivedanam//
(NārPR II.2.10cd–11)

[12] See De, VFM, pp. 129, 280–282, 370.

[13] BhBhP, p. 75.

[14] De, VFM, pp. 281–282.

the BVP, many of these other marks just mentioned appear as substitutions in one or another of the five lists. Altogether, we find the following substitutions: *stotra* or *stavana, dhyāna, naivedyabhojana* (=*nirmālyadhāraṇa*), *caraṇodakapāna, bhāvana* (devotion or meditation), and *varṇana.* Nonetheless, our text holds to the particular tradition of only nine defining marks.

More important than the number of characteristics are the views regarding the nature of the marks as a whole. There are two general problems here. First is the question of the interrelationship of the different devotional acts. Jīva Gosvāmin sees them as an ascending series of devotional stages.[15] It is important to note, in this respect, that he follows the order of the BhP.[16] The last three stages, then, are *dāsya,* followed by *sakhya,* and culminating in *ātmanivedana.*[17] The BhP may have intended its list of acts to represent ascending stages of devotion, though this is not entirely clear. The BVP, in any case, seems not to have this intention, judging from the apparently haphazard order of its different lists. Yet as we shall see, certain of the marks are given special attention.

The second question concerns the role or place of these devotional activities in the general scheme of *bhakti.* In the Caitanya school, various forms or levels of *bhakti* have been elaborated. Rūpa has distinguished two basic types, *sāmānyabhakti* (general devotion), and *uttamabhakti* (supreme devotion). *Uttamabhakti* is further differentiated into *sādhanabhakti, bhāvabhakti,* and *premabhakti,* in ascending order. *Sādhanabhakti* is realizable by external means, not by inward emotion (*bhāva*). *Sādhanabhakti* itself is twofold: *vaidhī* and *rāgānuga. Vaidhībhakti* is prompted entirely by scriptural injunction, not by attachment (*rāga*). The *vaidhībhakti* includes the various acts of devotion.[18] These acts thus occupy a rather low place in Rūpa's *bhakti*-stages. At the same time, apparently, the devotional acts persist in the higher

[15] De, VFM, pp. 280–283. Cf. Bhattacharya, "A Study of the Cult of Devotion," ALB, XXV, 602.

[16] Jīva adds two acts to those of the BhP, *śaraṇāpatti* and *gurusevā.* These appear as the first two stages. For *śaraṇāpatti* in the BVP, see below, p. 104.

[17] Cf. note 21 below.

[18] See De, VFM, pp. 126–129; cf. pp. 280–283, 370–371. Rūpa apparently includes *smaraṇa* under *rāgānugabhakti* (De, VFM, pp. 130–131), while Jīva includes it as one of the eleven elements of the *vaidhībhakti.*

stages of *bhakti,* even though the necessity of outward acts is dispensed with.[19]

The *vaidhībhakti* of the Caitanya school corresponds to the *maryādābhakti* of the Vallabha sect. The path of *maryādā,* or scriptural law, leads gradually to liberation. But the immediate attainment is through God's grace (*puṣṭi*) alone.[20] Further, Vallabha regarded the *maryādābhakti,* though once practicable, as no longer feasible in his own time. Liberation in the present day thus necessitates surrendering oneself entirely to God's grace. *Puṣṭi,* however, does not exclude the nine devotional acts; they are simply the natural result of *puṣṭi,* and not the means of liberation.[21]

We find then that there has been a tendency to subordinate the nine acts of *bhakti* to an extreme emotionalistic or self-surrendering love of God. Another kind of subordination is found in Śrīdhara's commentary on the BhP. In BhP III.29.8–12, *bhaktas* are classified as *tāmasa, rājasa, sāttvika,* and *nirguṇa.* Śrīdhara says that the devotion of each of the first three or *saguṇa bhaktas* has three stages, each of which in turn is connected with the nine devotional acts, so that *saguṇa-bhakti* is eighty-onefold. *Nirguṇabhakti,* however, is "onefold." Gail observes that Śrīdhara's motive for this scheme is clear: the multiplying of the second-rank *bhakti* forms illuminates more clearly the "onefold" *bhakti,* which is designated in the BhP itself as true recognition. Śrīdhara and the BhP thus tend to subordinate the nine devotional acts to an "intellectual" *bhakti* that stresses uni-

19 Cf. De, VFM, 272–273.

20 For the BVP's conception of grace, see chapter 6, section 2 below.

21 See Bhatt, "Vallabha," in HPEW, I, 352–355. Richard Barz gives the following summary of the nine devotional marks in Vallabha's teachings: "These nine steps are the general elements of the *Puṣṭimārga.* There is only one point at which Vallabhācārya's attitude towards these nine steps differs markedly from that of Rūpa Gosvāmī and other Vaiṣṇava *bhaktas:* Vallabhācārya makes the ninth and most difficult step the *ātma-nivedana,* the initial step in the *Puṣṭimārga.* Vallabhācārya begins with that attitude of mind which is, for other *bhaktas* not in his Sampradaya, the very apex of devotional achievement and the result of careful cultivation of the other eight steps over a long period of time. Evidently, Vallabhācārya saw the first eight steps of the practice of *bhakti* as being parts of the ninth, which would be the whole" (*Early Developments within the Bhakti Sect of Vallabhācārya,* p. 123). I am not sure I can fully agree with Barz's differentiation of Vallabha from other *bhaktas,* particularly the Caitanya school, for whom the nine steps certainly did not constitute the "apex of devotional achievement," as we have seen above. Cf. Parekh, *Sri Vallabhacharya,* pp. 237–239.

fying knowledge. Gail sees the BhP as differing from the Bengali Vaiṣṇavas as well as from the *sūtra* writers Nārada and Śāṇḍilya in its emphasis on mystical recognition of unity, rather than on love of God.[22] It should be remembered, however, that the difference is one of emphasis, not of absolute dichotomy. To see the role of the *bhakti*-marks in the BVP, let us look in some detail at several of these devotional acts.

a) *Arcana, sevana,* and *vandana*

Arcana, sevana (or *pādasevana,*[23] *pādasevā*[24]), and *vandana* relate to *devapūjā,* or the ritual worship of an image of the deity.[25] S. Bhattacharya suggests that these three marks may be of Tāntric origin.[26] Involved in the *devapūjā* is the purification of the celebrant by Vedic and Tāntric *mantras*, bathing, the offering of various articles of worship (*upacāra*), usually regarded as sixteen, and other rites already mentioned, such as *caranāmṛtapāna.*[27]

Many of these features of *pūjā* appear also in the BhP. But in the BhP, the relationship of *arcana, sevana,* and *vandana* to salvation is unclear, according to Gail. He shows that these three acts are connected with the fulfilment of desires, rather than with salvation. So long as personal desire remains, no real communion with God is possible. On the other hand, the true *bhakta,* who is free of personal desire, can do away with offerings and image worship: his devotional acts take place in his heart, where a spiritual image of Viṣṇu glows. This transformation from an outer to a spiritual offering is the fruit of the realization that God is immanent in one's own heart and in all beings. An external image of God becomes superfluous.[28]

The BVP also speaks of the true *bhakta* as free from personal desire, as we shall see below. Further, the true *bhakta* is one who

[22] BhBhP, p. 43. Cf. DBhP VII.37.4 ff. (See note 88 below.)
[23] PKh 36.73.
[24] BKh 6.15. Cf. PKh 27.141: *kṛṣṇapādāmbujārcana.*
[25] Cf. Gail, BhBhP, p. 75; De, VFM, pp. 281–282.
[26] "A Study of the Cult of Devotion," ALB, XXV, 602.
[27] For a list of the sixteen articles, see, for instance, BKh 26.90–91. The two preceding verses state that sometimes only twelve or five are offered to the deity, according to the resources of the devotee. According to De, Gopālabhaṭṭa says that the Tāntric Vaiṣṇavas have divided the *upacāras* into three groups, of five, ten, and sixteen ingredients, to accommodate the means of different devotees (VFM, p. 368).
[28] For Gail's analysis of *devapūjā* in the BhP, see BhBhP, pp. 79–86.

realizes Viṣṇu to exist equally in all creatures.[29] However, there is little tendency to suspend the outer forms of ritual. For instance, let us consider *naivedyabhojana,* which as we have seen is included under the notion of *arcana.* The BVP informs us that a person who does not eat the remnants of food offered to Hari, being void of *harisevā,* is impure to perform any rites.[30] Such a person, along with those void of *viṣṇupūjā* and others who neglect various rites, goes to hell.[31] The partaking of the remnants, on the other hand, purifies one of all sins.[32] Even eating the food offerings unknowingly frees one from the sins committed in seven births.[33] Finally, it is said:

> He who eats the remnants, bowing constantly to Hari,
> Who performs his *pūjā* or sings his praise with devotion, becomes equal to Viṣṇu.[34]

Such rites, of course, are not mere external acts but rooted in *bhakti* (*bhaktimūla*).[35]

The BVP in its attitude towards ceremonial worship thus differs from the BhP as well as the Caitanya school. In this respect, the BVP is closer to the Pāñcarātra Āgamas, which emphasize the necessity of such rituals.[36] The views of the BVP may also reflect its Tāntric orientation.

b) *Smaraṇa, kīrtana,* and *śravaṇa*

These three *bhakti*-marks, including the subsumed notions of *dhyāna, japa, stavana* and so forth, constitute an inner or mental cult complementing the concrete ritual just discussed.[37] Of the three basic marks, *smaraṇa* plays a particularly important role in our text.[38] It occurs also as *smṛti,* or in an inflected form of the

[29] See GKh 35.73.
[30] PKh 41.6.
[31] PKh 51.45–48.
[32] PKh 36.38.
[33] PKh 36.40. This is an interesting parallel to the BhP's views on *nāmakīrtana.* According to the BhP, even unintentional mention of the Lord's name leads to redemption. See BhP V.25.11; VI.1; and VI.2.7. BhP VI.1 contains the story of Ajāmila's redemption from sin by his accidental calling out to his son, whose name was Nārāyaṇa. Cf. Gail, BhBhP, p. 77.
[34] PKh 36.31.
[35] See, for instance, BKh 26.89.
[36] See De, VFM, p. 281.
[37] Cf. Gail, BhBhP, p. 75.
[38] Hacker has commented that whereas *smaraṇa* is only one of nine *bhakti*-marks in the BhP, it appears as the whole of *bhakti* in the ViP and Rāmānuja (*Prahlāda,* pp. 656–657).

root *smṛ*. It has four principal objects: the name of God, his *mantra*, his lotus-feet, and God himself.

Concerning the first, God has many names, but the most auspicious or sacred, of course, is Kṛṣṇa. Thus our text says that the fruit of remembering millions of names of the Lord is attained by remembering the one name of Kṛṣṇa.[39] As for the fruit of recalling God's name, let us consider the esoteric or mystical meaning and power of the word Kṛṣṇa. "Kṛṣi" (harvest), we are told, means *nirvāṇa;* the letter "n" means *mokṣa,* and the letter "a" means bestower; thus God (the bestower of *nirvāṇa* and *mokṣa*) is called by this name.[40] It is said that the pronunciation of the name has the same results as remembering or hearing it.[41] By the pronunciation of "K", the *bhakta* obtains *kaivalya* (emancipation), overcoming death and birth; "ṛ" bestows unequaled *dāsya* (servitude); "s" bestows *bhakti;* and "n" bestows dwelling with God and equality with him.[42] This kind of mystical etymology may well reflect Tāntric notions. We also find that remembering the name of God at the time of death leads to his abode.[43]

As for the second object of *smaraṇa,* the *mantra* of Viṣṇu or Kṛṣṇa, we are told that its recollection is the cause of purity of heart or mind (*manonairmalya*), and that by reflection or meditation (*upāsanā*) on Viṣṇu's *mantra,* the bonds of the heart are sundered, all doubts are removed, and *karma* destroyed.[44]

Kṛṣṇa's lotus-feet are the supreme refuge in the universe.[45] They are said to destroy birth, death, old age, sickness, sorrow, to uproot *karma,* and grant joy.[46] Thus it is natural that men in times of trouble remember them.[47] But the remembrance of or meditation on Kṛṣṇa's feet is also an act of supreme devotion, as is the case with the pious Ākrūra, who, filled with *bhakti,* constantly remembers the Lord's lotus-feet.[48]

All that has been said in reference to the name, *mantra,* and

[39] KJKh 13.62–63.
[40] KJKh 13.61–62.
[41] KJKh 13.63.
[42] KJKh 13.65–66. The text is perhaps corrupt, as the final letter "a" of Kṛṣṇa's name is omitted.
[43] PKh 10.77. Cf. BKh 3.50; PKh 14.38–39. This notion goes back at least to the *Gītā* (VIII.5). Cf. Edgerton, *The Bhagavad Gītā,* pp. 176–177.
[44] PKh 60.39–40.
[45] PKh 11.83.
[46] KJKh 128.8–9. Cf. GKh 46.9.
[47] E.g., KJKh 25.51.
[48] KJKh 66.36–37.

feet of Kṛṣṇa applies naturally to Kṛṣṇa in himself. Thus the remembrance of Kṛṣṇa gives fearlessness and well-being,[49] rescues men from misfortune,[50] delivers one from sin and protects one from temptation, especially sexual temptation.[51] The remembrance of God is closely associated with the idea of seeking his refuge, and may possibly be identified with one of the three forms of resorting to the Lord, by means of *dhyāna*.[52]

In the BhP, as Gail has noted, the effective power of *smaraṇa* is its capacity to merge the subject with the object of thought.[53] Thus in BhP XI.14.27, Kṛṣṇa says:

> The mind of him who meditates on worldly objects becomes attached to those objects.
> The mind of him who remembers me dissolves into me.

In our text, though, *smaraṇa* culminates not so much in the idea of mergence with God, but in "reciprocity." That is, not only does the true devotee remember God, but God remembers the devotee. Kṛṣṇa himself declares:

> [My *bhaktas*,] abandoning wife, son, and relatives, meditate on me day and night;
> And I . . . remember them constantly, day and night.[54]

Similarly it is said:

> Vaiṣṇavas meditate constantly on the lotus-feet of Govinda,
> And Govinda constantly meditates on them, in their presence.[55]

Kīrtana (*saṃkīrtana, utkīrtana*), is associated with the singing or praising of Kṛṣṇa, his deeds, and especially of his name and virtues. The fruits of *kīrtana* are said to be long life, freedom from sin, the overcoming of time, death, birth, passion, illness, and fear,

49 PKh 13.49.
50 PKh 37.40.
51 See KJKh 31.64; 32.3; 32.70, where Brahmā, afflicted by Kāma's arrows, remembers Hari. In KJKh 35.93, if one by accident sees a *parastrī*, he should remember Hari.
52 The other two are by means of speech, and in person. See PKh 13.48–49.
53 BhBhP, p. 72.
54 KJKh 6.58. Cf. BhP III.25.22 for the notion of the devotee abandoning his relatives.
55 BKh 11.44. Cf. NārPR I.2.36:
dhyāyante vaiṣṇavāḥ kṛṣṇaṃ kṛṣṇaś ca vaiṣṇavāṃstathā//

and the attaining of *sukha* (happiness), *mokṣa,* and *jīvanmukti.*[56]

Śravaṇa occupied an important place in the BhP, as is demonstrated by the example of King Parikṣit, who in his last week of life listens to the whole of the Purāṇa.[57] In the BVP, it is stated that whoever listens to the Purāṇa (BVP) with devotion attains *bhakti* and goes at death to Hari's abode.[58] It is further said that the hearing of one *adhyāya* produces the same fruit as the hearing of the whole.[59] *Śravaṇa* applies not only to the accounts of Kṛṣṇa's history and other sacred tales, but also to the hearing of his virtues, beauty, and name.[60] We may recall that the hearing of Kṛṣṇa's name is said to be equal to remembering or pronouncing it.[61] The idea of reciprocity associated with *smaraṇa* is also connected with *śravaṇa:*

> Upon hearing his own name and virtues, entirely agitated,
> Hari wanders, like a shadow, in the midst of his devotees.[62]

c) *Nivedana*

Surrender is the last, and perhaps the highest or supreme devotional act in the BhP. The terms used by the BhP are *ātmanivedana* and *ātmasamarpaṇa.*[63] According to Gail, it refers to the complete self-submission of the devotee to God, comparable to the *prapatti* doctrine of Rāmānuja.[64] In the BhP, the culmination of this submission is explained by Kṛṣṇa himself:

> When a mortal has abandoned all action (*tyaktasamastakarmā*), having surrendered his Self [to me], I wish to transform him.
> Attaining immortality, he is fit to become one Self with me.[65]

In the BVP, *nivedana* occurs in only three of the five lists, and in only one of these is it placed last.[66] It is referred to variously

[56] See PKh 3.62; 18.61; 27.21; and 27.110.
[57] Cf. Gail, BhBhP, p. 75.
[58] KJKh 133.68.
[59] BKh 1.64.
[60] See PKh 10.53 and KJKh 16.60–61.
[61] KJKh 13.62–63.
[62] KJKh 25.74.
[63] *Ātmasamarpaṇa* occurs in BhP VII.11.11.
[64] BhBhP, p. 60.
[65] BhP XI.29.34.
[66] It appears as the ninth mark in PKh 63.19. In KJKh 1.34 and BKh 6.16 it is eighth.

as *sarvanivedana* and *samarpaṇam ātmanaḥ*. *Samarpaṇa* elsewhere in the text is often connected with *karma*. This is similar to the notion of abandoning action that appears in the BhP passage just quoted. In KJKh 97.13, it is stated that whatever act (*karma*) is made over to Kṛṣṇa is auspicious, pure, and pleasing to the Lord. And in KJKh 25.30, the pious king Ambarīṣa is said to be an unstained agent (*kartā*), having surrendered all his acts to Kṛṣṇa (*sarvakarmasu kṛṣṇārpiteṣu*).[67]

As in the BhP, the notion of surrender in our text is associated with the idea of union with the Absolute. In PKh 36.69, it is said that a person having surrendered everything to Kṛṣṇa, dissolves or merges into the Supreme Brahman.[68] However, the next verse goes on to say that this state is not desired by Vaiṣṇavas, for it is void of service (*sevā*). We shall have occasion to refer again to this passage in our chapter on *mukti*, but what is important to note here is the apparent or implicit subordination of *samārpaṇa* to *sevā*. This term, as we shall see, is synonymous in our text with *dāsya*, the ninth mark listed in KJKh 1.34.

d) *Dāsya*

Dāsya in the BhP is the seventh of the nine marks. According to the commentator Śrīdhara, and Kāntimālā, *dāsya* means surrender of works (*karmārpaṇa*) to Viṣṇu.[69] In the BVP, *dāsya* may include this notion, even though surrender of works, as we have seen, appears in its own right as one of the nine *bhakti*-marks. What is more significant about *dāsya* in our text, however, is its close relation, and even identification, with *sevā* or *sevana*. For instance, in PKh 6.119, already quoted, the Vaiṣṇava desires not the fourfold *mukti* but *sevana*. The same idea is repeated in KJKh 84.45, with *dāsya* in place of *sevana*. Sevana, as already mentioned, is often connected with service to the Lord's feet (*pādasevana*). We find that *dāsya* also has this specific meaning, as in KJKh 13.193, where Garga asks for *dāsyaṃ padāmbuje*. Yet both terms seem to have a broader meaning as well.

Dāsya frequently appears in our text as a synonym for *bhakti*. In BKh 12.29, we find reference to *śrīkṛṣṇe bhaktidāsyam*, and in 12.36 to *bhaktir haridāsyam*. In BKh 18.45, a Vaiṣṇava is said

[67] We shall discuss further the nature of *karma* and *karmayoga* in our chapter below on *muktimārga* and *mukti*.

[68] *sarvaṃ kṛṣṇārpaṇaṃ kṛtvā pare brahmaṇi līyate//*

[69] See Hacker, *Prahlāda*, p. 657, and Gail, BhBhP, p. 59.

to attain *haribhaktiṃ harer dāsyam. Dāsya* at times is even considered as the fruit of *bhakti:*

> Through association with *bhaktas*, a thriving shoot [of the tree] of *bhakti* appears.
> Through seeing non-*bhaktas*, it dries up.
> It again blossoms forth from [the water of] conversation with Vaiṣṇavas.
> This shoot, indestructible, grows in every birth.
> When grown into a tree, it produces the fruit of *haridāsya.*[70]

And in KJKh 22.60, it is said that a virtuous man attains *bhakti* in this world, *dāsya* in the next.

What, we may ask, does *dāsya,* or *sevana,* signify in this highest sense? It is curious that *dāsya* occurs only once in the five lists in the BVP. To be sure, *sevā* or *sevana* appears in four, but twice it is connected with *pāda* and there is no indication in the lists themselves that would suggest that either *sevā* or *dāsya* holds an exalted position. In view of what has been said above, this apparent neglect, especially of *dāsya,* seems surprising. But let us look more carefully at the context in which these lists occur.

In introducing the list in PKh 27.141–143, our text enumerates many auspicious acts such as bathing at *tīrthas*, recitation of the four Vedas and so forth. The seed of these is said to be *kṛṣṇa-sevana,* described in the Purāṇas, the Vedas, and Itihāsas. The description that follows consists of the nine devotional acts. Regarding the list of marks appearing in BKh 6.15–16, Śiva asks Kṛṣṇa for a boon. His request is for uninterrupted *dāsya* to Kṛṣṇa. Śiva then names several acts, such as *japa, padasevana, dhyāna, pūjana, vandana,* and *kīrtana.* Finally, Śiva lists nine acts, repeating several of those he has just mentioned. He concludes, "Grant me, Lord, this boon, consisting of the *navadhā bhaktilakṣaṇa.*" This passage then apparently equates *dāsya* with the nine marks of *bhakti.*

These two examples strongly suggest that our text understands *sevana* or *dāsya* to consist of the nine devotional acts. The inclusion of *dāsya* or *sevana* in the nine does not necessarily invalidate

[70] GKh 8.76–78ab. Cf. also KJKh 21.221–226 and 111.12–14. The idea of *satsaṅga* (association with the good), incidentally, is already fully developed in the BhP. For discussion of the BhP's views on *satsaṅga,* see Gail, BhBhP, pp. 88–91.

this view, for these terms may then be understood in their more restricted sense. The identification of service with the devotional acts is an old Vaiṣṇava notion. In the BhP, as mentioned above, Prahlāda gives two lists of acts. One is simply called the *bhakti* of nine characteristics (*bhaktir navalakṣaṇā*), but the other is referred to as the six-limbed service (*saṃsevā ṣaḍaṅgā*). These lists themselves may well precede the BhP. Hacker comments that these two sets can hardly be the creation of the author (of the Prahlāda legend) of the BhP. Otherwise, he argues, there is no explanation of why their contents are similar in part, but one is called "service," the other "*bhakti*-characteristics." Hacker concludes that the two lists must have been collected by the poet, whose real contribution, apparently, was the emotionalistic conception of *bhakti*.[71] (We shall deal with this emotionalistic conception in the next section.) Hacker's comment suggests that service does not hold the supreme position in the BhP that it does in the BVP. Gail, though arguing along somewhat different lines from Hacker, asserts that in the BhP, bondage or service to Viṣṇu by no means constitutes the essence of *bhakti*, the peak of which is climbed by the knower.[72]

To summarize, the BVP does not view the nine *bhakti*-marks as an ascending series, but apparently as the constitutive parts of *dāsya*, in its highest sense. The various acts of service, including those of the concrete cult, are not suspended in favor of a "spiritual-intellectual" devotion, as sometimes happens in the BhP, nor subordinated to an extreme emotionalistic love of God, as among the Gosvāmins. *Dāsya* rather is the supreme devotion. It is not lacking in emotional content, however, as our next section will show.

2. *Preman:* ecstatic love

In the Caitanya school, as mentioned above, the *bhakti*-marks or outward acts of devotion are motivated by scriptural injunction, not by inner emotion. This outward *bhakti*, however, is a means to *bhāvabhakti*, which in turn may mature into the supreme *premabhakti*. The manifest signs of this *preman* or ecstatic love include weeping, erection of the hair, singing, dancing, laughing

[71] *Prahlāda*, p. 658.
[72] BhBhP, p. 40.

and so forth.[73] The roots of this emotionalistic *bhakti* can be traced back to the BhP and earlier.[74] In the BhP, we find that such emotional or ecstatic expressions of love are often the result of direct encounters with the Lord, as when Akrūra meets Kṛṣṇa.[75] They are also the response to devotional acts such as *pūjā*, or uttering the name of the Lord.[76] *Preman* in the BhP further has its eroticized aspect, described especially in *skandha* X. It is women who best exemplify this kind of devotion.[77]

In the BVP, we find that *preman* also occurs in an eroticized form. *Preman* characterizes especially Rādhā's feelings towards Kṛṣṇa.[78] She is frequently called, for instance, *kṛṣṇapremamayī*.[79] And she is said to have become *kṛṣṇapremādhidevatā* through *preman* and *sevā*.[80] Here we may note, by the way, the close association of service with *preman*. Rādhā in the BVP, as we shall see, does not serve as a model for man, however, at least in the erotic aspect. The true devotee is nonetheless moved by *preman*, though in a non-eroticized form.[81] Thus in KJKh 36.82, it is said that a *mahābhakta* weeps from an excess of *bhakti*, being agitated with love (*premavihvala*). And in KJKh 113.21, Śiva, having heard Pārvatī's praise of Kṛṣṇa, is *premavihvala:* his hair becomes erect as he himself breaks forth into praise of the Lord. Throughout the BVP the emotionalistic expression of *preman* is most often provoked by such acts as *smaraṇa, śravaṇa, dhyāna, kīrtana,* and *japa*.[82] In this, the BVP follows the BhP.

An apparent difference between the BVP and BhP concerns the

[73] De, VFM, p. 371.

[74] We may recall Hacker's comments above, that the real contribution of the BhP poet was apparently the emotionalistic conception of *bhakti*. Hacker asserts that the Prahlāda legend of the ViP emphasizes devotion more as an attitude of intellect than feeling (*Prahlāda*, p. 663). The BhP poet may well have drawn on older sources, however. Gail, for instance, suggests that the hair-erection motif may go back to BhG XI.14, where Arjuna stands before the awesome theophany of God (BhBhP, p. 94).

[75] BhP X.38.34–35.

[76] BhP II.3.24; V.7.11.

[77] See Gail, BhBhP, pp. 92–106.

[78] Cf. KJKh 19.18, where Kṛṣṇa is referred to as *rādhikāpremasindhu*.

[79] PKh 54.128; 54.176; 55.19; 55.45.

[80] PKh 7.99.

[81] Similar to *preman* is the term *sneha* (affection), which, however, seems to have fewer erotic connotations, and is associated especially with filial affection. Thus in PKh 10.54, Kṛṣṇa declares that the best Vaiṣṇava is one whose affection (*sneha*) goes beyond a son and is directed to God himself. Cf. PKh 20.24; 60.101.

[82] See PKh 6.118; 10.53–54; 28.1; 36.158–159, 56.57; KJKh 16.60–61.

final end or climax of *preman.* Gail has pointed to one example in the BhP where *preman* culminates in a state of non-duality, in which the beloved other is missing.[83] In another BhP passage, it is said that listening to the deeds and virtues of the Lord produces horripilation of the hair, stammering of the voice, and so forth, leading finally to the attainment of God, a state called by the wise the happiness of Brahmanirvāṇa.[84] The BVP, however, considers *nirvāṇa,* defined as merging into Brahman, to be an undesirable condition.[85]

3. Supreme devotion: desirelessness and *prīti*

In our discussion of *nivedana* above, we saw that action dedicated to Kṛṣṇa is pure and pleasing to him. Such action is free of personal desire. Thus in PKh 25.8, we are told:

> Unmotivated (*ahaitukī*) service to Viṣṇu, devoid of purpose (*saṃkalparahitā*),
> Uprooting *karma,* bestows *haribhakti.*

In the BhP, the term *ahaitukī* is applied to the highest or *nirguṇā bhakti.*[86] Śrīdhara glosses the term *ahaitukī* by *phalānusandhānaśūnyā* (void of seeking the fruits). The three lower or *saguṇā* grades of *bhakti* are connected with pride or purposefulness.[87] The *tāmasa bhakta,* according to the BhP, worships with arrogance or out of anger, seeing (himself) as separate (from others, or from God) (*bhinnadṛś*). The *rājasa bhakta* worships with the intention of gaining wealth and power, and also with the notion of individuality or separateness (*pṛthakbhāva*). Even the *sattvika bhakta,* surrendering his actions (*karma*), has a view to getting rid of *karma* and also clings to his individuality.[88] It is

[83] BhP I.6.16–18 (see BhBhP, pp. 92–93). According to BhP I.6.19, the devotee, when he loses sight of the beloved, is highly distressed.

[84] BhP VII.7.34–37. Cf. Hacker, *Prahlāda,* p. 663.

[85] PKh 36.69–70, already referred to above, in the discussion of *nivedana.* See also the next chapter, on *mukti.*

[86] BhP III.29.12. We have already referred to this classification of *bhakti* according to the *guṇas.* See p. 83 above.

[87] BhP III.29.8–10.

[88] A similar classification of the types of *bhakti* appears in DBhP VII.37.4 ff. The *nirguṇā bhakti* transcends the notion of difference, but at the same time, it is seen to consist of such acts as recitation of the Devī's name and deeds, worshipful singing and dancing, resulting in weeping, stammering, and erection of the hair. Compare this with Srīdhara's commentary mentioned above, pp. 83–4. The DBhP, however, goes on to subordinate even the *nirguṇā bhakti* to *jñāna* (see p. 101, note 9, below).

significant that the notion of individuality here is regarded, apparently, as the cause of pride and desire, and reflects an Advaitic viewpoint. Similarly in another classification of *bhaktas*, in BhP XI.2.45–48,[89] Hari himself declares that the best Bhāgavata sees the lordly nature of the Self in all beings, and all beings in the Lord, who is the Ātman. Further, such a devotee sees the universe as the *māyā* of Viṣṇu. The middling worshipper has love for the Lord, friendship for his followers, compassion for fools, and contempt for those who hate the Lord. The common devotee worships Hari as present in his image, but not in his votaries and other beings.[90]

In the BVP, we find a parallel classification of devotees in KJKh 84.41–51. The best *bhakta* engages his mind in *nāmaguṇakīrtana* and meditates on Kṛṣṇa's lotus-feet; his worship is *ahaitukī,* and he himself is devoid of intention (*saṃkalparahita*). In addition, he holds that there is no division or difference between women and men, and that there is no separation between all beings. The middling devotee also is free of purpose, performing *karma* without attachment, thus ridding himself of *karma.* He views Kṛṣṇa as the agent of all acts. The common worshipper has the same qualities but in diminished degree. It is interesting that the BVP has elaborated the idea of non-individuality and non-difference to encompass specifically the man-woman relationship. This evidently manifests the Tāntric orientation of our Purāṇa. The non-difference of men and women is clearly based on our text's doctrine of Prakṛti and her essential non-difference from the Male Principle of the universe.[91]

The BVP, like the BhP, also classifies devotees according to the *guṇas*. The classification is made with reference to the grandsons of Brahmā:

> The grandsons are of three types; some are gods, some Brahmans, and some demons.
> Those who are *sāttvika* are Brahmans, while the gods are *rājasika;*
> The demons are *tāmasika*. . . .

[89] Cf. Gail, BhBhP, pp. 39–41.

[90] In the Caitanya school, these are interpreted as three grades of *preman*. See De, VFM, p. 365.

[91] See, for instance, PKh 1.11, where it is said that, because Prakṛti has sprung from Kṛṣṇa's left side, a yogin makes no distinction between men and women. See also chapter 8 below.

. . . .

The Brahmans, devoted to Viṣṇu, are *mumukṣus* (desirous of *mokṣa*) and desire *dāsya*.
The gods are desirous of wealth, as also the *tāmasa* demons.
The *svadharma* of the Brahmans, who are free of desire (*niṣkāma*), is the pleasing worship (*arcana*) of Kṛṣṇa,
Who is qualityless and beyond even *prakṛti*.[92]

The idea of the *niṣkāma bhakta* appears elsewhere in our text:

Vaiṣṇavas are of two sorts, *sakāma* and *niṣkāma*.
The *niṣkāma bhakta* is better than the *sakāma*.
He who is *sakāma* must suffer [the fruits of] *karma;* he who is *niṣkāma* is free of affliction.[93]

According to PKh 26.37–38, Brahmans who are *haribhaktas* and *niṣkāma,* even if they do not follow their own duties (*svadharma*), go to Hari's abode on the strength of their *bhakti,* while Brahmans worshipping other gods, if neglecting *svadharma,* go to hell.[94] This is a logical extension of the view that the true *bhakta,* who does not desire the fruits of action and is thereby freed of *karma,* does not have to worry about becoming involved in either good or bad acts. The BVP, however, does not mean that the *bhakta* should act in any manner or forsake the acts of service to God. This will become clear when we look more carefully at the nature of the *niṣkāma bhakta.*

The term *niṣkāma* does not seem to mean the absence of all desires.[95] This is suggested by the following statement, regarding the motivation for ritual bathing:

On the part of the great Vaiṣṇavas, there is the desire for pleasing Kṛṣṇa (*śrīkṛṣṇaprītikāma*).
On the part of householders [in apparent contrast here to Vaiṣṇavas], there is the intention to get rid of their sins.[96]

The object of the Vaiṣṇavas' desire, *prīti,* is an important technical term, whose meaning we shall define more carefully in a moment. But first it should be noted that the desire for *prīti* pertains to

[92] PKh 60.46cd–47, 49–50.
[93] PKh 26.25cd–26. The Sanskrit text is given in Appendix A, section 2, along with the parallel verses from the DBhP.
[94] See Appendix A, section 2, for the Sanskrit text. Cf. PKh 29.25.
[95] Cf. the term *nirguṇa,* pp. 63 ff., above.
[96] BKh 26.59cd–60ab.

the *niṣkāma bhakta,* not the *sakāma bhakta.* This is made clear in PKh 10.41cd–42:

> On the part of all, indeed, there is intention, except for Vaiṣṇavas.
> Vaiṣṇavas, free of fruit-seeking (*phalasandhānarahita* [cf. Śrīdhara's definition above of *ahaitukī*]), are *jīvanmuktas.*
> They always desire love and devotion to me (*matprītibhaktikāma*) in all their acts.

And similarly in PKh 46.78cd: "The desires (*manorathāḥ*) of those without desires (*niḥspṛhāṇāṃ*) is for the lotus-feet of Śri Kṛṣṇa."

S. K. De has examined the concept of *prīti* or love in the Caitanya school.[97] According to his analysis, *prīti* is constituted of two elements, *sukha* and *prīyatā. Sukha,* or happiness, is based on personal satisfaction. *Prīyatā* involves *sukha,* but is primarily concerned with the happiness of the beloved person, regardless of personal satisfaction, and thus is not self-centered. De further says that *prīti* consists of service (*sevā*) to God, and is also referred to as *premabhakti.*

The conception of *prīti* in the BVP is similar in many respects to the above. To be sure, *prīti* often is used in a general sense, meaning "pleasure" or "delight," as in the phrase "*dhanādiṣu striyāṃ prītiḥ.*"[98] But when *prīti* is connected with Kṛṣṇa, the aspect of unselfishness is clearly present, as seen by our quotations above. *Prīti,* in this highest sense, helps to explain an apparent contradiction in our Purāṇa. It is said that whoever worships God but asks for a boon is deluded.[99] Yet throughout the text, pious devotees ask for the boon of *sevā,* or *dāsya.*[100] This boon, spoken of as the best of all boons,[101] is an exception, as it is prompted by *prīti* and thus is completely God-centered.

4. Householder and *saṃnyāsin*

With regard to the BVP's notion of the true devotee of God, at least one important problem remains. This concerns the status

[97] VFM, pp. 296 ff.
[98] PKh 46.78.
[99] BKh 14.44–45.
[100] E.g., Nanda asks for bondage and devotion in KJKh 21.135–136, and Garga seeks bondage to Kṛṣṇa's feet in KJKh 13.193.
[101] KJKh 97.8.

of the Vaiṣṇava as a householder or as an ascetic of some sort, especially the *saṃnyāsin,* but also the *vānaprastha, brahmacārin,* or *yati.* It is a problem frequently debated in our Purāṇa. In general, both the householder and *saṃnyāsin* are held up as ideals, as in KJKh 73.85, where Kṛṣṇa declares that among the stages of life, he himself is the householder, and among those endowed with discrimination, he is the *saṃnyāsin.* Regarding the *saṃnyāsin,* it is said that all his past and future *karma* is destroyed; he meditates upon God and in the end goes to God's abode.[102] The *saṃnyāsin* is not supposed to look upon the face of woman, stand in her presence, nor even touch the wooden figure of a woman.[103] The Vaiṣṇava is sometimes associated with *saṃnyāsins* and ascetics in apparent distinction from householders. For instance, in BKh 27.15, Vaiṣṇavas, *yatis*, and *brahmacārins* are differentiated from Śaivas, Śāktas, and householders.[104] And in PKh 10.54, it is said that those who have given over (*nyasta*) their homes and other possessions to God are the best Vaiṣṇavas. This "giving over," though, is not necessarily the physical renunciation and abandonment of the house, but may well be an inner surrendering or consignment of one's possessions to God.[105]

The final solution to the householder-*saṃnyāsin* problem is apparently found in *adhyāyas* 23 and 24 of the BKh. These chapters contain an interesting account of a quarrel between Brahmā and his son Nārada. The father is trying to persuade his son to marry and adopt the life of a householder. Nārada protests that marriage is only the root of evil, and that a wife obstructs *tapas, svarga, bhakti, mukti* and *karma.*[106] Brahmā gives a long reply, part of which is as follows:

[102] KJKh 83.84. For the duties of the *saṃnyāsin,* see KJKh 83.83 ff., and PKh 36.118 ff.; for those of the householder, see KJKh 84.1 ff.

[103] PKh 36.125–126.

[104] *Yatis* and *brahmacārins* are also frequently related to *saṃnyāsins* (e.g., KJKh 83.87; 83.100–101).

[105] Our text says that *saṃnyāsa* is one of five acts prohibited in the *kaliyuga* (KJKh 115.112–113). The other four prohibited acts are: *aśvamedha, gavālambha, palapaitṛka,* and *devareṇa sutotpatti. Saṃnyāsa* in this context, Ingalls has suggested to me, may refer not to world-renunciation, but rather to the giving over of a wife to another for the sake of obtaining superior offspring.

[106] BKh 23.20. For a more detailed analysis of the negative aspects of women in our Purāṇa, see pp. 181 ff. below.

At first one should be a householder, then a forest-dweller,
Then a *tapasvin* for the sake of *mokṣa.* This is the order according to *śruti.*
On the part of Vaiṣṇavas, there is worship (*arcā*) of Hari and austerity (*tapasyā*), according to *śruti.*
O Vaiṣṇava [Nārada], abide in a house and perform *kṛṣṇapadārcana.*
Of what use is *tapas* to that man for whom Hari exists inside [himself] and outside.

. . . .

Wherever *kṛṣṇasevana* is performed, [at that place there is] supreme *tapas.*[107]

Here we see that there is no need for the Vaiṣṇava to be outside the house. On the one hand, *tapas* is unnecessary for him; on the other, *sevana* is the highest *tapas.*

[107] BKh 23.20–22, 24ab.

6

Muktimārga and *Mukti*

1. *Bhakti, jñāna,* and *karma*

Bhakti (devotion), *jñāna* (knowledge), and *karma* (action) are the three traditional *mārgas* (paths) to liberation. In the preceding chapter, although the primary objective was to understand the BVP's conception of *bhakti,* it was necessary to broach the subject of *karma* and its relation to devotion. In this section, we shall attempt to define this relationship more precisely, as well as to analyze the relation of *bhakti* to the third traditional *mārga,* that of *jñāna.* We shall begin with the *bhakti-jñāna* relationship.

Our Purāṇa, for the most part, regards *jñāna* and *bhakti* either as complementary or identical. For instance, in PKh 46.72, it is said that "He is verily a *guru* who gives *jñāna* conjoined with *viṣṇubhakti.*" And in PKh 65.20, Durgā grants to a devotee *jñāna, bhakti* and *dāsya* to Kṛṣṇa. At times there is an apparent subordination of *jñāna* to *bhakti,* as in Kṛṣṇa's statement that:

> Those who are relatives of my devotees, of righteous minds and pure,
> Go by jewelled chariot to Goloka, hard to attain.
> Wherever they die, whether with *jñāna* or without,
> They are *jīvanmuktas*, purified by the mere presence of [my] devotees.[1]

[1] PKh 10.86–87.

This passage is not meant to denigrate *jñāna,* however, but to reveal the greatness of Kṛṣṇa's votaries. Elsewhere it is stated, in fact, that there is no *jñānin* better than a Vaiṣṇava.[2]

Most significantly, perhaps, *bhakti* is seen as the highest form of knowledge. In KJKh 110.6 ff., our Purāṇa divides knowledge into five kinds. The actual enumeration has become somewhat confused in the extant text, but apparently consists of the following: *yogātmaka* (knowledge of yoga, here associated with the Tāntric theory of the six *cakras*),[3] *viṣayātmaka* (worldly or sensual knowledge); *siddhyātmaka* (knowledge of divine or supernatural powers); *mokṣātmaka* (knowledge that leads to *mokṣa* or *nirvāṇa*); and *bhaktyātmaka* (knowledge whose essence is *bhakti*).[4] The *bhaktyātmaka* knowledge is referred to as the best (*śreṣṭha*) or supreme over all (*sarvapara*).

Since the highest knowledge is *bhakti,* we sometimes find *jñāna* defined as *kṛṣṇabhāvana* (love or devotion to Kṛṣṇa, or possibly meditation upon him).[5] *Jñāna* is also closely associated with, and perhaps identified with, *harisevana.*[6] But knowledge has not only this devotionalistic aspect. There is also its ontological or metaphysical side, for supreme knowledge is the realization that Hari or Kṛṣṇa is the one true reality, and that all else, appearing and disappearing, is deception.[7] It is important to note that these devotionalistic and metaphysical views of knowledge occur in the same verses, so that they are clearly regarded as two complementary aspects of *jñāna.* The same passage also ap-

[2] PKh 56.60.

[3] See p. 42 above.

[4] One may compare this fivefold division of knowledge with NārPR I.1.44 ff., where *rātra,* identified with *jñāna,* is said to be fivefold (and thus the name *pañcarātra* is explained). The first, called *jñāna paramatattva,* destroys birth, death and old age. The second, desired by *mumukṣus,* produces *mukti* and mergence into the feet of Hari. The third bestows *kṛṣṇabhakti* and *dāsya.* The fourth, called *yaugika,* yields all perfections (*siddhis*). The fifth is worldly knowledge (*vaiśayika*). The first two are considered as *sāttvika,* the third as *nairguṇya,* the fourth as *rājasika,* and the fifth as *tāmasa.*

[5] PKh 46.69.

[6] PKh 46.70.

[7] PKh 46.69–71. Cf. PKh 65.33ab:

sarveṣām īśvaraḥ kṛṣṇa iti jñānaṃ parātparam/

Cf. also PKh 10.55–56 (Kṛṣṇa speaking):

ābrahmastambhaparyantaṃ mattaḥ sarvaṃ carācaram/
sarveṣām aham eveśa itijñā vaiṣṇavottamaḥ//
asaṃkhyakoṭibrahmāṇḍaṃ brahmaviṣṇuśivādayaḥ/
pralaye mayi līyante cetijñā vaiṣṇavottamāḥ//

parently refers to this supreme knowledge as *kṛṣṇamārga.*[8] The BVP thus differs significantly from the Caitanya school, where there was less tendency to identify *jñāna* with *bhakti:* rather, the way of knowledge was regarded as a subordinate and insufficient means to the attainment of God.[9]

The relation of *jñāna* and *bhakti* to the remaining *mārga, karma,* is more complex. *Karma* refers to action in general, as well as to the consequence of that action borne by the doer. *Karma* also has the specific meaning of ceremonial rites as laid down by Vedic injunction and other religious or ascetic acts, such as vows (*vrata*), fasting (*anaśana*), austerity (*tapas*), charity (*dāna*), circumambulation (*pradakṣina*), and bathing at places of pilgrimage (*tīrthasnāna*). Such acts, we find, are contrasted both with knowledge and devotion. Thus in PKh 34.6, it is said that these acts "are not worth one sixteenth the gift of *jñāna.*" In PKh 27.139–143, there is reference to bathing, sacrifices, vows and so forth, and their fruits. The seed of all these fruits is said to be *kṛṣṇasevana,* which bestows *mukti.* It is this passage, as we noted above,[10] that defines *sevana* in terms of the nine *bhakti*-marks. We find here, then, an important differentiation between two kinds of acts: the general religious, ritual and ascetic acts on one side, and the specifically devotional acts to Kṛṣṇa on the other. The distinction between these two is brought out more clearly in KJKh 85.42–46. Kṛṣṇa names several of the standard meritorious acts such as *yajña* (sacrifice) and *tapas,* and concludes:

> By [such] action (*karma*) alone, men attain heaven,
> For *mokṣa* is not attained by action but just by service (*sevā*) to me.

It is also noteworthy that *sevā* here is contrasted with *karma.*

At issue, in part, is the traditional problem of action versus inaction, or *pravṛtti* and *nivṛtti.* These two paths are discussed in

[8] PKh 46.74.

[9] See De, VFM, pp. 270–272. It is interesting to compare also the views of the DBhP with those of the BVP. In DBhP VII.37.2–3, *bhaktiyoga* is said to be the easiest of the three traditional means. However, it is said further that the limit (*sīmā*) of this *bhakti* (and of *vairāgya*) is *jñāna* (VII.37.28). Even though a man performs *bhakti,* through the strength of his *prārabdha karma,* he does not at once attain knowledge of the Devī, but goes to her jewelled isle (verse 29), where he finally receives knowledge, without which *mokṣa* is impossible (verses 30–31).

[10] See p. 90 above.

a conversation between Indra and his *guru* Durvāsas. Indra first states:

> The *mārga* described in *śāstra* is twofold, O best of *munis*;
> One is the seed of worldly activity (*pravṛtti*), [the other] is the supreme cause of cessation or inactivity (*nivṛtti*).[11]

Concerning the path of worldy activity, it is elsewhere said that those who follow the *pravṛttipatha* take pleasure (*prīti*) in wealth and women.[12] In our text, wealth and women are frequently considered to be the two chief obstacles to salvation.[13] Returning to Indra's conversation, he declares that the *pravṛttivartman* (way of activity) is at first delightful, but later is filled with sorrow, leading to birth, death, and old age. After many births, through Kṛṣṇa's grace (*anugraha*), a man attains *satsaṅga* (good society, i.e., association with Kṛṣṇa's devotees) and is thereby enabled to see the *muktimārga*. Then, after several more births, through yoga, *tapas* and *anaśana*, a man finally attains the *muktimārga*.[14] Indra apparently equates *nivṛtti* with *muktimārga*, and considers such acts as *tapas* as a means to its attainment. Indra's preceptor, the sage Durvāsas, amplifies and modifies the views of his pupil. He asserts that while *dāna*, *tapas* and other action (*karma*) lead only to heaven, the real seed of *mokṣa* is the absence of intention (*saṃkalpābhāva*). If action which is *sāttvika* is performed without intention and is dedicated to Kṛṣṇa,[15] then one dissolves into the Supreme Brahman, in the state known as *nirvāṇa*.[16] *Nivṛtti*, then, apparently is not the absence of action, but the absence of intentionality, though leading ultimately to the cessation of activity along with individual existence in the final dissolution.

However, this state, Durvāsas declares, is not desired by the Vaiṣṇavas.[17] Durvāsas' explanation indicates that the *nivṛttimārga*, as well as the *pravṛttimārga* is not wholly adequate. This view is affirmed also in the passage dealing with the five kinds of knowledge, already mentioned. The fourth or *mokṣātmaka jñāna*, said to be the cause of *nirvāṇa*, is based on the *nivṛttimārga* and is not desired by *bhaktas*.[18]

[11] PKh 36.53.
[12] PKh 46.78.
[13] See below, pp. 181 ff., 189 ff.
[14] PKh 36.54–59.
[15] Cf. the section on *nivedana* in the preceding chapter, pp. 88–89.
[16] PKh 36.67–70.
[17] PKh 36.70.
[18] KJKh 110.14.

How, then, is the dichotomy between action and inaction resolved? It should be clear by now that the solution must be related to the notion of service (*sevā, sevana*). *Sevā,* as we have seen, is distinguished from action (*karma*), but it is not exactly the absence of action either, as it consists of the nine devotional acts. In this sense, it is the best of all action! Thus in PKh 36.82, Śiva declares that *śrīkṛṣṇapadasevana* is the best *jñāna,* the best *tapas,* and the best yoga.[19] Yet in PKh 36.85, it is said:

> Yogins, *siddhas*, *yatis* and *tapasvins*
> Must all experience their *karma,* but not those who serve Nārāyaṇa.

What, then, distinguishes *sevā* from *karma?* That is, what radically differentiates the acts of *sevā* from other acts, and why should the former alone be free of the consequences of *karma?*

Since the time of the *Gītā,* the problem of action and inaction has been resolved or transcended by the notion of not desiring the fruits of action and the dedication or surrender of one's actions to God.[20] Such actions are free of *karm*ic consequences. But in the BVP, as we have seen, the surrender of acts and the absence of desire or intention in themselves are not the final solution, for they lead only to *nirvāṇa.* What ultimately distinguishes *sevā* from even disinterested *karma* is that *sevā* is prompted by *prīti,* or the desire to please God.[21] We have already seen that desire for *kṛṣṇaprīti* transcends personal interest, since it is God-centered.[22] Similarly, action that is God-centered transcends all phenomenal *karma.* The BVP's views on the relation of *bhakti* and *sevā* to *karma* closely parallel those of the Caitanya school.[23]

2. The grace of God: impartiality and favoritism

An important problem related to the *muktimārga* concerns the role of God's grace (*anugraha, prasāda*). We have already seen that, according to Indra, it is God's grace or favor (*anugraha*)

[19] Cf. BKh 23.24, quoted in the previous chapter, p. 98.

[20] See BhG XVIII.57. Cf. V.10.

[21] The association of action with the pleasing of God is found also in *Śāṇḍilya* 63: "Even one act [such as repetition of the Lord's names], by pleasing the Lord, is effective" (*īśvaratuṣṭer eko 'pi balī*).

[22] See above, pp. 95–96.

[23] See De, VFM, pp. 269–270, 272–274.

that enables a man to attain *satsaṅga*.[24] *Satsaṅga* finally leads to *sevā* or *dāsya*.[25] *Dāsya* itself is often spoken of as a gift or boon (*vara*) from God.[26] It is by Kṛṣṇa's grace (*prasāda*) also that one attains pure *jñāna*.[27] Kṛṣṇa himself declares: "In whichever way people resort to me, in that same way I favor them."[28] This seems to suggest that a person must first resort to God before obtaining his grace. The resorting to God for refuge and its relation to God's grace, however, is not really elaborated by the BVP, in contrast to the Vaiṣṇava schools in general.[29]

Closely related to the problem of man's effort and divine grace is the matter of God's impartiality and favoritism. The idea of God's impartiality is founded in part on the ontological doctrine of his omnipresence. In KJKh 119.28ab, it is said, "There is the same nature (*samabhāva*) everywhere on the part of the Sarvātman, according to *śruti*." And in KJKh 120.55cd: "You [Kṛṣṇa] are the Ātman, the perfect Puruṣa; there is sameness (*samatā*) everywhere of yourself." The term *samatā* means not only "sameness," but also "impartiality." This meaning is brought out in KJKh 57.3, where Lakṣmī says that for the qualityless Sarvātman, there is *samatā* towards both a blade of grass and a mountain.

One aspect of this impartiality is the idea of fairness of judg-

24 PKh 36.57.

25 Cf. GKh 8.76–78, and p. 90, above.

26 KJKh 21.134–136; 73.84; 97.8. Cf. KJKh 31.9–11, where *dāsya* as a boon is given to a devotee by Brahmā.

27 PKh 36.111.

28 *ye yathā māṃ prapadyante tāṃ tathaiva bhajāmy aham//*
(PKh 13.29). This verse is identical with BhG IV. 11ab. Śaṃkara glosses *bhajāmi* with *anugṛhṇāmi*.

29 The doctrine of *śaraṇāgati* (*śaraṇāpatti, prapatti*) is closely related to the conception of grace in the Vaiṣṇava schools. (Regarding the doctrine in Rāmānuja's school, see Rangacharya, "Historical Evolution of Śrī-Vaiṣṇavism in South India," CHI, IV. 177–178; in Caitanya's, see De, VFM, pp. 280, 371; in Nimbārka's, see Chaudhuri, "Nimbārka," in HPEW I, 343; in Vallabha's, see Bhatt, "Vallabha," in HPEW I, 354.) In Rāmānuja's school especially, the question was raised whether *śaraṇāgati* depends in part on man's effort or solely on God's grace. The two main divisions of the school split, in large part, over this issue. In the BVP, the notion of Kṛṣṇa as the supreme refuge is quite common. He is referred to as the sole refuge of his devotees (*bhaktaikaśaraṇa:* BKh 8.34) and men and gods in times of danger often resort to him for protection. Fear, then, is one of the main motivating factors behind the seeking of refuge, according to our Purāṇa (e.g., PKh 13.18: Brahmā, Kaśyapa and the Sun go to Nārāyaṇa for protection through fear [*bhiyā*]). The notion of refuge, though, does not seem to play any technical theological role in connection with a doctrine of grace.

ment. For instance, in GKh 44.1 ff., Durgā asks Śiva to determine who was at fault in the quarrel between her son Gaṇeśa and Paraśurāma. She introduces her request by the statement that to the Lord, everything, from a blade of grass to a mountain, is equal.

The most important aspect of Kṛṣṇa's *samatā,* though, is not his fairness or justice to all, but his universal compassion. Thus in KJKh 25.133, Indra says that on the part of the Lord there is always equality of compassion (*kṛpayā samatā*) towards all beings. And in KJKh 15.80, it is said that Kṛṣṇa, who is able to make a blade of grass into a mountain and vice versa, possesses compassion (*kṛpā*) equally towards both the fit and unfit (*yogyāyogya*).[30] Throughout our text Kṛṣṇa's compassion is stressed. Frequently he is referred to as an ocean of mercy or compassion (*kṛpānidhi, dayānidhi, karuṇānidhi*) or as consisting of mercy (*kṛpāmaya*).[31] The universality of God's compassion, especially towards both the fit and unfit, clearly emphasizes the superiority of his grace over man's merit.

In KJKh 57.31, Kṛṣṇa himself declares his impartiality, but with an apparent qualification:

> On my part, there is *samatā* everywhere, towards a devotee, wife, or friend.
> Especially dear [though] is my devotee, dearer even than a wife.[32]

The idea of God being impartial to all beings and yet showing special favor to his devotees goes back to BhG IX.29.[33] In the BVP, the devotee is dearer to Kṛṣṇa than even Lakṣmī or Rādhā. Thus Kṛṣṇa declares to the gods:

> My real abode is not in Vaikuṇṭha or Goloka at the side of Rādhā.

[30] Cf. KJKh 22.57; cf. also BKh 14.13, where virtuous men in general are said to be equally compassionate to the fit and unfit. See also BKh 1.37, where the *guru* is said to be the same to the fit and unfit. Also, see KJKh 59.78 for the impartiality of the *saṃnyāsin.* Yama (Death) also is said to be impartial to all creatures (PKh 28.9).

[31] PKh 36.111; 59.65–66; 60.65; KJKh 22.61.

[32] *bhakte kalatre bandhau ca sarvatra samatā mama/*
viśeṣato 'timadbhaktaḥ kalatrātpara eva ca//

[33] BhG IX.29 reads:
samo 'haṃ sarvabhūteṣu na me dveṣyo 'sti na priyaḥ/
ye bhajanti tu māṃ bhaktyā mayi te teṣu cāpy aham//

Where my *bhaktas* reside, there I dwell day and night.
Rādhā, resting on my breast day and night, is dearer than my life,
You [gods] are dearer than life, [but even] Lakṣmī is not dearer than a *bhakta*.[34]

Similarly, it is said that Kṛṣṇa, even though despatching his disc Sudarśana for the protection of his devotees, is not free of anxiety and so abides at the side of his votaries.[35] In this connection, we find that Kṛṣṇa's devotee or servant is superior, in one sense, to the Lord. Kṛṣṇa explains to his foster father:

O Nanda, never is there misfortune for my devotee.
Sudarśana constantly protects him on all sides.
My *bhakta* is stronger than I: he is looked after while I am not.
I, the master, have no master, nor father or mother.[36]

God's special favor to his devotees is expressed in many other ways. It is said that Hari is pleased if his devotee is pleased,[37] and that he can be easily conquered or subdued (*atisādhya*) by his own votaries, but is rarely attained (*sudurlabha*) by others.[38] To favor his devotees he takes on a body or form (*bhaktānugrahavigraha*),[39] and is frequently spoken of as bestowing favor on his devotees (*bhaktānugrahakāraka*).[40] He is also referred to as having affection (specifically parental affection) for his votaries (*bhaktavatsala*).[41]

The impartiality towards all beings and the favoritism for his devotees represent the two sides of Kṛṣṇa's benevolence or grace. His compassion, in its impartiality, is not only universal and all-encompassing, but also beyond human effort and the distinctions

[34] KJKh 6.55–56.
[35] BKh 11.45. Cf. KJKh 6.54. Cf. also NārPR I.2.34:
datvā cakraṃ ca rakṣārthaṃ na niścinto janārdanaḥ/
svayaṃ tannikataṃ yāti taṃ draṣṭuṃ rakṣaṇāya ca//
And NārPR II.2.73:
evaṃ bhṛtyasya rakṣārthaṃ kṛṣṇo datvā sudarśanam/
tathāpi sustho na prītas taṃ tyaktum akṣamaḥ kṣaṇam//
[36] KJKh 74.20–21.
[37] KJKh 21.84.
[38] PKh 34.17.
[39] PKh 7.88.
[40] PKh 10.19.
[41] PKh 60.65.

of fit and unfit. At the same time, this compassion implies deep personal involvement on the part of the Lord. Through his grace, he binds himself to those who are committed to him. The paradoxical tension between impartiality and favoritism is not resolved in logical terms by the BVP. Both aspects of God's benevolence are simply experienced as true. The resulting paradox merely adds to the greatness of this benevolence, beyond human understanding as well as human effort.

3. *Mukti*

Two general notions of *mukti* (salvation or redemption) appear in the BVP. The first is the idea of mergence, especially the dissolution into the feet of God:

> Whoever at the time of death takes the water of the Śālagrama stone [a sacred stone pervaded by the presence of Viṣṇu],
> Is freed from all sin and goes to Viṣṇu's world.
> He attains *nirvāṇamukti,* and is released from the fruits of his *karma.*
> He then will dissolve into Viṣṇu's feet, without doubt.[42]

Similarly in PKh 34.67, it is said that "Vaiṣṇavas, filled with supreme bliss, [dissolve] into [Kṛṣṇa's] lotus-feet." This latter passage is significant, for the mergence takes place at the time of the *pralaya* (dissolution) of the universe, when everything, including the gods and men, dissolves back into Kṛṣṇa. *Pralaya* is the reversal of the evolutionary process, during which the Vaiṣṇavas emerged from Kṛṣṇa's feet.[43] Kṛṣṇa then is the beginning and end of all.

The above cosmogonic scheme, however, leads to a basic soteriological problem, for according to the usual Hindu conception, dissolution is not the final end but only one phase in an endless cycle of *pralayas* followed by new creations. The dissolution into Kṛṣṇa would seem to be merely a temporary stage before re-emergence. Thus it is said of the creator Brahmā that he disappears in the *prākṛtika laya* (natural dissolution), but reappears by the desire of the Lord.[44] And further:

[42] PKh 21.91–92.
[43] BKh 5.67–69.
[44] PKh 18.46. Cf. ViP I.5.65, where Brahmā, at the beginning of each *kalpa,* recreates the same world again and again.

In a blink [of Kṛṣṇa's] eye, dissolution occurs. . . .
In another blink creation again ensues.
How many creations are there? And how many dissolutions?
How many have come and gone? What man can count![45]

The BVP recognizes the soteriological difficulties arising from the theory of dissolution and re-creation. Accordingly, we find that there are certain exceptions to the general notion that everything perishes or dissolves back into Kṛṣṇa in the *pralaya*. For instance, it is said:

Brahmā, Viṣṇu, Śiva and other gods,
Seers and all embodied beings dissolve into Kṛṣṇa,
As well as Prakṛti. . . .
. . . .
Thus do all Brahmāṇḍas (universes) perish entirely.
Only Goloka and Vaikuṇṭha remain, with Kṛṣṇa and his attendants.[46]

And Kṛṣṇa says to Brahmā:

Those who dwell in Goloka are free from the wheel of time.
In dissolution, the entire universe is inundated with water.
Brahmā and others residing in other worlds now dissolve into me.[47]

The servants or attendants of Kṛṣṇa residing in his world are thus said to observe countless dissolutions.[48]

This brings us to the second notion of redemption in the BVP, that of becoming a servant (*pārṣada*) of Kṛṣṇa in Goloka. Let us look at a few passages in our text that bring out the contrast between the two kinds of *mukti*. In PKh 25.10–11, it is stated:

Mukti is twofold, as stated in *śruti,* all agree, O good lady.
One produces *nirvāṇa,* the other bestows *haribhakti* on men.
Vaiṣṇavas desire *mukti* in the form of *haribhakti.*
Other virtuous people desire *mukti* in the form of *nirvāṇa.*[49]

[45] PKh 7.80–81. Cf. PKh 36.176–177.
[46] PKh 7.76d–77, 79.
[47] PKh 11.134–135ab.
[48] PKh 10.77–78.
[49] The Sanskrit text is given in Appendix A, section 3, along with parallels from the DBhP.

Yama, the ruler of the dead, declares:

> In the uprooting of *karma, mukti* is said to be twofold,
> One has the form of *nirvāṇa,* the other is *sevā* to Kṛṣṇa, the Supreme Ātman.[50]

Nirvāṇamukti, in the passage quoted at the beginning of this section, was closely connected with dissolution into Viṣṇu's feet. In PKh 36.69–70, a passage already referred to in other contexts,[51] *nirvāṇa* is defined as dissolution into the Supreme Brahman, a state rejected by true Vaiṣṇavas as it is devoid of service.

Our text, as seen in the examples above, sometimes refers to *bhakti* or service as a form of *mukti,* but elsewhere it considers *bhakti* and *mukti* as distinct. *Mokṣa* once is even said to be destructive of devotion (*bhaktinirmathana*).[52] The following passage elaborates on this distinction:

> There are four kinds of *mukti* described by the Vedas.
> *Haribhakti* is foremost above them and is superior even to *mukti.*
> One [kind of *mukti*] bestows *sālokya* with Hari, the others provide *sārūpya,*
> *Sāmīpya,* and *nirvāṇa,* according to tradition.
>
> . . . .
>
> *Mukti* is devoid of *sevā, bhakti* increases *sevā;*
> This is the difference (*bheda*) between *bhakti* and *mukti.*[53]

Here we have named four kinds of *mukti.* Elsewhere our text also refers to five,[54] and even six kinds.

The six *mukti*s are *sārṣṭi, sālokya, sārūpya, sāmīpya, sāmya,* and *līnatā,* or *nirvāṇa.*[55] *Sārṣṭi* is attaining the power or condition

[50] PKh 26.19–20. See Appendix A, section 3.
[51] See above, pp. 89, 102.
[52] PKh 60.73.
[53] PKh 34.74cd–76ab, 78cd–79a. Cf. NārPR II.7.2–4:
līnatā haripādābje muktir ity abhidhīyate/
idam eva hi nirvāṇaṃ vaiṣṇavānām asammatam//
sālokyasārṣṭisāmīpyasārūpyam ity ataḥ kramāt/
bhogarūpaṃ ca sukhadam iti mukticatuṣṭayam//
śrīharerbhaktidāsyaṃ ca sarvamukteḥ paraṃ mune/
vaiṣnavānām abhimataṃ sārātsāraṃ parātparam//
[54] PKh 54.122 refers to *muktipañcaka* (Vaṅg; Veṅk 54.119, has *bhaktipañcaka,* evidently incorrect), and KJKh 97.8 mentions *pañcavidhā mukti.* The five kinds are not named in these passages.
[55] BKh 6.17.

of God.[56] Our text does not make clear how this differs from *sāmya* (equality). Possibly *sārṣṭi* and *sāmya* both refer to the devotee's sharing God's divine knowledge, splendor, and virtue.[57] *Sālokya* is the attainment of the same world as God, that is, Vaikuṇṭha or Goloka. All true devotees of Kṛṣṇa attain Goloka, carried there at death in a jewelled chariot according to the usual conception of our Purāṇa.[58] Kṛṣṇa himself declares that he bestows *sālokya* for the life of a Brahmā on those who remember his name.[59] Kṛṣṇa also says to his foster parents, Yaśodā and Nanda, that he will give them and the other residents of Gokula *sālokyamukti*.[60] *Sārūpya* is bearing the same form as the Lord. When a devotee of Kṛṣṇa dies, he sheds his human body, and going to Goloka, puts on a divine form. The form is that of a cowherd (*gopa*), dark-blue, with flute in hand, in other words, the supreme form of Kṛṣṇa.[61] Kṛṣṇa says that he first bestows *sārūpya* on a devotee and then makes him his attendant.[62] It is also said that the votary, attaining *sārūpya*, performs *sevā* and *dāsya*.[63] *Sāmīpya* is closeness or proximity to God. It is said of those who listen to the BVP that they put on Kṛṣṇa's form, go to Goloka, and become his *pārṣadas* in his presence (*samīpe*), doing *sevā*.[64] And a man who hears a hymn in praise of Kṛṣṇa goes to his side (*kṛṣṇāntike*).[65]

Līnatā or *nirvāṇa*, as seen above, is specifically related to the notion of mergence or dissolution into the Supreme. It is also called *aikya*, or oneness.[66] This form of *mukti*, outside our text, is often referred to as *sāyujya* (union or absorption into the deity).[67] It is unique among the forms of *mukti*, for it alone dissolves duality. Without duality, servant and master disappear and service is no longer possible. This perhaps explains why *nirvāṇa*

[56] In this connection, we may note that our Purāṇa often refers to a devotee's becoming *viṣṇutulya* (equal to Viṣṇu). (See PKh 55.58; 56.50; 67.9; 67.20; KJKh 5.124.)

[57] Cf. KJKh 36.15.

[58] BKh 20.45; 21.22.

[59] PKh 10.83; cf. 10.82.

[60] KJKh 126.6.

[61] See, for instance, PKh 20.21.

[62] PKh 10.80. Cf. 10.25.

[63] PKh 27.55; 27.65.

[64] KJKh 133.56.

[65] KJKh 5.126.

[66] PKh 18.40.

[67] E.g., BAP III.36.51 refers to *kṛṣṇasāyujya*.

is often singled out in contrast to *bhakti*. The other kinds of *mukti*, though often said to be not desired by the *bhakta*, are not in themselves opposed to *sevā*. We have just seen that they are often associated with servitude or the state of the *pārṣada*.[68] They are in part the necessary preconditions of service. The notion of *mukti* as mergence or dissolution, then, is deemed as inferior by our Purāṇa not only because of the soteriological problems related to the cosmological theory of *pralaya*, but most importantly because its monistic presuppositions undermine the *bhakti* ideal of *mukti* as *sevā*.[69] We see, then, that *sevā*, or *dāsya*, is both means and end, that *mukti* (in the highest sense) and *muktimārga* are identical. It follows that this highest *mukti* may be attained in this life. The true devotee, in fact, is frequently referred to as a *jīvanmukta*.[70] Accordingly, he has put off the bonds of the world, is free of good and bad *karma*, as well as of birth, death, time, fate, fear, misfortune, disease, passions, delusion and sin.[71] And he is joined with bliss.[72] At death, he retains his personal individuality, becoming a servant or attendant (*pārṣada, dāsa, kiṃkara*) of Kṛṣṇa in Goloka. Some of these attendants carry out such duties as guarding Kṛṣṇa's palace. Others sing the names and glories of Kṛṣṇa, meditate on his lotus-feet, and practice *japa*, thus continuing the service begun on earth.[73]

The BVP's views on the various kinds of *mukti*s and the state of supreme *mukti* are similar in many ways to those of the Caitanya school.[74] One significant difference, though, concerns the concept of *dāsya*. In the BVP, as we have seen,[75] *dāsya* is synonymous with *sevā*. In the Caitanya school, *sevā*, as complete servitude and submission to God, is regarded as the essential characteristic of *bhakti*.[76] *Sevā* is also identified with *prīti* and

[68] See also KJKh 22.59–60, where *sālokya, sārṣṭi*, and *sāmīpya* are mentioned along with *harer bhakti* and *dāsya*.

[69] Cf. this doctrine with that of the KūrP, where Śiva declares:
eṣā vimuktiḥ paramā mama sāyujyam uttamam/
nirvāṇaṃ brahmaṇā caikyaṃ kaivalyaṃ kavayo viduḥ//
(II.10.11).

[70] See preceding chapter, pp. 79–80.

[71] See, for instance, PKh 21.43; 22.38; 25.9; 36.114.

[72] PKh 36.114.

[73] See, for instance, the description of the inhabitants of Goloka in KJKh 4.137–138.

[74] See De, VFM, pp. 294–296.

[75] See pp. 89 ff., above.

[76] De, VFM, p. 279.

preman.[77] *Dāsya,* on the other hand, is one of the five devotional sentiments and merely one aspect of *bhakti.* The five devotional sentiments, or *rasas,* include *śānta* (humility and awe), *dāsya* (servitude), *sākhya* (friendship), *vātsalya* (parental affection), and *mādhurya* (erotic-mystical love).[78] These various sentiments are directly realized or experienced in service to the Lord in Goloka. The highest, most intense and intimate of the five is *mādhurya.* In the BVP, the erotic love of Rādhā and Kṛṣṇa is described in explicit detail and at great length, but as mentioned above,[79] Rādhā in her erotic aspects does not serve as a model for the human soul.[80] Man's highest aspiration and end is *dāsya* alone.

[77] *Ibid.,* pp. 297–298.
[78] For a concise description of the *rāsa* theory of the Caitanya school, see Dimock, *The Place of the Hidden Moon,* pp. 22–23.
[79] See chapter 5, p. 92.
[80] Cf. p. 196 below.

PART C

THE THEOLOGY OF RĀDHĀ AS PRAKṚTI

7

Some Theoretical and Historical Considerations

1. Aspects and implications of a feminine theology

Feminine deities, often but not always fertility goddesses, were a widespread phenomenon in man's early religious experience.[1] But the idea of female divinity was gradually neglected or rejected by many of the great historic religious traditions. Ultimate reality came to be conceived basically in terms of masculine forms (the Father, the King), or in terms of a formless and neuter Absolute. The Hindu tradition, however, while exceedingly creative in interpreting reality in both its masculine and neuter aspects, also developed the ritual, devotion, and theology of feminine divinity more profusely, and perhaps more profoundly, than any other major religious tradition. Hinduism thus preserves and constantly reaffirms one of man's earliest religious orientations to the universe, an orientation that particularly in the West seems to have been largely forgotten.[2] Ernest A. Payne asserts:

> India seems to be unique in showing a higher appreciation of goddesses in its later religious development than in its earlier. In most cases, also, the worship of the reproductive

[1] In the Indian case, one early goddess who was not primarily associated with fertility was Uṣas, or Dawn, the sovereign deity of dominion and wealth.

[2] Van der Leeuw cautions: "In no religion whatever is the mother or father completely lacking. Judaism and Islam have mercilessly expelled the mother, but to Christianity she returned as *mater gloriosa*" (*Religion in Essence and Manifestation,* I, 99).

> forces of Nature is a matter of ancient history. Today in China and Japan, as formerly in Greece and Rome, it has decayed as civilisation advanced, and has ceased to be an important constituent of religion. It is only in India, and to some extent in Tibet, which has been influenced by India, that such worship has continued unashamed until modern times.[3]

The BVP, belonging to India's later religious development, is rooted in the experience of the sacredness of both the masculine and feminine dimensions of life. The experience of the masculine aspect of ultimate reality underlies the Kṛṣṇaite theology of our text. We may refer to this Kṛṣṇaite theology as a "masculine theology." By this term we wish to include not only those conceptions of divinity that express aspects and functions of the deity that are more or less exclusively and unambiguously male (e.g., fatherhood), but also those conceptions that have been traditionally associated with male divinity but would seem to be applicable to female divinity as well (e.g., the Supreme Being as the source of all *avatāras*).[4]

[3] *Śāktas,* pp. 61–62. Payne's statement may be criticized on two accounts. His apparent equation of "appreciation of goddesses" with "worship of the reproductive forces of Nature" seems to overlook the many other facets of female deities (see note 1 above). Secondly, worship of a goddess, or goddesses, whether as Mother or otherwise, has not entirely "ceased to be an important constituent of religion" except in India. We may refer to Van der Leeuw's statement quoted in note 2 above, and to another comment of his: "Demeter and Isis are mothers; Mary, their successor, is mother and maiden. But despite the ideal of virginity, the church was just as little able to dispense with the mother's form as was later Buddhism in the case of Kwanyin in China and Kwannon in Japan" (*Religion in Essence and Manifestation,* I, 98).

[4] Such an inclusive definition of "masculine theology" hopefully obviates to some extent the problem of having to decide what qualities and roles are "truly" or "naturally" masculine or feminine. If one wished to concentrate exclusively on "natural" male or female aspects and functions, he would be faced not only with complex psychological and cross-cultural problems, but also with the problem of determining in the Indian or Hindu context what is considered to be masculine or feminine. For instance, to regard Kṛṣṇa's demon-killing function as part of a male "warrior-role" overlooks Durgā's bloody exploits. Yet the situation is complicated by the fact that in actual Indian society, men and not women have been the warriors. Another example concerns the supposed "passivity" of the female, a notion that is found not only in the West but in India as well. Yet, as we shall see, it is the female that comes to be regarded as the *śakti,* the energizing power of the inactive male. An additional problem is that the Indian context itself has not remained static, so that views of the nature of the masculine and feminine have undoubtedly changed.

The masculine or Kṛṣṇaite theology of the BVP, as we have seen, is based to a considerable extent on older conceptions of God within the Vaiṣṇava movement. The feminine theology of our Purāṇa is developed in large part around the figure of Rādhā as identified with Prakṛti, though "other" goddesses, especially Durgā, play a significant role as we shall soon see. This feminine theology, for the most part complementary to, rather than conflicting with, the masculine, is more innovative and creative, though it too builds on traditional concepts. It incorporates under new principles of synthesis a large number of diverse views and doctrines, many taken over from older masculine theological notions. It may be argued that only with the development of a mature feminine theology is masculine theology itself fulfilled.[5]

The feminine theology of the BVP has been maligned and misunderstood by both Indian and Western writers. R. G. Bhandarkar makes the following judgment:

> In the Brahmavaivarta-Purāṇa she [Rādhā] has been made to spring from the primordial body of Kṛṣṇa, forming its left side, and is eternally associated with him in his amorous sports in this world as well as the world of cows (Goloka). . . . The introduction of Rādhā's name and her elevation to a higher position even than Kṛṣṇa's operated as a degrading element in Vaiṣṇavism, not only because she was a woman, but also because she was originally a mistress of the cowherd god, and her amorous dealings were of an overt character.[6]

On a less moralistic, more philosophical level, Wilson asserts that the Purāṇic compilers,

[5] In this connection, we may refer back to Van der Leeuw's statement quoted in note 2 above, that no religion is completely lacking the mother or father. He elsewhere writes: "It is true that both male and female elements, and the dominance of either at any given period, play a great part in the structure of the idea of God. But there is too much of the feminine in every man, and of the masculine in every woman, for precedence to be conceded here to either the one or the other sex" (*Religion in Essence and Manifestation,* I, 178). Thus, it might be said that not only does the masculine require the feminine to be fully masculine and vice versa, but each in a way contains the other within itself.

[6] *Vaiṣṇavism, Śaivism,* p. 87. Bhandarkar elsewhere (p. 57) states that ". . . Rāmānuja's system is free from that repulsive form which Vaiṣṇavism assumes when Rādhā and other cowherdesses are introduced." Another Indian writer, A. K. Majumdar, refers to the account of Kṛṣṇa's division into two parts, the left half being Rādhā, as "puerile" ("Radha Cult," ABORI, XXXVI, 240).

> . . . confounding the instrument with the action, matter with the impulse by which it was animated, . . . have chosen to consider Prakŕiti also as the embodied manifestation of the divine will, as the act of creation, or the inherent power of creating, co-existing with the supreme. This seems to be the ruling idea in the Brahma Vaivartta. . . .[7]

Whether the BVP has confounded material, or instrumental, and efficient causality, or rather has perceived deeper subtleties and underlying unities, is worth pondering. In any case, the BVP is fully aware of the normal distinction of material (or instrumental) and efficient causality,[8] so that any "confounding" is in part, if not wholly, intentional.[9] Wilson goes on to state:

> The idea of personifying the divine agency, being once conceived, was extended [in the BVP] by an obvious analogy to similar cases, and the persons of the Hindu triad being equally susceptible of active energies, their energies were embodied as their respective Prakŕitis, Śaktis, or goddesses. From them the like accompaniment was conferred upon the

[7] "Analysis of the Puráńas," ESL, I, 100. This statement by Wilson, though rather insensitive in its use of such words as "confounding," correctly points out the association, if not actual identification, of the feminine principle with the "will" of the deity. The Goddess is often called the *icchāśakti* of God, that is, the energy or power of his will or desire. Such views would seem to call into question Van der Leeuw's assertion that the mother is "Form and Power" while the father is "Form and Will." He writes, "When he may no longer be the fructifier, the father may be the creator; the mother can only bear offspring. The father acts with power: the mother is merely potent. . . . The mother creates life: the father history. She is Form and Power: he Form and Will; . . ." (*Religion in Essence and Manifestation*, I, 100). It is clear that God's Will, as active in and creative of history, is strikingly different from the concept of *icchā*. But this makes only more apparent the problems posed by the sorts of polarity between the father and mother as suggested by Van der Leeuw. His analysis seems more appropriate to the Near East than to India.

[8] See pp. 124 ff., below.

[9] Payne has written, regarding the Śākta doctrine: "The self-existent Being is regarded as single, solitary, impersonal, quiescent, inactive. Once it becomes conscious and personal it is duplex and acts through an associated female principle, which is conceived as possessing a higher degree of activity and personality. *Śakti* is the instrumental cause, *Prakṛiti* the material cause, and Śiva the efficient cause of the world" (*Śāktas*, pp. 77–78). One may disagree in part with Payne's description of the Śākta doctrine, for the female principle is also an efficient cause, and the "self-existent Being" is often considered as female rather than male (or neuter). But Payne's description at least does not make what he describes appear as sheer foolishness, in contrast to Wilson.

> whole pantheon, and finally upon man; woman being regarded as portions of the primeval Prakŕiti. The whole being evidently a clumsy attempt to graft the distinction of the sexes as prevailing in earth, hell, and heaven, upon a metaphysical theory of the origin of the universe.[10]

We shall later examine in some detail the various doctrines referred to by Wilson. Let us here only state that the "attempt" of the BVP is not so evidently clumsy to this writer as to Wilson. Even more importantly, it is also not evident that the BVP was attempting "to graft the distinction of the sexes" upon anything, but rather, to elucidate the sexual aspects of reality in its various ramifications.

2. Prakṛti, Rādhā, Durgā

In the following chapters we shall have many occasions to investigate the historical origin and development of several facets of the Goddess doctrine in our text. In order to facilitate that task, we shall here present some brief introductory observations on certain key aspects of that development, beginning with the concept of Prakṛti. In the classical Sāṃkhya, as we have seen, Prakṛti was contrasted to Puruṣa, not as woman to man, but as matter to spirit. And these two principles were regarded as ultimately distinct. We may recall that in ViP I.2.23–24, Viṣṇu is apparently identified with Brahman, Puṃs, and Pradhāna, and in the BVP, in GKh 32.33–34, Kṛṣṇa is said to be Prakṛti, Puṃs and beyond both, and to bear the form of a man, woman and eunuch. It is significant that the ViP uses the neuter term *pradhāna*, rather than the feminine *prakṛti*. Both terms in the Sāṃkhya are used to designate the material cause of the universe. The primary point of the ViP passage, then, seems to be the identification of Viṣṇu, the Supreme Brahman, with the efficient and material causes of the universe. The gender of the different principles is largely irrelevant, or at least not emphasized. To be sure, the ViP says that *pradhāna* is also known as *prakṛti*,[11] and refers to *prakṛti* as *jagadyoni* (womb of the world),[12] but the sexual aspects and possibilities of *prakṛti* are left largely undeveloped.

[10] "Analysis of the Puráńas," ESL, I, 101.
[11] ViP I.2.19.
[12] ViP I.2.21.

Prakṛti or *pradhāna* is regarded mainly as the source of material evolution, beginning with *mahat, ahaṃkāra,* the subtle elements and so forth.[13] Yet the seeds for an enlarged interpretation of *prakṛti's* sexual role are clearly present in the ViP, as for instance, in the notion that the various elements derived from *prakṛti* combine together to form a cosmic egg.[14] The cosmic egg, as we shall see, plays an important role in our Purāṇa.[15]

In the BVP, the older notions of *prakṛti* persist, though in altered form. She is still associated with the three *guṇas*,[16] and is referred to as pre-eminent (*pradhāna*) in creation, an apparent pun on the word *pradhāna,* meaning also material cause.[17] And in BKh 3.4 ff., we find the evolution or manifestation of the three *guṇas* from the primordial Puṃs, followed by *mahat, ahaṃkāra,* the subtle and gross elements. *Prakṛti,* though, is not specifically mentioned in the passage.

We also find *prakṛti* often referred to as *mūlaprakṛtir īśvarī,* the Goddess, Primordial Nature.[18] She is now contrasted with Puruṣa, not primarily as matter to spirit, but as woman to man. Thus in PKh 12.17cd, it is stated: "As woman and man [constitute] one body, so do Puruṣa and Prakṛti." We see here also an emphasis on the unity of the two.

Prakṛti, as we shall see, was personified, feminized, and divinized long before the final composition of the BVP. This development occurred in part by the identification of various goddesses with Prakṛti. Durgā was early associated with Prakṛti, and at a much later time, Rādhā too was identified with Nature.[19] Perhaps because of this, Prakṛti, though personified, was not really "personalized." By this I mean that Prakṛti, while conceived as a conscious being, as a queen or goddess (*īśvarī*), was not really endowed with a distinctive personality or individuality. She has no concrete image or form, and almost no "history," that is, no specific stories or legends in which she, as a distinctive being,

[13] ViP I.2.34 ff.

[14] ViP I.2.51 ff. For an analysis of the various sexual aspects of the cosmogony in ViP I.2, see Penner, "Cosmogony as Myth in the Vishnu Purāṇa," *History of Religions,* V, 283–299; esp. pp. 289–294.

[15] See below, pp. 172 ff.

[16] See, for instance, PKh 1.6, where the three syllables of her name, *pra, kṛ,* and *ti,* are identified with *sattva, rajas,* and *tamas.*

[17] PKh 1.7.

[18] E.g., PKh 1.12.

[19] See below, pp. 148, 154–155.

plays a role. Her "personality," to the extent that it does exist, is borrowed as it were from the goddesses with whom she is identified. But this fact also allowed her to transcend in a sense the other goddesses. Thus, a common conception of our Purāṇa, particularly of the PKh, is that Prakṛti is the One female principle of the universe, which then divides into or becomes manifest as the various goddesses.[20] In PKh 4.1, these goddesses themselves are referred to as *prakṛtis*, though the use of *prakṛti* in the plural is perhaps limited to this one verse in the BVP.[21]

Prakṛti, though essentially related to all goddesses, is identified especially with Durgā and Rādhā in our text. This double identification of Prakṛti is explained in the following way:

> She who merges into Kṛṣṇa's breast is the Goddess Primordial Nature.
> The Śāktas[22] call her Durgā, the eternal Viṣṇumāyā.
> Vaiṣṇavas call her Mahālakṣmī, the supreme Rādhā.[23]

This passage does not mean that Rādhā and Durgā are merely names of Prakṛti, for as suggested above, they are also the fully personalized aspects of Prakṛti. But even further, Rādhā and Durgā at times are each regarded as the supreme feminine principle of the universe, and then Prakṛti appears as an epithet or aspect of them. Thus in PKh 2.68, Durgā is referred to as *mūlaprakṛtir īśvarī*, as is Rādhā in PKh 55.18.[24]

The identification of both Durgā and Rādhā with Prakṛti is not an inconsistency but rather points to the essential identity of the two goddesses. In many places of the text, it is said that Rādhā is Durgā and that Durgā is Rādhā.[25] In KJKh 124.39 ff., we find

[20] We shall discuss this view in some detail below, pp. 142 ff.

[21] In PKh 4.1, Nārada asks Nārāyaṇa:
adhunā prakṛtīnāṃ ca vyāsaṃ varṇaya bho prabho//
In classical Sāmkhya, *prakṛti* was one, but this was not the earliest form of the doctrine. Earlier notions were that *prakṛti* was eightfold (e.g., BhG VII.4), or that there were eight *prakṛtis* (see Johnston, *Early Sāṃkhya*, pp. 25–29).

[22] The Veṅk reads *santo,* but notes *śāktā* is a variant reading (PKh 54.89). Ānand reads *santo.* Vaṅg has *śāktā* (PKh 54.92).

[23] PKh 54.88cd-89ab, 91ab. We shall deal with the relationship of Rādhā and Lakṣmī later.

[24] Cf. PadP, V.70.4, where Rādhikā is referred to as Mūlaprakṛti.

[25] E.g., PKh 55.52 (for Rādhā as Durgā); 65.25 (for Durgā as Rādhā). In addition, it may be noted, both Rādhā and Durgā are identified with many of the other goddesses, such as Lakṣmī, Vāṇī, Gaṅgā, and so forth (for Rādhā, see PKh 55.50 ff.; for Durgā, KJKh 129.94 ff.).

an account of a meeting between the two. After embracing and kissing each other, Durgā says to Rādhā:

> Always my heart and life [is concentrated] on you, as yours on me,
> For there is no difference between us, like Śakti and Puruṣa.[26]

Nonetheless, just as the BVP ultimately favors Kṛṣṇa over Śiva, so also is Rādhā favored over Durgā. Durgā's subordination, however, is even less pronounced and explicit than Śiva's. Further, in many cases, the "Rādhāism" of our text seems to be directly based upon theological notions originally pertaining to Durgā. Accordingly, our study of Rādhā as Prakṛti in the following chapters will make frequent use of theological motifs and ideas connected with Durgā.

[26] KJKh 124.43. Cf. BAP III.42.48, in which Rādhā says to Durgā: *tvaṃ cāhamāvayor devi bhedo naivāsti kaścana/*

8

Prakṛti and Supreme Reality

The relationship of Prakṛti to the Supreme Reality constitutes one of the fundamental theological problems of the BVP. This problem has been dealt with in two basic ways. One approach, relatively the more direct, has recourse to a number of analogies or relational models. The importance of these models can be judged by their constant recurrence throughout all sections of the text. The second approach involves the various epithets applied to Prakṛti and the Supreme.

1. Analogies and Relational Models

The several analogies and relational models may be considered under four main types: (1) efficient and material cause, (2) substance and attribute, (3) support and supported, or container and contained (*ādhāra* and *ādheya*), and (4) soul (Ātman) and body. No one model in itself can comprehend the whole reality, but each can illuminate certain essential facets of it. We should therefore pay attention to the specific aspects of the analogies that are emphasized in each case, in order to understand the limitations as well as the broader implications of the models. Often our text gives a series of analogies in which examples from two or more of the above four types are included, and sometimes the analogies themselves are mixed, but for the sake of analysis we shall deal with each separately, as far as possible.

a) *Efficient and material cause*

Prakṛti, as we have seen, has traditionally been regarded as the material cause of the universe. In our Purāṇa, the efficient cause is usually identified with Brahmā, the creator, or with Kṛṣṇa. The relationship of the efficient and material causes is illustrated by two standard analogies, often appearing together as in PKh 2.8–9:

> Without gold, a goldsmith is unable to make an earring;
> Without clay, a potter is not able to make a jar;
> And just so is Brahmā unable to create the world without her [Prakṛti].
> She in essence is the energy of all; with her, he is ever endowed with energy.[1]

Brahmā, then, like any other artisan, requires the raw materials of his craft in order to create. In similar fashion, Kṛṣṇa himself declares to Rādhā:

> As a potter with clay is always able to make a pot,
> So am I with you, who are Prakṛti, able to create the world.
> Without you, I cannot move and am ever powerless.
> You in essence are the energy of all; come to me.[2]

Clay and gold, as is well known, are frequently used images in Indian philosophy. In CU VI.1.4–5, they serve to illustrate the underlying unity of all existence. The modification of clay or gold into specific forms (such as jars or earrings) is merely a name, while the reality is the substance itself. In the CU examples, however, there is no potter or goldsmith, and the general viewpoint is non-theistic. With the inclusion of an artisan or agent, a theistic element is introduced. At the same time, a dualistic viewpoint tends to replace the earlier monistic emphasis, for God, as artisan, is set over against the world or matter.

The examples of CU VI.1.4–5 are indirectly referred to in BS II.1.14,[3] regarding the non-difference of cause and effect (Brahman and world). The BS, in II.1.24–25, raises the problem of the cause, as agent, needing instruments (as a potter requires a

1 Cf. NārPR II.6.28cd–29:
sṛṣṭibījasvarūpā sā [prakṛti] na hi sṛṣṭis tayā vinā//
vinā mṛdaṃ ghaṭaṃ kartuṃ kulālaś ca na ca kṣamaḥ/
vinā svarṇaṃ svarṇakāraḥ kuṇḍalaṃ kartum askṣamaḥ//

2 PKh 55.86–87.

3 Cf. Ghate, *The Vedānta,* p. 73.

wheel and clay). The BS itself apparently denies the applicability to Brahman of the artisan analogy. The transformation of Brahman into the world is compared to milk, which by itself turns into curds (BS II.1.24). Nimbārka, Rāmānuja, and Vallabha, as well as Śaṃkara, in commenting on II.1.24–25, all affirm that Brahman needs no instruments but creates the world by Its own power of will,[4] thereby confirming the rejection of the artisan analogy.[5] We see, then, that there has been resistance to the inclusion of the potter in the clay analogy even by theistic thinkers, because of the accompanying dualistic implications.

The acceptance of the potter and goldsmith in the analogies of the BVP might seem to imply a dualistic view of Brahman and Prakṛti. But the purpose of the analogies in the BVP is not so much to suggest an ultimate ontological dualism, but rather to show the absolutely essential and necessary role that Prakṛti plays in creation.[6]

More problematic for our Purāṇa, however, is an implicit subordination of Prakṛti to Puruṣa or Kṛṣṇa in such analogies. This is brought out in the following passage, in which the neuter Brahman represents the Supreme:

> Not what is created by the potter, but just the clay is eternal.
> Not what is created by the goldsmith, but just the gold is enduring.
> Eternal is that supreme Brahman, and eternal is Prakṛti, so it is held.
> Of the two, there is equal pre-eminence according to some.
> But the potter and goldsmith gather the clay and the gold,
> While the clay and the gold are unable to fetch the [artisans].

[4] *Ibid.*, p. 75.

[5] For example, Nimbārka states succinctly:
kumbhakārādīnām anekopakaraṇopasaṃhāradarśanād bahyopakaraṇarahitaṃ brahma na jagatkāraṇam iti cen na yataḥ kṣīravat kāryākareṇa brahma pariṇamate svāsādhāraṇaśaktimattvāt// (*Vedāntapārijātasaurabham*, II.1.23. [corresponds to II.1.24 in most editions of the BS.])
Cf. Chaudhuri, "The Nimbārka School of Vedānta," CHI, III, 333–335, 340.

[6] Cf. KJKh 67.80 (Kṛṣṇa speaking to Rādhā):
yathā tvaṃ ca tathāhaṃ ca samau prakṛtipuruṣau/
na hi sṛṣṭir bhaved devi dvayor ekataraṃ vinā//

Therefore Brahman is superior to Prakṛti,
Some say, even though the two are eternal.
Still others say that Brahman himself is Prakṛti and Puṃs.
Or that Brahman is distinct from Prakṛti.[7]

Since the artisan is the active and conscious agent, while the raw material is purely passive matter to be worked upon, the logical implication is that Brahman is the superior principle.[8] Yet this passage does not press the ontological implications to a definite conclusion. Instead, the succeeding verses define the nature of Brahman and Prakṛti and their mutual interaction in the following way:

Brahman is the supreme abode, the cause of all causes;
This is one definition of Brahman according to scripture.
And Brahman is the Self of all, unstained, in the form of witness,
Pervading all, the source of all; this too is a definition according to scripture.
Prakṛti is the energy of that Brahman, in essence the seed of all,
Whence Brahman becomes endowed with energy. This is the definition of Prakṛti.[9]

It becomes clear, then, that the analogies of potter and clay, goldsmith and gold, do not express the full truth. For while clay and gold are passive materials, Prakṛti represents not only matter but energy. The analogies of the artisan and his working materials appear many times in our text,[10] and almost all refer to Prakṛti's

[7] BKh 28.29–33.

[8] Gilbert Cope makes the following interesting comment on potter and pot analogies in the Bible: "In Genesis 2, in the account of the creation of Adam, God is depicted as a clay-modeller or potter who 'generates' man from the moist earth: this metaphor is fairly frequent in the Bible and is wonderfully explicit in Isaiah:

'O Lord, thou art our father;
We are the clay, and thou art our potter.'

Here we have complete reversal of the primary situation in which the potter was the *mother,* for it is recognized that pot-making originated as a feminine occupation" (*Symbolism in the Bible and the Church,* pp. 132–133). It seems that India also has reversed the "primary situation."

[9] BKh 28.34–36.

[10] In addition to those already cited: GKh 7.70–71; 40.60–61; KJKh 6.220–221; 15.59–60; 67.74–76. Cf. PKh 59.19–20.

energy as the generative power of the Supreme and stress the helplessness of the Supreme without her. It is as energy, incidentally, that Prakṛti begins to overcome the ontological dualism between herself and the Supreme, for as energy, she is possessed by, or unites with, the Supreme for the sake of all activity. Prakṛti's energetic aspect will be brought out more clearly in the second type of analogy.

b) *Substance and Attribute*

Let us begin by quoting three examples of this relational model. In PKh 2.7 it is stated:

> As burning [inheres] in fire, beauty in the moon and lotus, brilliance in the sun,
> Eternally united, never separated (*na bhinnā*), so is Prakṛti in Ātman.

The second example, with Prakṛti and Brahman:

> As the energy of burning [inheres] in fire, brilliance in the sun, O Muni,
> As whiteness in milk and coolness in water,
> As sound in the sky and smell in the earth, ever,
> So are *nirguṇa* Brahman and *nirguṇā*[11] *Prakṛti*.[12]

And Kṛṣṇa says to his foster father:

> As whiteness inheres in milk, with no difference (*na . . . bheda*) between them,
> As coolness in water, as burning in fire,
> As sound in space, as smell in earth, O King,
> As beauty in the moon, as brilliance in the sun,
> . . . so am I with Rādhā.[13]

[11] For *nirguṇā* as an epithet of Prakṛti, see below, pp. 134–135.

[12] BKh 28.23cd–25ab.

[13] KJKh 73.48–50ab. The last line (50ab) in both Veṅk and Ānand seems a bit confused. The Ānand is apparently the better reading. Cf. NārPR II.6.23–24:

jale satyasvarūpā sā [*prakṛti*] *gandharūpā ca bhūmiṣu/*
śabdarūpā ca nabhasi śobhārūpī niśākare//
prabhārūpā bhāskare sā nṛpendreṣu ca sarvataḥ/
vahnau sā dāhikā śaktiḥ sarvaśaktiś ca janteṣu
[text misprints *jantaṣu*]//

It is of interest to note that in BhG VII.8–9, Kṛṣṇa declares that he is taste in water, light in the moon and sun, sound in space, smell in earth, brilliance in fire. The BhG thus reflects a basically masculine-oriented theology.

The clear intent of these analogies is to show the inseparability and non-difference of Prakṛti and the Supreme. This relationship of non-difference, however, does not necessarily mean an absolute identity, for the analogies imply rather a "non-difference in difference" (*bhedābheda*). Absolute identity would preclude any real relationship, while an attribute inheres within its substance.

In this regard, one might suppose that "substance" has ontological priority over "attribute." But from the viewpoint of the BVP, as we shall see shortly, it almost appears that the attribute is superior. Yet as with the analogies of efficient and material cause, the implications of the substance-attribute model with regard to the question of Prakṛti's or Kṛṣṇa's ontological superiority are not stressed. Indeed, in one case, the analogy is actually reversed, Rādhā being identified with the substance and Kṛṣṇa with the attribute. Kṛṣṇa says to Rādhā:

> As you are, so am I; there is certainly no difference between us.
> As whiteness inheres in milk, as burning in fire, my fair Lady,
> As smell in earth, so do I inhere in you always.[14]

The primary purpose here is to show the inseparability of Rādhā and Kṛṣṇa, not to prove her superiority. This reversal of the analogy is an exception, and perhaps is influenced by the analogies of *ādhāra* and *ādheya*, to be discussed below, in which Kṛṣṇa rests on or in Prakṛti. In the substance-attribute analogies, Kṛṣṇa more properly is represented by substance and Prakṛti by attribute.

Let us look more closely at the specific analogy of burning and fire. In some cases, it is not mere "burning" (*dāhikā*), but the "power of burning" (*dāhikāśakti*) that is said to inhere in fire, as in the second of the three examples quoted at the beginning of this section. In PKh 55.88ab, Kṛṣṇa says to Rādhā: "You are the energy of burning in fire; fire is powerless without you." Prakṛti, or Rādhā, then, is not merely an inseparable attribute, but the activating energy of the substance, without whom the substance cannot carry out its proper function. It is important to note that we are no longer dealing merely with an analogy, for Rādhā herself *is* the *śakti* of fire.

[14] KJKh 15.59cd–60.

The relational model of burning and fire most clearly brings out Prakṛti's energizing role, but even in the other examples, Prakṛti represents a kind of power to make manifest the essential character or nature of the substance. Thus, following the verse just quoted above, Kṛṣṇa says:

> You [Rādhā] are the beauty in the moon; without you, it is not beautiful.
> You are the brilliance in the sun; without you, it has no brilliance.[15]

And in another passage, in which Prakṛti is identified with Durgā, it is stated:

> She [Durgā] is the burning in fire, the brilliance in the sun,
> The beauty in the moon and in the lotuses, exceedingly fair;
> She is the essence of all energy in Śrī Kṛṣṇa, the Supreme Self,
> By whom the Self is endowed with energy, as well as the world,
> And without whom the whole world, though living, is as though dead.[16]

The shift from analogy to identity applies not only to Prakṛti but to Kṛṣṇa as well. In KJKh 67.67cd–70ab, Kṛṣṇa says to Rādhā:

> By a portion I am fire and you are burning . . .
> With you I am powerful; without you I am unable to burn.
> By a portion I am the brilliant sun; you are the cause of the brilliance.
> With you I blaze forth; without you I cannot illuminate.
> By a portion I am the moon, you are its grace, Rohiṇī;
> With you I captivate the mind, without you I have no beauty.

The actual identification of Kṛṣṇa and Prakṛti with substance and attribute emphasizes and makes explicit the essential energizing role of Prakṛti and Kṛṣṇa's dependence upon her.

An additional aspect of the substance-attribute model is found in KJKh 42.27:

[15] PKh 55.88cd–89ab.
[16] PKh 2.74cd–76.

By whom milk became white and water was made cool, long ago,
And fire was made to burn, obeisance to him, to Kṛṣṇa.

The implications of this verse are significant, for it suggests that the inseparability of substance and attribute, or of Kṛṣṇa himself and Rādhā, ultimately depends upon his will.

c) *Adhāra* and *ādheya*

In most Vaiṣṇava works, Kṛṣṇa is commonly referred to as the *ādhāra,* the support or foundation, of the universe, who is himself *nirādhāra,* without any support. For instance, the ascetic Aṣṭāvakra praises Kṛṣṇa in the following way:

[The tree of the world process or *saṃsāra* grows from] the sprout of Prakṛti.
You [Kṛṣṇa] are its support, you who are without support, the support of all. Reverence to you.[17]

Elsewhere, Kṛṣṇa says to Rādhā:

By a fraction I am Śeṣa [the world-supporting serpent], and by a portion you are Earth;
On my head, fair lady, I bear you, the support of crops.[18]

In these examples, Prakṛti, or Rādhā, is the *ādheya,* or that which is to be supported. Let us compare with these the following passage (again, Kṛṣṇa is speaking to Rādhā):

Behold, my fair lady, the whole universe is constituted of supports and the supported.
There is nothing supported without a support.
The flower supports the fruit, the shoot supports the flower.

[17] KJKh 29.47. In 29.44cd, Kṛṣṇa is referred to as the tree of *saṃsāra,* its seed, and its fruit. The tree has three branches, Brahmā, Viṣṇu, and Śiva, with the Vedas as branches and acts of asceticism as flowers (29.46). The next line reads:

saṃsāraviphalā [or *saṃsārā viphalā* in Ānand] *eva prakṛtyaṅkuram eva ca/*

The meaning of *saṃsāraviphalā* is unclear to me. Cf. BhP III.9.16:

yo vā ahaṃ ca girīśaś ca vibhuḥ svayaṃ ca sthityudbhavapralayahetava ātmamūlam/
bhittvā tripād vavṛdha eka uruprarohas tasmai namo bhagavate bhuvanadrumāya//

[18] KJKh 67.76cd–77ab.

> The branch supports the shoot, the tree itself supports the branch.
> The sprout supports (grows into) the tree, being endowed with the power of life.
> The seed supports the sprout, the earth supports the seed.
> Śeṣa supports the earth, the tortoise supports Śeṣa.
> Wind supports tortoise, and I support the wind.
> You are my support; I rest upon you always.[19]

Here we see a reversal of the first examples. Kṛṣṇa is still the support of the universe, but Prakṛti is no longer connected with the tree of *saṃsāra* or with the earth. Rather, she now is regarded as the ultimate support of Kṛṣṇa himself. Throughout the BVP, Prakṛti is usually identified with the *ādhāra,* and Kṛṣṇa with the *ādheya.*

Adhāra means not only "support," in the sense of an underlying prop or foundation, but also "receptacle," "vessel," or "container." Thus, *sarvādhāra* may have the meaning, "receptacle of the universe," or "that within which all is contained." As applied to Prakṛti, the two senses of *ādhāra* bring out her supportive and her creative functions. Her supportive role we have already seen in part, as the prop of Kṛṣṇa. She is also the nourisher and sustainer of the universe. As container, she is the receptable or womb in which the seed of the universe is implanted. This twofold aspect of *ādhāra* is brought out in the following passage, with regard to the human level of existence:

> From man arises the seed, from the seed the continuation of offspring.
> Woman, a portion of Prakṛti, is the *ādhāra* of both [the receptacle of the seed, the support of the offspring].[20]

With Prakṛti as *ādhāra* in the form of womb, Kṛṣṇa is *ādheya* in the form of seed. He declares to Rādhā: "You are the *ādhāra* of creation, and I have the form of the seed."[21] Kṛṣṇa therefore rests within Prakṛti as the seed or germ of the universe. But it is not only in this cosmogonic context that Prakṛti is the container or receptacle of Kṛṣṇa, for it is also said: "In relation to the Ātman [Kṛṣṇa], you [Rādhā] are the body, for you are its *ādhāra* (con-

[19] KJKh 6.208–212ab.
[20] KJKh 6.214.
[21] KJKh 15.62.

tainer)."[22] The model of soul and body appears, then, to be merely a special case of the *ādhāra-ādheya* relationship, yet it seems sufficiently important in itself to merit separate treatment.

d) *Ātman and body*

In the case of the Ātman and body relational model, analogy gives way almost completely to identification. The Ātman-body relationship may be understood on at least two levels: the cosmological and the ultimate. The cosmological aspect is expressed in GKh 7.73cd: "Prakṛti is the container [i.e. body] of all, and I [Kṛṣṇa] am the Ātman of all, in all creatures." The second level concerns the relationship of Rādhā and Kṛṣṇa in itself. Kṛṣṇa is her Ātman, and she his body. These two levels are closely interrelated, for the cosmological aspect is the manifestation or reflection of the ultimate. Their interrelationship is suggested in the following passage, in which Kṛṣṇa says to Rādhā:

> . . . [you] have the form of the body of embodied beings;
> You always are my *ādhāra* and I am your Ātman, in mutual interdependence (*parasparam*).[23]

The Ātman-body relational model would seem to emphasize more Rādhā's dependence upon Kṛṣṇa, for the Ātman is usually thought of as eternal and independent, while the body dies when the Ātman departs. Thus Rādhā says to Kṛṣṇa:

> You are the Ātman of all. . . .
> As a body abandoned by the Ātman, so am I without you.
> You are my life; I am dead without you.[24]

Yet Rādhā is also eternal:

> As Ātman itself is eternal, so are you [Rādhā], Prakṛti herself,
> Endowed with all energy, the eternal container of all.[25]

The Ātman-body relationship in our Purāṇa is meant to show the *mutual* dependence of Rādhā and Kṛṣṇa. For instance, in PKh 59.17, a householder without a wife is said to be like the *jīva* without *śakti,* the Ātman without body, the *ādheya* without *ādhāra,* and the Lord without Prakṛti. The Ātman without the

[22] KJKh 15.105.
[23] KJKh 67.79.
[24] KJKh 67.13–14ab. Cf. KJKh 68.27–28; 95.6.
[25] KJKh 6.221.

body is powerless. Thus in PKh 3.38, it is said: "So long as the Ātman remains in the body, so long is it endowed with *śakti.*" And further, just as with the substance-attribute analogy, so may the Ātman-body relation of Kṛṣṇa and Rādhā be reversed. Kṛṣṇa says to her, for example: "You are my Ātman, mind and life; I bear (*vahāmi*) merely the body."[26] Nonetheless, Kṛṣṇa is normally identified with the Ātman and Rādhā with the body. Their mutual interdependence and inseparability is clearly the point of the following words of Kṛṣṇa to Rādhā:

> Without the body, where is Ātman? And where is the body without the Ātman?
> Both are pre-eminent, O Goddess; without you now, whence would come the world?
> Nowhere is there separation of us, the two seeds of the world, O Rādhā.
> Where there is Ātman, there also is body; there is no separation. . . .[27]

In summary, the relational models of the BVP stress Prakṛti's creative and activating roles, and the mutual dependence and inseparability of Prakṛti and Kṛṣṇa.[28] Their cosmological-cosmogonical relation is precisely defined, but the purely ontological question of their ultimate relative status is not completely answered. At times, Prakṛti is apparently subordinated to Kṛṣṇa, yet there is a recurring tendency to regard her as at least his equal.

[26] KJKh 2.11ab. In the *Skanda Purāṇa,* Kṛṣṇa is referred to as Ātmārāma, and it is explained that Rādhikā is the Ātman of the Ātmārāma (B. Majumdar, *Kṛṣṇa in History and Legend,* pp. 185–186).

[27] KJKh 6.215–216.

[28] Similar relational models are found in ViP I.8.15–32, explaining the relationship of Śrī to Viṣṇu. For instance, it is said that he is the creator, she the creation; she is the earth, he the support (I.8.18ab); he is the sun, she its radiance (I.8.22ab); he is the moon, she its undiminishing beauty (I.8.24ab); she is the light and he the lamp; she is the creeper and he the tree (I.8.29). Hazra has shown that I.8.15–32 is a late addition to the ViP (*Purāṇic Records,* pp. 21–22). And in BhP VI.19.10–12, it is said that Viṣṇu and Śrī are the rulers and ultimate cause of the universe; she is the subtle *prakṛti, māyā,* and *śakti,* while he is her controller as *puruṣa;* he is the Ātman of all embodied beings, she is the body, its senses and recipient vessels (*śarīrendriyāśayā*); she is "name and form," he is their cause (*pratyaya*) and support (*upāśraya*). Cf. Rukmani, *A Critical Study of the Bhāgavata Purāṇa,* pp. 125–126.)

2. Epithets of Prakṛti

We may recall that Kṛṣṇa's supreme and transcendent nature was indicated in several ways: by identification with Paraṃbrahman, Paramātman, Paramapuruṣa; by the ascription of various negative and positive attributes; and by paradox.[29] Let us see to what extent Prakṛti participates in these different aspects of transcendency, according to our Purāṇa.

In PKh 1.10, Prakṛti is referred to as *brahmasvarūpā,* in PKh 64.31 as *parabrahmasvarūpā,* and in KJKh 94.71 as *brahmasvarūpā paramā.*[30] The adjunct *-svarūpa* may indicate only similarity, and the above epithets would then mean that Prakṛti is like Brahman. But *svarūpa* may also signify "natural or true form or condition." In this case, the epithets would mean that Prakṛti's true nature is the Supreme Brahman, or that she is the true form of Brahman. From the context of the epithets, it seems that identification rather than mere similarity is the intent of our Purāṇa. In one instance, Prakṛti, as Durgā, is apparently regarded as superior to Brahman, for she is said to uphold the Paraṃbrahman.[31]

Prakṛti, traditionally associated with the three *guṇas*, is referred to in the BVP as *triguṇātmikā* (having the three *guṇas* as her essence),[32] or simply as *triguṇā* (possessing the three *guṇas*).[33] Yet like Brahman, she is also *nirguṇā.*[34] Sometimes she is referred to simply as *nirguṇā* (without *saguṇā* or *triguṇā, et cetera*), as in PKh 54.92, where she is called the *nirguṇā śakti* of the *nirguṇa* (Kṛṣṇa).[35] Elsewhere, *nirguṇā* and *saguṇā* appear together as epithets of Prakṛti.[36] An explanation of the relationship of these two aspects is given in PKh 55.77, where Kṛṣṇa says to Rādhā:

[29] See above, pp. 63 ff.

[30] These epithets also occur in KJKh 43.74; 47.10; and 88.16.

[31] KJKh 88.18 reads in part:

. . . *brahma paraṃ tvaṃ* [*Durgā*] *bibharṣi sanātani//*

The passage in which this verse occurs is quoted at length below: see p. 136 and note 41.

[32] PKh 2.68.

[33] BKh 28.26, and PKh 64.14.

[34] BKh 28.24; this verse is translated above: see p. 127 and note 12.

[35] Cf. PKh 54.90ab:

buddhyadhiṣṭhātṛdevīṃ ca śrīkṛṣṇasyaiva nirguṇām/

In Vaṅg, the last part of the line reads: *kṛṣṇasya nirguṇātmikām* (54.93b), and in Ānand: *kṛṣṇasya triguṇātmikām* (54.90b).

[36] E.g., PKh 64.11 and KJKh 129.85.

. . . you are the Goddess Mūlaprakṛti,
You are *saguṇā* by a fraction (*kalā*), but in yourself you are *nirguṇā* alone.

As for Atman and Paramātman, we have already seen one instance in the soul-body relational model where Kṛṣṇa is identified with the body and Rādhā with the Ātman.[37] Like the epithet Brahman, Ātman is often associated with Prakṛti with the adjuncts *-svarūpā,* or *-svarūpiṇī.* Thus in KJKh 129.85, Prakṛti, as Pārvatī, is referred to as *parabrahmasvarūpā . . . paramātmasvarūpiṇī.* And inKJKh 43.74, Śiva addresses Durgā as *brahmasvarūpe . . . parātmasvarūpe.* Rādhā, in PKh 1.51 is called *ātmasvarūpiṇī.*

It has been noted previously that Kṛṣṇa's relation to Puruṣa is variously conceived.[38] Sometimes he is identified with Puruṣa, sometimes he is regarded as superior to Puruṣa as well as to Prakṛti. Thus in KJKh 43.58cd–60, the following views are put forth regarding Brahman or the Bhagavat:

The Bhagavat, self-willed, brings about transformation by his desire (*icchā*).
His power of desire (*icchāśakti*) is the eternal Prakṛti, mother of the universe.
Some people say the eternal light of Brahman is one.
Others say Brahman is twofold, attended by Prakṛti.
Yet others say the One is beyond Māyā and Puruṣa.

In GKh 7.49 ff., the gods and sages are discussing the relative status of Puruṣa and Prakṛti. Pārvatī asserts that in the Vedas, Puruṣa is superior to Prakṛti. Bṛhaspati replies that without both Puruṣa and Prakṛti creation is impossible, and that Kṛṣṇa has created both, so the two are equal. Pārvatī rejoins:

Kṛṣṇa, who is the creator of all, by a portion becomes *saguṇa* as the Puṃs.
Therefore Puṃs is greater than Prakṛti, not vice versa.[39]

Kṛṣṇa also, we may recall, is identified with masculine, feminine, and neuter.[40]

37 KJKh 2.11.
38 See above, p. 66.
39 GKh 7.52. Cf. BKh 28.25, where it is said that Brahman, for creation, by a portion becomes Puruṣa and *saguṇa.*
40 GKh 32.34; KJKh 113.31.

Let us compare these views of Kṛṣṇa with the following eulogy of Durgā offered by Śiva:

> Through *māyā,* you assume manhood (*puruṣatva*), and through *māyā* you are Prakṛti herself.
> You are beyond both, eternal, supporting the Supreme Brahman.
>
> . . . .
>
> O Goddess, you have the form of a woman; you are the excellent Puruṣa (*atipuruṣa*); and you are a eunuch.[41]

And in KJKh 94.7ab, Uddhava says to Rādhā: "You indeed are Rādhā, you are Kṛṣṇa; you are Puṃs and Prakṛti, supreme."

Turning now to the various attributes ascribed to Prakṛti in herself, we find the following negative descriptions: without form,[42] indescribable,[43] unstained,[44] without desire,[45] without egotism,[46] incomparable,[47] without beginning or end,[48] and without support.[49] *Nirguṇā,* of course, may be included in the list of negative descriptions, though it is not really an "attribute." Positive attributes include: supreme,[50] the true or real,[51] eternal,[52] self-willed,[53] supreme bliss,[54] omniscient,[55] the power of knowledge,[56] and having the form of light.[57]

[41] KJKh 88.18, 27ab. We may compare this with Devī's position in the KūrP. It is said: "Some people say that you [Devī] are Prakṛti [and] beyond Prakṛti/ . . . In you are *pradhāna* and *puruṣa* . . ." (I.12.209cd, 210cd). She is also said to be *prakṛteḥ parastāt* (I.12.229), and to be the one Puruṣa of all men (I.12.220).

[42] *nirākārā* (PKh 1.51).

[43] *anirvacanīyā* (GKh 45.21).

[44] *nirliptā* (PKh 1.51).

[45] *nirīhā* (PKh 1.51).

[46] *nirahaṃkārā* (PKh 1.51).

[47] *nirupamā* (PKh 11.34).

[48] *ādyantarahitā* (PKh 11.34).

[49] *nirāśrayā* (PKh 66.10).

[50] *parā* (PKh 64.1); *paramā* (PKh 66.9); *parātparā* (PKh 64.50).

[51] *satyā* (PKh 64.11). We may recall that Kṛṣṇa is regarded as *satya,* while all from Brahmā to a blade of grass is seen as *mithyā.* In PKh 57.15, Durgā, as Prakṛti, is called *satyasvarūpā,* in contrast to the *ābrahmastambhaparyanta* which is *mithyā* and *kṛtrima.*

[52] *nityā* (PKh 1.10); *sanātanī* (PKh 1.10).

[53] *svecchāmayī* (PKh 64.11).

[54] *paramānandarūpā* (PKh 1.43; 1.48); *paramāhlādarūpā* (PKh 1.50); *paramānandarūpiṇī* (KJKh 43.74).

[55] *sarvajñā* (PKh 54.179; 66.10).

[56] *jñānaśakti* (PKh 5.17).

[57] *jyotirūpā* (PKh 55.78).

The paradoxical expression of Prakṛti's transcendent nature, though minimal, is still present in the BVP. The pair of epithets, *nirguṇā* and *saguṇā*, retains something of a paradoxical quality, despite the usual philosophical explanation of their relation in terms of pre-creation and creation. The paradoxical nature of Prakṛti is especially evident in that her transcendent nature is *nirguṇā*, yet her essence is regarded as constituted of the three *guṇas* (*triguṇātmikā*). Further, *māyā* cannot be used to explain away paradoxes in her case, for she herself is Māyā.[58] Parallel to *nirguṇā* and *saguṇā* are the terms *nirākārā* and *sākārā*. Prakṛti's *sākārā* nature is usually, if not always, subordinated to her *nirākārā* aspect. For instance, it is said of Durgā: "You are endowed with form through the *guṇas* and formless through the absence of *guṇas*."[59] And Kṛṣṇa says to Rādhā: "Being a mass of light (*jyotīrūpā*), you are formless, taking on a body to favor your devotees."[60] Such explanations, however, we wish to stress, do not completely interpret out Prakṛti's paradoxical nature. For in some instances, the BVP allows paradoxes to stand, as in PKh 65.24, where Prakṛti is called *nityā* (eternal) and *anityā* (transient).

* * * * *

By now it should be clear that all the various means used to indicate Kṛṣṇa's transcendent nature have also been applied to Prakṛti. The similarity of Prakṛti in herself to Kṛṣṇa in himself may be rather perplexing to those who wish to determine the superiority of one or the other. Indeed, according to our Purāṇa, it is an indeterminable problem. Brahmā, for instance, says to Rādhā:

> You have arisen from the left half of Kṛṣṇa's body, equal to Kṛṣṇa in all ways.[61]
> Is that Śrī Kṛṣṇa you, Rādhā? Or are you, Rādhā, Hari himself?
> This matter has not been determined by me in the Vedas; by whom can it be ascertained?

[58] Cf. pp. 73–74, above.
[59] KJKh 88.17.
[60] PKh 55.78ab. Missing is the notion that a form of Prakṛti exists within the mass of light. Cf. the views of Kṛṣṇa, pp. 70–71, above.
[61] For the notion of Rādhā arising from Kṛṣṇa's body, see below, pp. 154–157, 170–172.

. . . .

> By whom can it be determined, whether you are a portion of him, or he is a portion of you?[62]

We have already referred to Uddhava's statement that Rādhā is Kṛṣṇa and Kṛṣṇa is Rādhā. Uddhava goes on to say that neither in Purāṇa nor in *śruti* is a distinction made between Rādhā and Mādhava.[63] Rādhā herself says to Kṛṣṇa:

> I have been constructed by someone out of half your body;
> Therefore there is no difference between us, and my heart is in you.
> Just as my Self (Ātman), heart, and life has been placed in you,
> So has your Self, heart, and life been placed in me.[64]

And Kṛṣṇa says to her:

> There is no difference between us, for we always are of one body.[65]

In this connection, it may be noted that not only is Rādhā referred to as *kṛṣṇavāmāṅgasambhūtā*,[66] but also Kṛṣṇa in his turn is called *rādhikāṅga*.[67] The indeterminability of the gender of the ultimate reality is perhaps best illustrated by the following account of Brahmā's vision of Kṛṣṇa in Goloka:

> At one moment, there was just one Kṛṣṇa with only one Rādhā.
> At another moment, on every seat, there was a Kṛṣṇa, each with a Rādhā.

62 KJKh 15.101–102ab, 107ab.
63 KJKh 94.7.
64 KJKh 6.202–203.
65 KJKh 6.67. Cf. NārPR II.3.67cd, referring to Rādhā and Kṛṣṇa:
ekāṅgo hi tanor bhedo dugdhadhāraṇyayor yathā//
Cf. also PadP V.75.44cd–46 (Kṛṣṇa speaking):
ahaṃ ca lalitā devī rādhikā yā ca gīyate//
ahaṃ ca vāsudevākhyo nityaṃ kāmakalātmakaḥ/
satyaṃ yoṣitvarūpo 'haṃ yoṣic cāhaṃ sanātanī//
ahaṃ ca lalitā devī puṃrūpā kṛṣṇavigrahā/
āvayor antaraṃ nāsti satyaṃ satyaṃ hi nārada//
And cf. BAP III.42.47:
prakṛtiḥ puruṣaś cobhāv anyonyāśrayavigrahau/
dvidhā bhinnau prākaśete prapañce 'smin yathā tathā//
66 KJKh 17.221.
67 KJKh 13.78.

Kṛṣṇa was bearing the form of Rādhā; his wife bore the form of Kṛṣṇa.
Brahmā was unable to realize whether [the Supreme] has the form of a woman or the form of a man.[68]

It is evident that there is a strong tendency in the BVP to raise Prakṛti to equality with, if not superiority to, Kṛṣṇa. Nonetheless, our Purāṇa is not quite prepared to commit itself to the view that Prakṛti is ontologically superior to Kṛṣṇa. Underlying all of the theology of Prakṛti or Rādhā is the notion that she arises from Kṛṣṇa in the beginning and dissolves back into him at the end of the cosmic eon.[69] In one place, it is said:

As the Bhagavat is eternal, so is Bhagavatī [Prakṛti].
Through her *māyā,* in natural dissolution, she disappears then into the Lord.[70]

Even in this passage, there is an implicit ontological subordination of Prakṛti to Kṛṣṇa. This subordination is indirectly revealed by the fact that throughout the BVP, it is Prakṛti's equality with Kṛṣṇa that is in question, not his with her.

[68] PKh 11.110–111.
[69] We have already quoted examples asserting Rādhā's origin from Kṛṣṇa's body. For the dissolution of Prakṛti back into Kṛṣṇa, see for example PKh 54.87–88; 54.94.
[70] PKh 57.14.

9

Prakṛti: Her Cosmogonic Role

In our text, as we have seen, Prakṛti ultimately is subordinated to Kṛṣṇa, the Supreme and Final Reality. Her significance, however, lies not so much in her ultimate ontological status, but in her dynamic aspect, as the *śakti* of Kṛṣṇa. In this aspect, she plays two main roles: cosmogonic and redemptive. Her importance for the first has been briefly suggested in the analysis of her relationship to the Supreme, and here we shall examine in detail this function. In the next chapter, we shall deal with her redemptive activity and its relation to her cosmogonic role.

Prakṛti's cosmogonic activity is described in the first three *adhyāyas* of the PKh. These chapters were apparently added as an introduction to the remaining chapters of the PKh and thus belong to the latest recast of the text.[1] This introduction consists

[1] It is of interest that at the beginning of PKh 4, there appears a "table of contents" of the rest of the chapters in the *khaṇḍa*. Nārāyaṇa, in response to Nārada's request to narrate at length the deeds and forms of worship of the goddesses derived from Nature, replies:

Durgā, who is the mother of Gaṇeśa, Rādhā, Lakṣmī,
 Sarasvatī,
And Sāvitrī are the five forms of Prakṛti at the
 beginning of creation. (4.4)
Their worship (*pūjā*), glory (*prabhāva*), power
 (*prasiddha*), supreme majesty (*paramādbhūta*),
Their deeds, like nectar, the cause of all good, (4.5)
The auspicious history of the parts and fractions
 of Prakṛti,
The whole I shall tell you, O Brahman, listen with
 care: (4.6)

of two parts, chapter one, and chapters two and three. Each part gives a different account of Prakṛti's cosmogonic functions, though both begin in a similar fashion. Nature's origin is described in the first *adhyāya* as follows:

> Through yoga, the Ātman in the act of creation became twofold;
> The right half became Puṃs, the left half Prakṛti.[2]

The second *adhyāya* states:

> The self-willed [Kṛṣṇa], by his own desire, became twofold;
> The left half was in the form of a woman; the right half, a man.[3]

The two accounts diverge from this point on. Chapter one describes what may be called Prakṛti's divisional manifestation in the process of creation, beginning with her division into five

---

> Vāṇī, Vasundharā, Gaṅgā, Ṣaṣṭhī, Maṅgalacaṇḍikā,
> Tulasī, Mānasī, Nidrā, Svadhā Svāhā, and Dakṣiṇā, (4.7)
> . . . .
> Their history in brief, bestowing merit, an ornament to *śruti,*
> I shall tell you, along with the lovely account of the fruits of *karma;* (4.9)
> And the great, extensive history of Durgā and Rādhā,
> I shall afterwards relate in succession, in brief form: hear! (4.10)

The "account of the fruits of *karma*" (4.9) refers to the story of Sāvitrī and her dialogue with Yama, who discourses at length on this topic. We find, then, that the above passage gives a fairly accurate description of the present contents of the rest of the PKh. The following goddesses are dealt with in the PKh: Vāṇī or Sarasvatī (*adhyāyas* 4–6), Vasundharā (8–9), Gaṅgā (10–12), Tulsi (13–22), Sāvitrī (23–34), Lakṣmī (35–39), Svāhā (40), Svadhā (41), Dakṣinā (42), Ṣaṣṭhī (43), Maṅgalacaṇḍikā (44), Manasā (45–46), Surabhi (47), Rādhā (48–56), Durgā (57–67). It would seem probable, then, that chapter 4 (except for the first five or six verses) was once the actual beginning of the PKh. This is further indicated by the fact that verses 7, 9–10 seem to disregard the notion of the five goddesses or five main forms of Prakṛti, mentioned in verse 4. Verse 4 is identical with PKh 1.1, where it seems originally to have belonged. The introductory chapters 1–3 thus provided an overall theological framework giving unity to the various accounts of the goddesses dealt with in the succeeding chapters.

[2] *yogenātmā sṛṣṭividhau dvidhārūpo babhūva saḥ/*
pumāṃś ca dakṣinārddhāṅgo vāmāṅgaḥ prakṛtiḥ smṛtaḥ// (PKh 1.9)

[3] *svecchāmayaḥ svecchayā ca dvidhārūpo babhūva ha/*
strīrūpā vāmabhāgāṃśād dakṣiṇāṃśaḥ pumān smṛtaḥ// (PKh 2.29)

main forms. The second part deals with Prakṛti's sexual role, or creation by copulation.

Two points may be noted here. First, both accounts are introduced by Nārada's questioning of Nārāyaṇa regarding the reasons for Prakṛti's original manifestation and division into five parts.[4] But these questions seem to be an appropriate introduction only to the first account, the creation by copulation having little to do with the five forms of nature. The second point is that within chapters two and three, there is a clear interruption, from 2.54 to the end of the *adhyāya* (2.90). The account of creation by copulation continues at 3.1. The section 2.54–2.90 deals with the origin of various gods and goddesses from Kṛṣṇa's body. We shall have occasion to return to this passage. Let us begin, though, by looking at the doctrine of Nature's divisional manifestation.

1. Divisional manifestation

a) *The doctrine according to PKh 1*

The divisional manifestation of Nature is briefly described as follows:[5]

> By the desire of the self-willed Kṛṣṇa to create,
> The goddess Mūlaprakṛti suddenly became manifest;
> By his command she became fivefold through division in the act of creation;
> Or rather, out of consideration for her devotees, she assumed a form for their sake.[6]

Prakṛti's fivefold form consists of five important goddesses of the Hindu pantheon: Durgā, Rādhā, Lakṣmī, Sarasvatī, and Sāvitrī.[7]

[4] PKh 1.1–3 and 2.1–4.

[5] Cf. Wilson, *Sects*, pp. 244–246.

[6] *svecchāmayasyecchayā ca śrīkṛṣṇasya sisṛkṣayā/*
sā 'virbabhūva sahasā mūlaprakṛtir īśvarī//
tadājñayā pañcavidhā sṛṣṭikarmaṇi bhedataḥ/
atha bhaktānurodhād vā bhaktānugrahavigrahā//
(PKh 1.12–13)

The term "*bhaktānugrahavigraha*" is commonly applied to Kṛṣṇa, Śiva, Rādhā, and other major deities throughout the BVP. Cf. p. 106 above.

[7] *gaṇeśajananī durgā rādhā lakṣmīḥ sarasvatī/*
sāvitrī vai sṛṣṭividhau prakṛtiḥ pañcadhā smṛtā//
(PKh 1.1)

This verse is identical with PKh 4.4. Cf. note 1 above.

There are further divisions of Prakṛti, essentially numberless. All female beings, divine or mortal, are regarded as *aṃśas* (parts), *kalās* (fractions), or *kalāṃśāṃśas* (parts of parts of fractions), of Prakṛti.[8] Certain goddesses are *pradhānāṃśas* (chief parts);[9] a multitude of lesser female deities, including the village goddesses, are *kalās*.[10] Women are *kalāṃśāṃśasamudbhūtā* (sprung from parts of parts of a fraction).[11] In PKh 1, the five principal forms of Prakṛti in themselves are not referred to by such terms as *aṃśa,* all of which clearly subordinate the fraction or part to the whole. Apparently a closer affinity, and perhaps actual identification, is intended between Prakṛti and her main forms. The latter possibility is suggested by the following line: "The five goddesses are proclaimed as perfectly complete (*paripūrṇatamā*) [manifestations of Prakṛti]."[12]

We may recall that the terms *kalā* and *aṃśa* are also used in our text with reference to the *avatāras* of Kṛṣṇa, and he in himself is designated as *paripūrṇatama.*[13] In the *avatāra* doctrine of later Vaiṣṇavism, we may note, there were held to be three *mukhya avatāras* (chief incarnations): (1) *pūrṇāvatāra* (complete incarnation), (2) *aṃśāvatāra* (major-partial incarnation), and (3) *kalāvatāra* (minor-partial incarnation).[14] In Tāntric

[8] *aṃśarūpā kalārūpā kalāṃśāṃśasamudbhavā//*
prakṛteḥ prativiśvaṃ ca rūpaṃ syāt sarvayoṣitaḥ/
(PKh 1.59–60)

This text seems somewhat corrupt. The Vaṅg seems better, but the best reading, I think, appears in the parallel text of the DBhP:
aṃśarūpāḥ kalārūpāḥ kalāṃśāṃśāṃśasambhavāḥ/
prakṛteḥ prativiśveṣu devyaś ca sarvayoṣitaḥ//
(IX.1.58)

Cf. Wilson, *Sects,* p. 245, note 3, for yet another reading.

[9] The series of *pradhānāṃśas* begins at PKh 1.61 and includes the following: Gaṅgā, Tulasī, Manasā, Ṣaṣṭhī, Maṅgalacaṇḍikā, Kālī, and Vasundharā.

[10] The *kalās* begin at PKh 1.100 and end with the statement:
yā yāś ca grāmadevyas tāḥ sarvāś ca prakṛteḥ kalāḥ//
(PKh 1.142)

[11] PKh 1.143. These terms are not precisely systematized throughout the PKh. For instance, in 2.71, women are called *aṃśāṃśakalās* (of Durgā); and in 48.41, goddesses are referred to as *aṃśāṃśakalās* (of Rādhā).

[12] *paripūrṇatamāḥ pañcavidhā devyaḥ prakīrttitaḥ//*
(PKh 1.60)

[13] See above, pp. 60–61.

[14] This is according to Grierson's scheme based on Śrīdhara's and Jīva Gosvāmin's commentaries on the BhP, and on the *Bhaktamālā* of Nābhādāsa (17th century). See Grierson, "Gleanings from the Bhakta-mala," JRAS 1909, pp. 625–626. See also De, "Sects and Sectarian Worship in the Mahabharata," *Our Heritage,* I, 21. Cf. p. 61, above.

texts, the personified *śaktis*, on the analogy of the types of *avatāras* (of male deities), were classified as *pūrṇā śakti, aṃśarūpiṇī, kalārūpiṇī,* and *kalāṃśarūpiṇī.*[15] Mortal women were included in the last. In our text, the second goddess Lakṣmī is referred to as the *śaktir dvitīyā,*[16] so by extension, the five goddesses may be considered as *paripūrṇatamā śaktis*. They are not *avatāras* of Prakṛti, but rather her fully complete energies, arising immediately after she herself became manifest. They may, of course, descend to earth as *avatāras*, as is made clear by Nārada's request to hear about the *avatāra* of each,[17] and by the brief reference to Rādhā's descent as the daughter of Vṛṣabhānu.[18] The standard means of incarnation in the rest of the PKh is by an *aṃśa* or *kalā* of the deity involved.[19]

This analysis of Prakṛti's divisional manifestation has led not so much to a discussion of cosmogony but of incarnation. The only creation has been that of all female beings, from goddesses to women. Let us reconsider the cosmogonic aspect and Kṛṣṇa's creative desire, *sisṛkṣā*.[20] This term is found in a similar context in the BhP:

> The Lord assumed the form of *puruṣa,* along with *mahat* and the rest,
> Consisting of sixteen parts [the eleven *indriyas* and five *bhūtas*] in the beginning, through the desire to create the world (*lokasisṛkṣayā*).[21]

Prakṛti, though not actually named, is represented by the principles of *mahat* and so forth. Nature appears here as a non-personified concept. Nonetheless, certain important similarities exist between this passage and the first *adhyāya* of the PKh. In the

[15] See Monier-Williams, *Brāhmanism and Hindūism,* p. 187.

[16] PKh 1.30.

[17] PKh 1.3.

[18] PKh 1.54.

[19] The actual term *avatāra* is relatively infrequent in the PKh. It does occur, as we have seen, in 1.3 and 1.54. In 49.32, there is reference to Kṛṣṇa's *bhārāvataraṇa*. Most commonly, though it is said that the gods or goddesses "go to Bhārata" or "attain human birth" and so forth.

[20] See note 6 above, first line.

[21] *jagṛhe pauruṣaṃ rūpaṃ bhagavān mahadādibhiḥ/*
sambhūtaṃ ṣoḍaśakalam ādau lokasisṛkṣayā// (I.3.1)

Cf. *Kumārasambhava* II.7:
strīpuṃsāv ātmabhāgau te bhinnamūrteḥ sisṛkṣayā/
prasūtibhājaḥ sargasya tāv eva pitarau smṛtau//

BhP, the cosmogonic ideas, though more detailed, are still subordinated to the *avatāra* theme, for the verse quoted above is part of an introduction to the enumeration of twenty-two *avatāras* of Viṣṇu. And just as in the PKh all female beings are derived from parts of Prakṛti, so in the BhP a few verses later on: "By the parts of the parts [of Kṛṣṇa] gods, animals, men and so forth are created."[22]

In the BhP, the connection between creation and the *avatāras* seems to be the creative activity of many of the latter, which complements the protective functions of the other *avatāras*. In the PKh, however, the forms and parts of Nature have almost no creative or cosmogonic role. At this point, let us recall that Prakṛti became fivefold not only through the command of Kṛṣṇa, desiring to create, but also out of Prakṛti's consideration for her devotees. The first *adhyāya* of the PKh appears to be much more concerned with this second explanation. The five goddesses are individually described and eulogized, followed by an enumeration of the lesser goddesses. The five goddesses are all said to be worshipped in India,[23] and the chapter concludes with a brief account of the history of their worship. It seems, then, that cosmogonic notions have been largely overshadowed by the devotional purposes of the chapter.

Although our primary purpose so far has been to describe the doctrine of Nature's divisional manifestation as found in PKh 1, it has seemed helpful in explaining some of its features to refer to other literature and the ideas of various schools. Such comparisons have shown that the PKh has taken over many older notions concerning Viṣṇu and Kṛṣṇa and applied them to Prakṛti and her parts. Let us now attempt a more thorough historical analysis of one aspect of the doctrine. Our investigation will be guided by one of Nārada's own questions to Nārāyaṇa: how did Nature, consisting of the three *guṇas*, become fivefold in the act of creation?[24] We shall, of course, be seeking an historical answer

[22] *yasyāṃśāṃśena sṛjyante devatiryannarādayaḥ/*
Cf. BhP I.3.28–29:
ṛṣayo manavo devā manuputrā mahaujasaḥ/
kalāḥ sarve harer eva saprajāpatayas tathā//
ete cāṃśakalāḥ puṃsaḥ kṛṣṇas tu bhagavān svayam/

[23] *evaṃ nigaditaṃ sarvaṃ prakṛter bhedapañcakam/*
sāḥ sarvāḥ pūjitāḥ pṛthvyāṃ puṇyakṣetre ca bhārate//
(PKh 1.150)
Cf. PKh 1.163, where all the *kalās* of Nature are said to be worshipped.

[24] PKh 2.2–3. Cf. PKh 1.2.

rather than a theological one such as given by Nārāyaṇa. In so doing, we shall attempt to throw light not only on some of the curious features of our text mentioned at the beginning of this chapter, but also on the development of important doctrines in the Kṛṣṇaite sects.

b) *Historical development of the five main forms of Prakṛti*

Of the five goddesses, four, Durgā, Lakṣmī, Sarasvatī, and Sāvitrī, are ancient, going back to Vedic and Upaniṣadic times.[25] Rādhā, however, is a late-comer to the Hindu pantheon.[26] She makes her appearance probably no earlier than the third or fourth centuries of the Christian era, and even then seemingly only as a human figure.[27] Possibly only after the eleventh century does she finally attain the stature of a goddess.[28] Let us be-

[25] Sarasvatī appears in the RV both as a sacred river and as a river goddess. In RV II.41.16, she is invoked as: *ámbitame nádītame dévitame sarasvatī.* (Cf. Gupta, "Conception of Sarasvatī in the Purāṇas," *Purāṇa,* IV, 56.) Sāvitrī, the name of the famous hymn to the sun (Savitṛ) in RV III.62.10, also called Gāyatrī, early became a full goddess in her own right. In the MBh she at times holds a higher place, apparently, than Sarasvatī, with whom she is closely related (see Carpenter, *Theism in Medieval India,* p. 278). Lakṣmī, though not appearing as a goddess in the RV (see Monier-Williams, *Brāhmanism and Hindūism,* p. 182), finds a place in later Vedic literature, in the *White Yajur Veda,* and ŚB (see Sh. Dasgupta, *Aspects of Indian Religious Thought,* p. 58. Cf. Gonda, *Aspects of Early Viṣṇuism,* pp. 213–215). Durgā (as Durgi) appears in the *Taittirīya Āraṇyaka* (see Sh. Dasgupta, *Aspects of Indian Religious Thought,* p. 64, and Karmarkar, *The Vrātya or Dravidian Systems,* p. 99).

[26] Wilson writes: "The fifth division of the original Prakŕiti, was Rādhā, . . . unquestionably a modern intruder into the Hindu Pantheon" (*Sects,* p. 245). One might better use the metaphor of a late-arriving guest of honor than an intruder.

[27] The earliest known reference to Rādhā apparently is in the *Gāthāsaptaśatī* (*or Gāhāsattasaī*) attributed to Hāla. This work has been dated as early as the first century A.D. (Mehta, *Mirabai,* p. 100). A. K. Majumdar suggests that Hāla may have lived in the second century A.D. ("Rādhā Cult," ABORI, XXXVI, 234). The seventh-century writer Bāṇabhaṭṭa alludes to the *Gāthāsaptaśatī.* B. Majumdar points out, however, that there are several recensions of the *Gāthāsaptaśatī* and that some post seventh-century material has been included (*Kṛṣṇa in History and Legend,* p. 166, note 7), so that the reference to Rādhā may be after Bāṇabhatta. Certainly, though, by the eighth century A.D., there are definite references to Rādhā (cf. Pandey and Zide, "Sūrdās and His Krishna-*bhakti,*" *Krishna: Myths, Rites and Attitudes,* p. 182; and B. Majumdar, *Kṛṣṇa in History and Legend,* p. 170).

[28] B. Majumdar states, with reference to the eighth-century work, *Veṇīsaṃhāra,* of Bhaṭṭa Nārāyaṇa, which mentions Rādhā and Kṛṣṇa in its

gin this historical inquiry by pointing out certain features in the early development of the goddess cults that seem important for the present study and quickly move into the later history and evolution of our doctrine.

It seems that originally some of the goddesses were not associated with male consorts. Very early, however, Durgā was considered to be the wife of Śiva;[29] and Karmarkar asserts: "Thus if Śiva had his spouse, all other Aryan gods also must have one each."[30] The goddesses, though, were often attached to more gods than one. For instance, Lakṣmī was often said to be the wife of Dharma, Kubera, Indra and others, and only in the youngest parts of the MBh was Lakṣmī, or Śrī, recognized as the wife of Nārāyaṇa-Viṣṇu.[31] And the gods might have more than one wife. Thus Sāvitrī and Sarasvatī came to be associated primarily with Brahmā.

---

opening, benedictory verse: "Some scholars think that, though Kṛṣṇa is here definitely regarded as a divinity, Rādhā was a mere lady-love of his. There are hundreds of benedictory verses in which the blessings of Śiva have been invoked and some incident reflecting his love for Pārvatī has been mentioned. Nobody suggests that in such passages Pārvatī is not to be regarded as a goddess" (*Kṛṣṇa in History and Legend,* p. 170). The distinction between human and divine in Hindu thought is often indeterminate or fluid, and Majumdar's remarks warn us against too quickly presupposing Rādhā to be *merely* a human figure in the early works referring to her. A. K. Majumdar's study of the Rādhā cult, we may mention in particular, seems to go too far in assuming that the divinization of Rādhā occurred only after the twelfth century. He assumes that Jayadeva's erotic treatment of Rādhā "would not have been possible if at that time there had been anything approaching a Rādhā cult; it would have been a sacrilege. It may be taken therefore that even at the end of the twelfth century Rādhā was not worshipped" ("Rādhā Cult," ABORI, XXXVI, 241). He goes on to say that before the end of the fifteenth century, there is clear evidence of Rādhā-worship (*ibid.,* p. 242). However, we may point out that already Nimbārka, usually assigned to the twelfth century, offers praise to Vṛṣabhānu's daughter (Rādhā), whom he refers to as *devī* (for the actual verse, see note 79 below).

Nonetheless, B. Majumdar perhaps is too extreme in suggesting that Rādhā was already regarded as a goddess in the eighth century. Unlike Durgā or Pārvatī, Rādhā's origin, as one of the *gopīs*, points to a human status, any divine aspect being at most implicit. The explicit recognition of Rādhā's divinity appears possibly for the first time with Nimbārka.

[29] In the *Taittirīya Āraṇyaka,* Ambikā or Umā is the wife of Rudra (see Karmarkar, *The Vrātya or Dravidian Systems,* p. 99). Ambikā here is also identified with Durgā (or more precisely, Durgi).

[30] *The Vrātya or Dravidian Systems,* p. 99.

[31] See Gonda, *Aspects of Early Viṣṇuism,* pp. 222–225, and Jaiswal, *The Origin and Development of Vaiṣṇavism,* pp. 96–101.

One of the most important developments in the goddess cults was the identification of the goddesses with *prakṛti,* as well as with the *śakti*s of their consorts. In the *Viṣṇudharmottara,* dated by Hazra between A.D. 400 and 500,[32] Lakṣmī is called *vaiṣṇavī śakti,* and Viṣṇu and Śrī are identified with *puruṣa* and *prakṛti.*[33] Such developments not only allowed the goddesses to take on important cosmogonic functions, but also resulted in the ascription of the three *guṇa*s of *prakṛti* to *śakti,* often identified with one or another of the goddesses. Thus in the *Ahirbudhnya Saṃhitā* (ca. sixth century A.D.), a central creative energy, called *māyāśakti* or *mūlaprakṛti,* produces a "*guṇa*-body" consisting of *sattva, rajas,* and *tamas.*[34] These are associated with Viṣṇu, Brahmā, and Rudra respectively, along with their *śakti*s Lakṣmī, Sarasvatī, and Gaurī. The gods of the *trimūrti,* incidentally, had been associated for some time with the *triguṇa* doctrine.[35]

These ideas quickly found their way into Purāṇic literature. The *Kriyāyogasāra,* an Upapurāṇa perhaps of the ninth or tenth century, states that in creation, Mahāviṣṇu appears as Brahmā, Viṣṇu, and Rudra. His *ādyā prakṛti* (primal nature) then becomes manifest as Brāhmī, Lakṣmī, and Ambikā to help the three gods accomplish the work of creation.[36]

In the VarP, the *triśakti* idea is further developed and systematized. This is found in a section called the *triśaktimāhātmya,* constituting chapters 90–96, which Hazra states is a Śākta document from the rather indefinite period A.D. 800–1400.[37] Here the original goddess (called Devī, but apparently meaning only "goddess" and not specifically identified with Durgā) is referred to as *trikalā* (having three parts)[38] and *trivarṇā* (having three colors).[39] When she becomes threefold, her three forms are white, red, and black.[40] The white form is Brāhmī, and is active in creation; the red form is Vaiṣṇavī and protects the universe;

[32] *Studies in the Upapurāṇas,* I, 212.
[33] See Jaiswal, *The Origin and Development of Vaiṣṇavism,* p. 109.
[34] See Schrader, *Introduction to the Pāñcarātra,* pp. 62, 67.
[35] See, for instance, *Maitrāyaṇīya Upaniṣad* V.2; cf. *Kumārasambhava* II.4, 6; VII.44. Cf. also Hopkins, *Great Epic of India,* pp. 183–184, esp. note 1 on p. 184.
[36] See Hazra, *Studies in the Upapurāṇas,* I, 269 and 273.
[37] *Purāṇic Records,* pp. 101, 105.
[38] VarP 90.25.
[39] VarP 90.27.
[40] VarP 90.28.

the black is Raudrī and destroys the world.[41] Further, the white form is *sāttvikī*, the red is *rājasī*, the black is *tāmasī*,[42] and are the *śaktis* of Brahmā, Viṣṇu, and Śiva respectively.[43]

The above examples indicate that the triadic division of primordial nature into three *śaktis* according to the *guṇas* and identified with one or another form of Lakṣmī, Sarasvatī, and Durgā, was quite popular. But there was also another tendency, less concerned with systematic schematization, to identify one goddess with as many other goddesses as possible, thereby adding to the former's glory. Thus in the famous *Devīmāhātmya* of the MārkP, dated by Pargiter as no later than the ninth century A.D. and probably from the fifth or sixth,[44] the goddess Caṇḍī (another name of Durgā) is eulogized as the supreme primal nature[45] and is variously identified with Sāvitrī,[46] Śrī[47] or Lakṣmī,[48] Sarasvatī,[49] and many others. She is the one supreme goddess, as all other goddesses, Brahmāṇī and so forth, merge into her.[50] All women, in fact, are parts of the Devī.[51] The *Devīmāhātmya* thus foreshadows many ideas of the PKh.

In the KūrP, there is another *devīmāhātmya*, constituting chapter twelve of the first part.[52] In the preceding chapter, it is

41 VarP 90.29–32.

42 VarP 96.63–64.

43 VarP 96.72–74. The ascription of *sattvaguṇa* to Brahmā and *rajoguṇa* to Viṣṇu is very peculiar. The normal Purāṇic scheme equates Brahmā with *rajas* and Viṣṇu with *sattva*.

44 *The Mārkaṇḍeya Purāṇa*, Introduction, p. XX. Hazra affirms this dating (*Purāṇic Records*, p. 12).

45 *paramā prakṛtis . . . ādyā* (MārkP LXXXI.63).

46 MārkP LXXXI.55.

47 MārkP LXXXIV.10.

48 MārkP XCI.20.

49 MārkP XCI.21.

50 *tataḥ samastās tā devyo brahmāṇīpramukhā layam/*
tasyā devyās tanau jagmur ekaivāsīt tadāmbikā//
(MārkP XC.4)

Cf. MārkP LXXXVIII.11, where the goddesses, as *śaktis*, emanate from the gods.

51 *vidyāḥ samastās tava devi bhedāḥ* [another reading: *aṃśāḥ*] *striyaḥ samastāḥ sakalā jagatsu//*
(MārkP XCI.5)

Pargiter notes that the Bombay Ed. reads:
striyaḥ samastāḥ sakalam jagac ca//
(*The Mārkaṅḍeya Purāṇa*, p. 512)

52 Chapter twelve refers to itself in verse 313 as *devyā māhātmyakīrtanam*, and in verse 325 as *devyā māhātmyam uttamam*.

related how Śiva divides himself into two, *puruṣatva* ("maleness") and *strītva* ("female-ness"). The *strītva* apparently is identified with the great goddess Devī, arising from half the body of Śiva, and known also as Śivā, Satī, and Haimavatī.[53] This notion of a god splitting into male and female parts, the latter being his consort, comes to be applied to Kṛṣṇa and Rādhā, as we shall see. In chapter twelve, Devī is called Primordial Nature[54] and the controller of nature and *puruṣa*.[55] She is the *paramā śakti* (supreme energy).[56] She is the mother of Brahmā, Viṣṇu, and Śiva,[57] and the spouse of each.[58] She is also the mother of the three *śaktis*.[59] Finally, she is identified with Sāvitrī, Kamalā, Lakṣmī, Śrī, Gaṅgā, Sarasvatī, and many others.[60]

Before we turn to the BVP itself, let us first consider some special characteristics or features of our four ancient goddesses. This concerns their association or identification with certain parts of the body. Sarasvatī, from early times closely related to Sāvitrī as a goddess of speech and learning, Mother of the Vedas, and

53 *saiṣā maheśvarī devī śaṃkarārddhaśarīriṇī//*
śivā satī haimavatī . . . / (KūrP I.11.13–14)

54 *mūlaprakṛtir īśvarī* (KūrP I.12.69).

55 *pradhānapuruṣeśvarī* (KūrP I.12.68 and 75).

56 KūrP I.12.48.

57 *brahmeśaviṣṇujananī* (KūrP I.12.86).

58 *brahmaviṣṇuśivapriyā* (KūrP I.12.129).

59 *triśaktijananī* (KūrP I.12.175).

60 KūrP I.12.92–93. This *devīmāhātmya* apparently belongs to a later revision of the originally Pāñcarātra KūrP. Hazra has shown that the KūrP has passed through two main stages, the original KūrP (ca. 550–650) being revised and added to by the Pāśupatas around the beginning of the eighth century (*Purāṇic Records,* pp. 58, 71). Hazra draws attention to the anti-Tāntric attitudes of these Pāśupatas and their condemnation of the *śāstras* of the Tāntra influenced schools of the Kāpālas, Bhairavas, Yāmalas, Vāmas, and others (*ibid.,* p. 67). One such condemnation appears near the end of the KūrP *devīmāhātmya* (I.12.262–3). This might suggest that the whole chapter may belong to the Pāśupata recast, but such does not appear to be the case. The actual praise of the Devī concludes around verse 243 or 244, and only in the following verses is Pāśupata influence evident. Further, in the eulogy proper, there are many Tāntric elements, as in I.12.128, where the Devī is called *kuṇḍalinī.* The KūrP *devīmāhātmya* may well have originated in Śaivite Śākta circles similar to that responsible for the MārkP *Devīmāhātmya.* The historical relationship of the two texts is unclear. However, there are at least some hints of close interaction. For instance, in KūrP I.1.34, Lakṣmī is Viṣṇu's *śakti,* by whom the world is supported (*yayedaṃ dhāryate jagat*). In the MārkP *Devīmāhātmya,* XCIII.1, it is the Devī by whom the world is supported (*yayedaṃ dhāryate jagat*).

so forth,[61] has long been associated with the tongue or mouth. In the PadP and MatP, she is said to live in the mouth or mouths of Brahmā.[62] In the MBh, Sarasvatī is referred to as Kṛṣṇa-Viṣṇu's tongue.[63] In our own Purāṇa, this conception is quite common, as in KJKh 94.110, where Sarasvatī is said to dwell in the tongue of Kṛṣṇa.[64] Durgā has long been identified with a series of feminine nouns, such as *cetanā* (consciousness), *nidrā* (sleep), *kṣudhā* (hunger), and *chāyā* (shadow).[65] One such term that seems to have been especially associated with Durgā was *buddhi* (intellect). Her identification with *buddhi* already appears four times in the MārkP *Devīmāhātmya*[66] and once in the KūrP *devīmāhātmya.*[67] Throughout the BVP, Durgā is closely associated with *buddhi.* In some places, after the fashion of the MārkP, she is identified with a long series of feminine nouns that includes *buddhi.*[68] But often the intellect is singled out as one of her chief characteristics, and she is referred to as *buddhirūpā,* or as the presiding deity of intellect.[69] As for Lakṣmī, as early as the *Viṣṇudharmottara* she was thought of as dwelling in the breast of Viṣṇu.[70] And in KJKh 41.74, it is said: *vakṣaḥsthalodbhavā lakṣmīḥ* (Lakṣmī is sprung from [Kṛṣṇa's] breast). The relevance of these features of the goddesses for our present inquiry will become clear shortly.

The three goddesses popularized by the old triadic scheme, along with Sāvitrī, are frequently associated together in the BVP. One especially interesting occurrence is in chapters 3–4 of the

61 Cf. Carpenter, *Theism in Medieval India,* p. 278.

62 Gupta quotes the following with citations: *brahmāsye tu sarasvatī* (PadP V.29.216) and *brahmāsyeṣu sarasvatī* (MatP 13.52). The PadP reference (to Ānand), however, is incorrect, and I have been unable to trace it. Cf. Gupta, "Conception of Sarasvatī in the Purāṇas," *Purāṇa,* IV, 71.

63 *devī jihvā sarasvatī* (Bombay: VI.65.61 = Critical: VI.61.56). See Gonda, *Aspects of Early Viṣṇuism,* p. 228. See also Chatterjee, "Some Aspects of Sarasvatī," in *Foreigners in Ancient India and Lakṣmī and Sarasvatī in Art and Literature* (Sircar, ed.), p. 149.

64 *jihvāyāṃ ca sarasvatī.* Cf. KJKh 35.11; 41.73.

65 See MārkP LXXXV.11 ff.

66 MārkP LXXXI.60; LXXXIV.4; LXXXV.14; XCI.7.

67 KūrP I.12.117.

68 E.g., PKh 1.19–20; KJKh 43.78 ff.

69 E.g., GKh 45.4; KJKh 41.78; 86.97; 109.20.

70 *lakṣmim āvāhayiṣyāmi viṣṇor vakṣasi saṃsthitām/*
(*Viṣṇudharmottara* III.106.30)

BKh, in which Kṛṣṇa is represented as the primordial god, from the parts of whose body the other deities emanated. The account briefly is as follows. At the beginning of creation, from the right side of Kṛṣṇa, who is called *puṃs,* there were manifested (*āvirbabhūvuḥ*) the three *guṇas* followed by the principles of nature. Next the four-armed Nārāyaṇa became manifest, who at once eulogized Kṛṣṇa. The five-faced Śiva then appeared from Kṛṣṇa's left side and proceeded to praise him. Afterwards, from the navel-lotus of Kṛṣṇa, there arose an ancient anchorite with water-pot in hand, four-faced, the creator of the world, the husband of the Mother of the Vedas (*vedaprasū* = Sāvitrī?), the beloved of Sarasvatī. He, of course, is Brahmā. He too worshipped Kṛṣṇa. One last god, Dharma, then emerged from Kṛṣṇa's breast.[71] Dharma's wife, Mūrti, arose from his left side. The emanation of gods from Kṛṣṇa was followed by that of the goddesses. Sarasvatī next was manifested from his mouth (*mukha*), Mahālakṣmī from his heart (*manas*), Durgā from his intellect (*buddhi*), who is also called the goddess Mūlaprakṛti and ruler of all *śakti*s, and Sāvitrī from his tongue-tip (*rasanāgra*). Each gave praise to Kṛṣṇa and then sat down on a jewelled throne. The account of the origin of these goddesses thus appears to be based on the analogy of their husbands' emanations from Kṛṣṇa's body, each goddess being derived from a part of Kṛṣṇa with which she had been especially associated, as we have just shown.[72]

It has been pointed out that the BVP is not the work of a single age, but is rather a compilation of legends and doctrines composed at different times. Chapters 3 and 4 of the BKh seem to belong to one of the earlier layers of our text. This is indicated first of all by the fact that Rādhā is not mentioned therein. I suggest, then, that BKh 3–4 reflects a stage in Kṛṣṇaite Vaiṣṇavism when Kṛṣṇa had attained absolute supremacy, even above Nārāyaṇa or Viṣṇu, but his beloved Rādhā had not yet attained

71 The idea of gods deriving from the primordial being goes back to the famous *Puruṣa Sūkta* of RV X.90, in which the four castes, the gods Indra and Agni, and so forth, arise out of the sacrifice of the *puruṣa*. In a *puruṣasūkta* of the BhP, it is stated: *devā nārāyaṇāṅgajāḥ* (BhP II.5.15). Cf. pp. 32–33 above.

72 The connection of Lakṣmī with *manas* is somewhat problematic. But I think it is clear that *manas* here should mean heart rather than mind, for later on Kāma is said to arise from Kṛṣṇa's *mānasaḥ* (BKh 4.6).

importance as a goddess. Further evidence for the early age (relative to the final compilation of the BVP) of BKh 3–4 will be forthcoming.

During the time BKh 3–4 was being composed or shortly thereafter, certain independent developments were taking place with regards to some of the individual goddesses. Let us first consider the closely related pair, Sarasvatī and Sāvitrī. In BKh 3–4, Sarasvatī is considered as the wife of Brahmā, for he is referred to as *sarasvatīkānta* (BKh 3.33). Sāvitrī, too, is perhaps regarded as a spouse of Brahmā, for he is also referred to as *vedaprasūpati* (BKh 3.33).[73] In any case, throughout the BVP, Sāvitrī is considered almost exclusively to be a wife of Brahmā. This is not the case with Sarasvatī, who is often regarded as the consort of Nārāyaṇa. In the legend of Sarasvatī in PKh 4–6, it is stated that she was given originally by Kṛṣṇa to Nārāyaṇa, and she then became a co-wife of Lakṣmī and Gaṅgā. Sarasvatī and Gaṅgā became involved in a jealous fight and cursed each other to descend to earth as rivers. Nārāyaṇa, tired of their quarreling, ordered them to go to Brahmā and Śiva respectively. The two goddesses then were filled with remorse and begged for mercy, but Nārāyaṇa's orders, and the curses, could not go unfulfilled. A compromise was reached, whereby, in the case of Sarasvatī, she would go to earth as a river by a *kalā,* to Brahmā by half an *aṃśa,* and remain herself (*svayam*) with Nārāyaṇa.[74] In this way her old relationship to Brahmā is still recognized and harmonized with her new status as the wife of Nārāyaṇa. A somewhat different explanation is found in GKh 42.59:

> Sarasvatī, having issued from the mouth of Kṛṣṇa, became twofold:
> As Sāvitrī, she is the wife of Brahmā; as herself she is [the wife] of Nārāyaṇa.[75]

Only in the earliest layers of the BVP, it seems, then, is Sarasvatī regarded as simply the consort of Brahmā.

A more important development concerns Lakṣmī and Rādhā.

[73] *Vedaprasū* may possibly refer to Sarasvatī, but in BKh 4.5, Sāvitrī is specifically called *śrutiprasū*.

[74] PKh 6.85.

[75] The Sanskrit is given in note 97 below.

As mentioned above, Rādhā attained divine status perhaps only as late as the twelfth century. As Kṛṣṇa's beloved, she soon came to be associated and identified with Viṣṇu's consort Lakṣmī. Thus, in the *Śrikṛṣṇakīrtana* of Caṇḍīdāsa (fourteenth century), it is related how the gods, having requested Nārāyaṇa to destroy the demon Kaṃsa, received two hairs from him, one to be born as Kṛṣṇa, the other as Balarāma.[76] The gods then requested Lakṣmī to be born as Rādhā, to be a companion for Kṛṣṇa. Here, Rādhā is implicitly subordinated to Lakṣmī, but Rādhā was quickly becoming Lakṣmī's equal or even superior, just as Kṛṣṇa had risen above Viṣṇu. A new explanation of Rādhā's relationship to Lakṣmī was required, and we find such an explanation in the BVP. In PKh 35.4, it is stated that at the beginning of creation, in the Rāsamaṇḍala, a goddess sprang from Kṛṣṇa's left side.[77] This goddess, unnamed, then divided into two parts, equal in every respect. The left side was Mahālakṣmī, the right Rādhikā.[78] Meanwhile, Kṛṣṇa also became twofold, his left side becoming the four-armed Nārāyaṇa, his right side the two-armed Kṛṣṇa. Lakṣmī and Rādhā became their respective consorts. In PKh 48.29–47, a similar account is given, with certain elaborations. It is related, for instance, that from the hair-pores of Rādhā and Kṛṣṇa there emerged the *gopīs* and *ballavas* (cowherds) respectively. Further, it is specifically stated that the goddess splitting off from Kṛṣṇa's left side at the beginning of creation was Rādhā.[79] Possibly, this goddess, often simply called Prakṛti, was

[76] For this summary, I have relied on A. K. Majumdar, "Rādhā Cult," ABORI, XXXVI, 243. The story of Viṣṇu's or Nārāyaṇa's two hairs goes back to MBh I.189.31 (Critical Ed.).

[77] *sṛṣṭer ādau purā brahman kṛṣṇasya paramātmanaḥ/*
devī vāmāṃśasambhūtā cāsīt sā rāsamaṇḍale//

[78] *tad-*[= *devī-*]*vāmāṃśā mahālakṣmīr dakṣiṇāṃśā ca rādhikā/* (PKh 35.10)

[79] *etasminn antare durge dvidhārūpo babhūva saḥ/*
dakṣiṇāṅgaṃ ca śrīkṛṣṇo vāmārddhāṅgā ca rādhikā//

Cf. notes 2 and 3 above. The association of Rādhā with Kṛṣṇa's left side goes back at least to Nimbārka, who says that Vṛṣabhānu's daughter (Rādhā) shines with delight on Kṛṣṇa's left side (or limb):

aṅge tu vāme vṛṣabhānujāṃ mudā virājamānām anurūpasaubhagām/
sakhīsahasraiḥ parisevitāṃ sadā smarema devīṃ sakaleṣṭakāmadām// (*Daśaślokī* 5)

With Nimbārka, though, Kṛṣṇa's left side is apparently not regarded as the source or origin of Rādhā, a notion that probably only arose after Rādhā became "Tāntricized," as by the Sahajiyā poet Caṇḍīdāsa.

not originally identified with either Lakṣmī or Rādhā.[80] But in any case, the latter soon attained pre-eminence and her identification with Prakṛti was established.

These independent developments regarding the individual goddesses have been incorporated into chapters 5 and 6 of the BKh. That BKh 5–6 did not originally follow *adhyāyas* 3 and 4 seems highly probable, since the narrative of Brahmā's creation of the world from the marrow of Madhu and Kaitabha, beginning in chapter 4, is interrupted by 5 and 6 and continues in 7.[81] In BKh 5, it is related how Rādhā split off from Kṛṣṇa's left side in the Rāsamaṇḍala. She is also associated with Kṛṣṇa's vital breaths or life (*prāṇas*). She is said to be the presiding deity of his life and to have arisen from his *prāṇas*, thereby becoming dearer to him than his life.[82] The emergence of the cowmaids and cowherds from Rādhā's and Kṛṣṇa's hair-pores is also mentioned. In BKh 6.1, Kṛṣṇa gives Mahālakṣmī and Sarasvatī to Nārāyaṇa. The association of Sarasvatī with Nārāyaṇa rather than with Brahmā is further indication that BKh 5–6 is later than 3–4.

If we consider BKh 3–6 as a whole, the resulting synthesis of early and later doctrines in effect introduces Rādhā into the privileged circle of goddesses emanating from Kṛṣṇa's body at the beginning of creation. In this connection, we may note an interesting passage in PKh 34, where the manifestation of the five goddesses is reversed in an account of the dissolution of the universe: Durgā merges into Kṛṣṇa's intellect; Lakṣmī, with various goddesses and the *gopīs*, dissolves into Rādhā, and Rādhā into Kṛṣṇa's *prāṇas*; and finally, Sāvitrī merges into Sarasvatī with the Vedas, and Sarasvatī into Kṛṣṇa's tongue.[83]

Returning to BKh 3–6, there would seem to be two problems or inadequacies in its synthesis of old and new doctrines, at least from the viewpoint of the final redactors of the BVP. First, the notion of Lakṣmī's origin from Rādhā's left side apparently has had to be omitted, as Lakṣmī has already arisen from Kṛṣṇa's heart. Second, Rādhā is implicitly subordinated not only to

[80] Prakṛti, for Nimbārka, was merely primal matter and not yet identified with Rādhā (cf. Chaudhuri, "The Nimbārka School of Vedānta," CHI, III, 339). It is unclear as to when Rādhā became identified with Prakṛti.

[81] See p. 32 above.

[82] BKh 5.27.

[83] PKh 34.62–65. The Sanskrit text is given in Appendix A, section 4, along with the parallel text from the DBhP.

Lakṣmī, but to all the other gods and goddesses who had previously emanated from Kṛṣṇa.

Another synthesis which attempts to resolve these problems is found, I suggest, in the section PKh 2.54–90, which as pointed out above, seems to interrupt the account of Prakṛti's creation by copulation. In 2.29, as part of the copulative cosmogony, Kṛṣṇa by his own desire splits into two parts, his left side becoming female, his right side male. Then in 2.54, after the copulative act of the two parts, there arises from the tongue-tip of the female, called Devī, the goddess Sarasvatī.[84] It is then stated that "she," in the context apparently referring to Sarasvatī, becomes twofold, her left half becoming Kamalā, her right half Rādhā.[85] Kṛṣṇa also, again, divides into two, his right half becoming two-armed (Kṛṣṇa), his left half four-armed (Nārāyaṇa).[86] Kṛṣṇa then tells Sarasvatī to be Nārāyaṇa's wife, and gives Lakṣmī to him as well. From the hair-pores of Rādhā and Kṛṣṇa emerge the cowmaids and cowherds. Soon thereafter, Durgā arises from Kṛṣṇa's body (*deha*) and is given a jewelled throne in front of Kṛṣṇa.[87] Next a four-faced being, an ascetic with water-pot in hand, arises with his wife from Kṛṣṇa's navel-lotus.[88] This clearly is Brahmā and his wife Sāvitrī. Together they praise Kṛṣṇa. Finally, Kṛṣṇa divides into two, the left half becoming Mahādeva (Śiva), the right half Kṛṣṇa.[89] Śiva also eulogizes the Supreme.

In this synthesis of PKh 2.54–90, it seems probable that the Devī who divides into Rādhā and Kamalā originally referred to Prakṛti, or Rādhā herself, but not to Sarasvatī, on the basis of the examples already cited. It also appears that Sarasvatī's origin from Prakṛti's tongue-tip has been transferred from Kṛṣṇa's. If we take these two changes into account, then PKh 2.54–90 reveals how the doctrine of Rādhā's splitting into Lakṣmī and Rādhā (as found in PKh 35.4 ff., and 48.29 ff.) was incorporated into the framework of BKh 3–4. To illustrate this, let us diagram the various accounts:

[84] The Sanskrit text for this and the following citations may be found in Appendix C, which gives the PKh text (in parallel with the NārP).
[85] PKh 2.56.
[86] PKh 2.57.
[87] PKh 2.66, 79.
[88] PKh 2.80–81.
[89] PKh 2.84.

BKh 3–4:

The three *guṇas* [Prakṛti]

Kṛṣṇa

- Nārāyaṇa (from Kṛṣṇa's side)
- Śiva (from the left side)
- Brahmā (from the navel-lotus)
- Dharma (from the breast)
- Sarasvatī (from the mouth)
- Lakṣmī (from the heart)
- Durgā (from the intellect)
- Sāvitrī (from the tongue-tip)

PKh 35.4 ff.; 48.29 ff.:

Kṛṣṇa

- Prakṛti (= Rādhā)
  - Lakṣmī (from the left side)
  - Rādhā (from the right side)
- Puṃs (= Kṛṣṇa)
  - Kṛṣṇa (the right side)
  - Nārāyana (the left side)

PKh 2.54–90 (with the two slight revisions):

Kṛṣṇa

- Prakṛti
  - Lakṣmī (from the left side)
  - Rādhā (from the right side)
  - Sarasvatī (from the tongue-tip)
- Puṃs
  - Kṛṣṇa (the right side)
  - Nārāyana (the left side)
  - Durgā (from the body)
  - Brahmā, Sāvitrī (from the navel-lotus)
  - Śiva (from the left side)

The discrepancies between BKh 3–4 and PKh 2.54–90, especially with regards to the different order of appearance of the deities, in large part may be explained by the necessary accommodation to the Rādhā-Lakṣmī account in the PKh version. Other differences can perhaps be explained on the hypothesis that one or the other of the extant narratives was based on older, somewhat different models. But the over-all correspondence, in addition to the literal agreement of many smaller details such as occur in the descriptions of the gods and goddesses, strongly suggests that PKh 2.54–90 is indeed based on BKh 3–4, or some version thereof.[90]

In any case, PKh 2.54–90 has provided us with the goddesses who are the five main forms of Prakṛti, though they are not yet referred to as such. That this is the source of the finally systematized doctrine of PKh 1 is already indicated by Nārada's introductory questions at the beginning of *adhyāya* 2, asking how Nature became fivefold. Only if this refers to 2.54–90 does it have any relevance. The most conclusive evidence, though, is found not in the BVP but in the NārP, which we have already shown is familiar with the extant BVP.[91] The passage in question seems sufficiently important to quote at length:

> Nārada said:
> "O Brahman [Sanatkumāra], you have related the rules enjoined by the Tantras
> And the greatness of Kṛṣṇa's *mantras* also described therein. (I.83.5)
> There the goddess Rādhikā, foremost of all, has been spoken of;
> The history of the descents of her parts (*aṃśāvatāras*), along with her *mantra*, (6)
> Is narrated in the Tantras; please tell me that, omniscient one. I have come to you for refuge." (7ab)
>
> . . . .
>
> Having heard the words of the magnanimous Nārada, (8cd)
> Sanatkumāra, remembering the lotus-feet of Rādhā, replied:
> "Listen, Nārada, I will describe the origin of Rādhā's parts (*aṃśas*), (9)
> The supreme wonder of her energies (*śaktis*), along with the means of perfecting her *mantra*.

[90] For a comparison of the textual similarities, see Appendix B.

[91] See pp. 26–27, above.

This Rādhā, who I said arose from half the body of Kṛṣṇa, (10)
Dwells eternally in Goloka as the wife of Kṛṣṇa,
Resting in the middle of the orb of light, both visible and invisible in her essence. (11)
One time, O best of sages, while Kṛṣṇa was resting with her,
From his left side came forth Nārāyaṇa himself. (12)
From Rādhā's left side, Mahālakṣmī became manifest.
Then Kṛṣṇa, giving Mahālakṣmī to Nārāyaṇa, (13)
Sent them off to Vaikuṇṭha, to constantly protect [the universe].
Then from the hair-pores of the Lord of Goloka, O sage, (14)
There arose countless cowherds, equal in splendour and age.
All of them, as dear [to Kṛṣṇa] as his life, became attendants of the Lord. (15)
From Rādhā's hair-pores, there came into being cowmaidens
On all sides, equal to Rādhā, [yet] her servants, of gentle speech. (16)
At this time, O Brahman, suddenly from Kṛṣṇa's body (*deha*),
There became manifest Durgā, Viṣṇu's Māyā, eternal, (17)
The source of goddesses, the divine Mūlaprakṛti,
Most perfect (*paripūrṇatamā*), lustrous in essence, having the nature of the three *guṇas*, (18)
With a thousand arms and many weapons, three-eyed,
The eternal seed of the tree of *saṃsāra*. (19)
The Lord of Rādhikā presented to her a jewelled throne.
At that time, there, the four-faced (Brahmā), with his wife, (20)
The best of knowers (*jñānins*), a glorious being (*puṃs*), reciting the syllable "Om,"
Carrying a water-pot, an ascetic, came forth from the navel of Hari [Kṛṣṇa]. (21)
With his wife Sāvitrī, he praised the Lord of all [Kṛṣṇa]
And sat down on a lovely seat at the command of the Lord, O sage. (22)
Then Kṛṣṇa, O great one, became twofold,
His left side becoming Mahādeva [Śiva], his right half Lord of the *gopis* [Kṛṣṇa]. (23)
This left half, five-faced and three-eyed, the best of sages,

Having praised Kṛṣṇa, with his permission sat down in front of Hari. (24)
Then Kṛṣṇa said to the four-faced [Brahmā], 'O Lord, bring about creation,
Abiding in Satyaloka constantly. Go, remembering me always.' (25)
Thus addressed by Hari and bowing to the ruler of the world,
He [Brahmā] left with his wife and brought about creation, (26)
From his mind and body;[92] he is our father, O best of *munis*.
After that, Kṛṣṇa declared to the five-faced [Śiva], O great-minded one, (27)
'Take Durgā, O Lord of the universe, and practice austerities in Śivaloka
For as long as creation endures. At its end, destroy the worlds on all sides.' (28)
He, too, bowing to Kṛṣṇa, went to Śivaloka.
Then in the next moment, O Brahman, from the mouth of Kṛṣṇa, the supreme Ātman, (29)
Sarasvatī arose, carrying a lute and book.
The Bhagavat ordered her: 'Go to Vaikuṇṭha, my dear. (30)
Remain by Lakṣmī's side, taking refuge in the four-armed [Nārāyaṇa].'
She also bowed to Kṛṣṇa and went to Nārāyaṇa. (31)
Thus for the sake of creation, Rādhā became fivefold.
The *mantras*, *dhyānas*, worship and so forth of these [five] fully complete manifestations (*pūrṇasvarūpa*), (32)
I will tell you: listen, O best of Brahmans." (33a)

The similarity of this passage to PKh 2.54–90 is apparent. In Appendix C, the two passages have been placed in parallel to show the many literal identities. The most important point in the NārP account is that it explicitly states that it is a description of the

[92] The Sanskrit reads:
sṛṣṭiṃ . . . mānasīṃ kalpadaihikīm
This "mental" and "corporeal" creation apparently refers to Brahmā's creating various beings from his mind and body. Cf. BhP III.12.27:
manaso dehataś cedaṃ jajñe viśvakṛto jagat//
Cf. also BhP III.10.1:
[Brahmā] *prajāḥ sasarja katidhā daihikīr mānasīr vibhuḥ//*
The meaning of *kalpa* in the NārP account I cannot explain.

origin of Rādhā's five *aṃśas*, though in fact, their actual origin is from Kṛṣṇa, not from Rādhā. The NārP seems to prove conclusively that the synthesis of PKh 2.54–90 is indeed the source of the doctrine of Prakṛti's, or Rādhā's, five parts.

The NārP account in certain ways appears to be an older version than PKh 2.54–90. A glance at Appendix C shows that the NārP, though discarding much of the descriptions of the goddesses, their clothing and so forth found in PKh 2.54–90, retains the more original legend of Sarasvatī arising from Kṛṣṇa's mouth. She is also introduced in a more appropriate place, not being confused with Lakṣmī's arising from Rādhā's left half. Further, PKh 2.60, which mentions the barrenness of Lakṣmī and Sarasvatī since they are parts of Rādhā, has reference to PKh 2.50–53 (in the copulative cosmogony), where Rādhā and all her parts are cursed by Kṛṣṇa to be forever childless. PKh 2.60 has no parallel version in NārP, and indicates that when PKh 2.54–90 was inserted into chapters 2–3, it was modified to fit the context. Finally, NārP I.83.14ab; 25–29ab, may be a part of the original synthesis, even though not paralleled in PKh 2.54–90.[93] In these verses, Nārāyaṇa, Brahmā, and Śiva with their consorts go to their respective worlds to engage in the works of preservation, creation, and destruction. These verses, if part of the original, apparently became superfluous in PKh 2.54–90 when it was inserted into chapters 2–3, for in chapter 3 the three gods are assigned these functions anyway. Regarding the reason for this insertion of PKh 2.54–90, since both the doctrine of the divisional manifestation and the copulative cosmogony begin with Kṛṣṇa's division into male and female, the two accounts came to be regarded as complementary and as elaborating two different facets of cosmogonic development.

Before leaving the NārP version, we may note that it uses the word *aṃśa* with reference to the five forms of Rādhā.[94] Similarly in PKh 2.60, Lakṣmī and Sarasvatī are referred to as *aṃśas* of Rādhā. As we have remarked above, the term *aṃśa* is not used in connection with the five main forms of Prakṛti in PKh 1. Rather, in PKh 1.60, they are referred to as *paripūrṇatamā*. In

[93] In the case of 14ab, PKh 2.59cd is an approximate parallel, but the latter has no reference to the protection-motif, which is the main cosmogonic function of Nārāyaṇa and his wives.

[94] NārP I.83.6 and 9.

NārP I.83.32, Rādhā's five forms are called *pūrṇasvarūpa,* apparently foreshadowing PKh 1.[95]

We can see, then, that PKh 1 represents the culmination of a long process in the evolution of the feminine theology of Prakṛti. The goddesses now derive only indirectly from Kṛṣṇa, for their immediate origin is from Prakṛti herself. In addition, there is no longer any reference to the other gods.

Let us now look at various references or parallels to the doctrine of PKh 1, both in other parts of the BVP and in other works. The last *adhyāya* (30) of the BKh, in the concluding verses (18–21), summarizes the doctrine as it appears in PKh 1, and serves as an introduction to it. The last three chapters of the BKh, incidentally, on the nature of Kṛṣṇa and his relation to Prakṛti, seem to belong to the latest parts of the BVP. In the GKh, there are three passages that refer to Prakṛti's five forms.[96] Two of the passages refer to Sarasvatī not only as one of the main forms of Prakṛti, but also as arising from Kṛṣṇa's mouth, thus reflecting an earlier stage in the development of the doctrine.[97] All the passages are evidently late additions to the GKh, for they have little to do with the story of Paraśurāma or Gaṇeśa. The KJKh also contains a number of references to Prakṛti's five forms. In KJKh 67.51cd–52ab, Kṛṣṇa declares to Rādhā:

> The subtle Prakṛti is a fraction of me, having a fivefold form: Sarasvatī, Kamalā, Durgā, you, and the mother of the Vedas [Sāvitrī].[98]

And in KJKh 27.107, Rādhā adores Kṛṣṇa, "by worshipping whose feet I [Rādhā] have become Sarasvatī, Lakṣmī, Durgā, Gaṅgā, and Sāvitrī."[99] This passage does not actually refer to Rādhā's

[95] In NārP I.83.18 and PKh 2.68, Durgā is referred to as *paripūrṇatamā.*

[96] The first reference is in GKh 40.61–68, which begins:
sā [Prakṛti] ca śaktiḥ sṛṣṭikāle pañcadhā ceśvarecchayā/
rādhā padmā ca sāvitrī durgā devī sarasvatī// (40.61)
The other references to the five forms of Prakṛti in the GKh appear in 42.56 ff. and 45.27 ff.

[97] In GKh 40.66, it is stated:
kṛṣṇakaṇṭhodbhavā sā syād yā ca devī sarasvatī//
See also GKh 42.59:
sarasvatī dvidhā bhutvā kṛṣṇasya mukhanirgatā/
sāvitrī bramaṇaḥ kāntā svayaṃ nārāyaṇasya ca//

[98] *madaṃśā prakṛtiḥ sūkṣmā sā ca mūrtyā ca pañcadhā//*
sarasvatī ca kamalā durgā tvaṃ cāpi vedasūḥ/

[99] *ahaṃ sarasvatī lakṣmīr durgā gaṅgā śrutiprasūḥ/*
yasya pādārcanān nityaṃ pūjyā tasmai namonamaḥ//

becoming fivefold, but apparently has the notion in mind. It is noteworthy, at any rate, that Gaṅgā here has replaced Rādhā as one of the forms. This passage thus emphasizes that Rādhā is not merely a first among equals, but ontologically elevated beyond the other goddesses. Finally in KJKh 129.96, we find the brief statement: "By your [Kṛṣṇa's] command, I have become fivefold, in the form of the fivefold Prakṛti."[100] The speaker, however, is Durgā, not Rādhā.

It is clear, then, that the doctrine of the five forms of Prakṛti belongs to one of the latest recasts of the BVP, references to it having been inserted into several of the older legends. But the final compilers, it seems, were not bound to any rigid and systematic scheme. On the one hand, not only Rādhā, but Durgā as well came to be associated with the original Prakṛti. In view of the latter's long identification with Mūlaprakṛti,[101] and the close relationship of Durgā with Rādhā in the BVP, this seems only natural. On the other hand, just as the old triadic division of Prakṛti was often transcended by identifying the original Devī with several goddesses, so here the same trend seems to have overcome any attempt to freeze the fivefold division of Prakṛti into an absolutely standard form. Thus in PKh 55, Rādhā, called the Mūlaprakṛti, is identified with Mahālakṣmī, Bhāratī (Sarasvatī), Pārvatī, Sāvitrī, and also with Tulasī, Gaṅgā, Vasundharā.[102] PKh 65 has a passage similar to the last, except that Durgā here is the Mūlaprakṛti.[103]

[100] *tavājñayā pañcadhāhaṃ pañcaprakṛtirūpiṇi/*

[101] E.g., in KūrP I.12.69, Durgā is called *mūlaprakṛtir īśvarī.*

[102] . . . *tvaṃ* [Rādhā] *mūlaprakṛtir īśvarī/*

. . . .

mahālakṣmīś ca vaikuṇṭhe bhāratī ca satāṃ prasūḥ/
puṇyakṣetre bhārate ca satī tvaṃ pārvatī tathā//
tulasī puṇyarūpā ca gaṅgā bhuvanapāvanī/
brahmaloke ca sāvitrī kalayā tvaṃ vasundharā//
goloke rādhikā tvam ca sarvagopālakeśvarī/
(PKh 55.77b, 79–81ab)

[103] Durgā identifies herself as:
. . . *mūlaprakṛtir īśvarī//*
puṇye vṛndāvane ramye goloke rāsamaṇḍale/
rādhā prāṇādhikā 'haṃ ca kṛṣṇasya paramātmanaḥ//
ahaṃ durgā viṣṇumāyā buddhyadhiṣṭhātṛdevatā/
ahaṃ lakṣmīś ca vaikuṇṭhe svayaṃ devī sarasvatī//
sāvitrī vedamātā 'haṃ brahmāṇī brahmalokataḥ/
ahaṃ gaṅgā ca tulasī sarvādhārā vasundharā//
(PKh 65.24d–27)

Turning to other works, we have seen that the NārP contains the account of PKh 2.54–90 with some minor differences. The DBhP in the ninth *skandha* gives nearly an exact copy of the PKh chapters. However, at times, the DBhP reverses the ontological priority of Kṛṣṇa and Devī, so that Kṛṣṇa arises from her, and she divides into the two-armed and four-armed forms.[104] In the NārPR, II.3.50 ff., we find the following account:

> The previously unknown (*apūrvam*) story of Rādhā is secret and hard to obtain.
> It gives *mukti* at once, is pure, the essence of the Vedas, bestowing merit.
> Just as Śrī Kṛṣṇa is esssentially Brahman, beyond Prakṛti,
> So is [she] essentially Brahman, unstained, beyond Prakṛti.
> Just as he is *saguṇa* in time, in accordance with *karma,*
> So through *karma* [she] is Prakṛti, whose essence is the three *guṇas*.
> In the vital breaths and tongues of that supreme Lord,
> In his intellect and heart, Prakṛti resides by her yoga.
> She becomes manifest and disappears in time, O Nārada.
> She is not created but eternal, the form of truth, like Hari.
> The goddess who presides over his life has the form of Rādhā, O *muni.*
> The goddess who presides over his tongue is Sarasvatī herself.
> The goddess who presides over his intellect is Durgā, destroying all misfortune.
>
> . . . .
>
> The goddess presiding over his heart is Sāvitrī among the Brahmaṇas [?]
> The celebrated Mahālakṣmī has arisen from Rādhā's left side,
> The presiding deity of the wealth of the Lord, O Nārada.
>
> . . . .
>
> The goddess Mahālakṣmī herself is the wife of him who dwells in Vaikuṇṭha.
> Sāvitrī is the wife of Brahmā in Brahmaloka, free of disease.
> Sarasvatī became twofold, formerly, through Hari's command,
> [Becoming] Sarasvatī and Bhāratī through her yoga, being an accomplished yogin.

[104] See Appendix A, section 4.

Bhāratī is the wife of Brahmā; Sarasvatī the wife of Viṣṇu.
The goddess [Rādhā] presides over the Rāsa [circular dance of Kṛṣṇa with the *gopīs*], the Queen of the Rāsa herself formerly;
In Vṛndāvana this goddess is most perfect (*paripūrṇatamā*) and virtuous.[105]

This passage contains many parallels to the BVP, as in the idea of Sarasvatī becoming twofold. The goddesses, except for Mahālakṣmī, are closely associated with the parts of Kṛṣṇa's body, yet they are all subsumed under the notion of Prakṛti. Further, the first four lines identify Rādhā with Prakṛti, indicating that the goddesses are really forms of Rādhā. In NārPR II.3.37, it is explicitly stated that the wives of the gods are parts and fractions of Rādhā.[106] It is significant that the NārPR account of the five forms of Prakṛti, or Rādhā, occurs immediately after the narration of Rādhā and Kṛṣṇa's cosmogonic copulative act, which parallels the copulative cosmogony of PKh 2–3 (yet to be considered). As stated earlier, the NārPR is apparently younger than our BVP, for it names the *khaṇḍas* of the extant BVP.[107] The NārPR doctrine of Prakṛti's five forms, therefore, is probably derived from the BVP, or some version of it, rather than vice versa.

In another late work, the *Mahābhāgavata Purāṇa*, it is stated:

The third, supreme knowledge, is she who herself became fivefold:
Gaṅgā, Durgā, Sāvitrī, Lakṣmī, and Sarasvatī.[108]

The "supreme knowledge" (*parā vidyā*) is one of the three parts into which Prakṛti initially divides herself, Māyā and Paramā being the other two. Māyā is responsible for the creation of *saṃsāra*, Paramā is the energizing power, and Vidyā destroys *saṃsāra*.[109] The doctrine in the *Mahābhāgavata Purāṇa* is highly systematized, for the five forms of Vidyā are an addition to the three initial forms of Prakṛti. This suggests a later development of the

105 NārPR II.3.50–56ab, 59cd–60, 62cd–65.
106 *yasyāś* [= *rādhāyāś*] *cāṃśāṃśakalayā babhūvur devayoṣitaḥ//*
107 See above, p. 26.
108 *sā tṛtīyā parā vidyā pañcadhā yābhavat svayam/*
gaṅgā durgā ca sāvitrī lakṣmī caiva sarasvatī//
(quoted by Avalon in *Principles of Tantra,* I. 253)
109 See Avalon, *Principles of Tantra,* I. 253.

more simple version of the PKh.[110] What is most interesting, though, is the substitution of Gaṅgā for Rādhā, an intriguing parallel to KJKh 27.107, discussed above.

Not only was the doctrine of Prakṛti's or Rādhā's five forms not rigidly adhered to in the BVP itself, but also in the PadP, we find the following elaboration of Rādhā's forms:

> The goddess said to be made from Kṛṣṇa, Rādhikā, the supreme deity,
> Representing all prosperity, is in essence the delight (*āhlāda*) of Kṛṣṇa.
> Thus, O Brahman, by the wise she is called bliss (*hlādinī*).
> Durgā and others, whose natures consist of the three *guṇas*, are the millionth parts of her fractions.
> She in person is Mahālakṣmī when Kṛṣṇa is the Lord Nārāyaṇa.
> There is not the slightest difference between them, O best of sages.
> She is Durgā when Hari is Rudra; when Kṛṣṇa is Śakra, she is Śacī;
> She is Sāvitrī when Hari is Brahmā, Dhūmorṇā when Hari is Yama.[111]

The historical relation of this text to the BVP is uncertain, though clearly it shares many of the same basic ideas. I suggest that the PadP passage is later than the BVP since Durgā and the other goddesses are only infinitesimal parts of Rādhā, thus indicating a more extreme elevation of Rādhā than that found in our text.

To recapitulate, we may point out four main stages in the development of the doctrine of Prakṛti's five forms. The first stage consisted of two related but somewhat opposed trends. On the

[110] Hazra has dated the *Mahābhāgavata Purāṇa* as not later than the twelfth century ("The Mahābhāgavata-purāṇa," IHQ, XXVIII, 27). But A. K. Majumdar suggests that parts of it may be later ("Rādhā Cult," ABORI, XXXVI, 247).

[111] *devī kṛṣṇamayī proktā rādhikā paradevatā/*
sarvalakṣmīsvarūpā sā kṛṣṇāhlādasvarūpiṇī//
tataḥ sā procyate vipra hlādinīti manīṣibhiḥ/
tatkalākoṭikoṭyaṃśā durgādyas triguṇātmikāḥ//
sā tu sākṣān mahālakṣmīḥ kṛṣno nārāyaṇaḥ prabhuḥ/
naitayor vidyate bhedaḥ svalpo 'pi munisattama//
iyaṃ durgā harī rudraḥ kṛṣṇaḥ śakra iyaṃ śacī/
sāvitrīyaṃ harir brahmā dhūmorṇā 'sau yamo hariḥ//
(PadP V.82.53–56)

one hand, there was the identification of one or another goddess, usually Lakṣmī or Durgā, with Prakṛti. This resulted in the tripartite division of the primordial goddess according to the three *guṇas*, identified with Lakṣmī, Sarasvatī, and Durgā, the consorts of the three gods active in the creation, preservation, and destruction of the universe. On the other hand, there was the identification of the primordial goddess with a multitude of other goddesses. Thus we often find Durgā identified with Lakṣmī, Sarasvatī and several others, including Sāvitrī, who was closely associated with Sarasvatī as Brahmā's wife. This first stage, then, served to popularize four of the five main forms of Prakṛti, frequently in a cosmogonic context. The second stage, appearing in the early parts of the BKh, saw the creation or emanation of the four goddesses from Kṛṣṇa's body. In the next stage, Rādhā, who had already been derived independently from Kṛṣṇa's left side, was included among the other four. Finally, Kṛṣṇa was replaced by Prakṛti, often identified with Rādhā, as the immediate source of the five goddesses. We have also seen that the BVP's doctrine of Prakṛti's or Rādhā's five forms found its way into a number of late works, though often in modified versions.

The development of the doctrine of Prakṛti's divisional manifestation, as pointed out earlier, involved the incorporation of older masculine theological ideas. That is, many notions originally associated with male divinity were transferred to Prakṛti and her forms. This was the case, for example, with the *aṃśa* and *avatāra* theories, the *triguṇa-trimūrti* correspondence in connection with the cosmological roles of creation, preservation, and destruction, and the idea of deities emanating from the primordial being. In most instances these notions were traditionally, rather than inherently or innately, masculine features and were readily adaptable to a feminine theology. Yet precisely because of this, the doctrine of divisional manifestation, for the most part, did not emphasize or develop specifically feminine characteristics. Consequently, it could attain little more than an imitative parity with the masculine models. The situation is different with the copulative cosmogony, to which we now turn.

2. Creation by copulation

A copulative cosmogony seems especially suited to a feminine theology. At the same time, such a cosmogony allows for a fuller development of masculine theological notions. We shall begin our analysis by summarizing the doctrine as it appears in our text.

a) *The doctrine according to PKh 2–3*

Kṛṣṇa in the beginning was alone but desirous of creating.[112] As already mentioned, he divides himself into two parts, male and female.[113] Kṛṣṇa, as the male, looks upon the damsel, full of grace, charm and beauty. He, the abode of sexual love (*kāmādhāra*), is filled with carnal desire (*mahākāma*).[114] The woman herself is desirous of her lover (*kāntakāmukī*).[115] Kṛṣṇa, as if the incarnation of coition itself, embraces her in various ways for the lifetime of a Brahmā.[116] At last fatigued, he discharges his seed (*vīrya*) into her womb (*yoni*) at an auspicious moment.[117]

There are two important side products of the copulative act. From the woman's exhausted limbs, perspiration (*śramajala*) flows forth and forms the cosmic waters which support the universe.[118] From her labored breathing (*niḥśvāsa*) arises the cosmic wind (*vāyu*) which supports the waters (literally, "everything").[119] Vāyu, personified as the wind god, now gives birth from his left side to a damsel who becomes his wife and bears five sons, the five vital breaths of all creatures.[120] The presiding deity of the waters, Varuṇa, next arises, and from his left side, his wife Varuṇānī.[121]

Returning to the main account, the original female, referred to as Kṛṣṇa's *śakti,* bears his seed (*garbha*) for a hundred *manvantaras.*[122] She is also called the presiding deity of Kṛṣṇa's life, dearer than his life, and other epithets commonly associated with Rādhā, but no explicit identification with her is made. This

[112] *sa kṛṣṇaḥ sarvasṛṣṭyādau sisṛkṣus tv eka eva ca/* (PKh 2.28)
[113] PKh 2.29. See footnote 3 above.
[114] PKh 2.30.
[115] PKh 2.36.
[116] *nānāprakāraśṛṅgāraṃ śṛṅgāro mūrtimān iva/*
cakāra suklasambhogaṃ yāvad vai brahmaṇo vayaḥ//
(PKh 2.39)
[117] *tataḥ sa ca pariśrāntas tasyā yonau jagatpitā/*
cakāra vīryādhānaṃ ca nityānāndaḥ śubhakṣaṇe//
(PKh 2.40)
[118] *tadādhāraśramajalaṃ tatsarvaṃ . . .//*(PKh 2.42)
[119] *sa ca niḥśvāsavāyuś ca sarvādhāro babhūva ha/* (PKh 2.43)
[120] PKh 2.42cd–45.
[121] PKh 2.46.
[122] PKh 2.47.

damsel eventually gives birth to a golden egg (*aṇḍaṃ suvarṇābham*), the supreme abode or receptacle of the universe.[123] For some unexplained reason, the woman is aggrieved in her heart and casts the egg angrily into the cosmic waters.[124] Kṛṣṇa, seeing her abandon the egg, curses her to be forevermore barren, as well as all her *aṃśas*.[125]

The copulative cosmogony is interrupted at this point by the section PKh 2.54–90, discussed above. In 3.1, the egg, having lain in the waters for a lifetime of Brahmā, splits into two parts. Inside is a child, crying from hunger, abandoned by his parents.[126] He is the lord of many universes (*naikabrahmāṇḍanātha*),[127] is known as the Mahāvirāṭ or Mahāviṣṇu, and is a sixteenth part of Kṛṣṇa's might (*tejas*). In each of the child's hair-pores exists a universe,[128] and to each universe there belongs a Brahmā, Viṣṇu and Śiva.[129]

The Mahāvirāṭ, weeping, meditates on Kṛṣṇa, who appears to him and consoles him.[130] Kṛṣṇa promises the Mahāvirāṭ that he shall be the support of all worlds until their dissolution.[131] Further, Brahmā will emerge from the Virāṭ's navel, and the eleven Rudras, by an *aṃśa* of Śiva, from Brahmā's forehead.[132] Kṛṣṇa then goes to heaven and orders Brahmā and Śiva, or the Rudras, to take their births in the forementioned manner, for the sake of the creation and destruction of the universe.[133] Meanwhile, the Mahāvirāṭ has been reduced in size. In the navel-lotus of this small Virāṭ (*kṣudro virāṭ*) Brahmā is born.[134] He then brings about creation, beginning with the production of the mind-born sons Sanaka and others.[135] After the eleven Rudras emerge from Brahmā's forehead, he then creates heaven, earth, the nether

[123] *suṣāvāṇḍaṃ suvarṇābhaṃ viśvādhārālayaṃ param//* (PKh 2.49)

[124] PKh 2.50.

[125] PKh 2.51–53.

[126] PKh 3.2–3a.

[127] PKh 3.3b. Vaṅg reads: *brahmāṇḍāsaṃkhyanāthaḥ*. The notion of several cosmic eggs, here called *brahmāṇḍas,* is found in earlier Purāṇas: ViP II.7.27; LiṅgaP I.87.19; and BhP VI.16.37 (cf. Agrawala, *Matsya Purāṇa,* p. 19).

[128] *pratyekaṃ romakūpeṣu viśvāni nikhilāni ca/* (PKh 3.6)

[129] PKh 3.8.

[130] PKh 3.21–24.

[131] PKh 3.25a.

[132] PKh 42b–43. Cf. ViP I.7.10.

[133] PKh 3.47–49.

[134] PKh 3.51b–53a.

[135] PKh 3.57b–58a.

world, and all that is animate and inanimate, in the navel of the small Virāṭ.[136]

In the above account, four ancient cosmogonic notions have been taken over and assimilated to the new theme of Rādhā and Kṛṣṇa's love-making, as the original creative act. The four older notions relate to: (1) the primordial androgyny, (2) the golden egg, (3) the cosmic elements, water and wind, and (4) Brahmā's creative activity. In order to see more clearly the special characteristics and significance of the new synthesis, we shall briefly examine certain historical aspects of each of the older cosmogonic ideas.

b) *Historical roots of the copulative cosmogony*

i) The primordial androgyny. We have already seen in the KūrP that Devī was regarded as constituting half the body of Śiva.[137] The idea of an androgynous being is much older than the KūrP, however. One of the earliest references is in BU I.4.1–5, where, in the beginning of creation, Ātman, in the form of *puruṣa,* desired a second and grew into a being resembling a man and woman in embrace. After splitting into two parts, the man united with the woman, whence came mankind. The woman then fled, hiding herself by becoming a cow. But he became a bull, united with her, and cows were produced. She then became a horse, a goat, and so forth, till all animate creation was begotten.

The motif of the woman's fleeing is related to the notion that she is in some sense the male's daughter and thus fearful of incest. The idea of the father desiring and uniting with his daughter occurs already in the RV.[138] In the earliest sources, there is mention only of a father (*pitṛ*) and a daughter (*duhitṛ*).[139] The father was soon identified with Prajāpati, his daughter with Vāc (Speech), Uṣas (Dawn), or the sky.[140] In the Purāṇas, Prajāpati becomes Brahmā, his daughter Vāc, Gāyatrī, or Sarasvatī.[141] The legend of Brahmā's desire for his daughter is told in our own text, in KJKh 35. The usual Purāṇic

[136] PKh 3.60.

[137] See p. 150 above and note 53.

[138] RV X.61.5–7; I.71.5; I.164.33. See Sh. Dasgupta, *Obscure Religious Cults,* p. 335; Agrawala, *Matsya Purāṇa,* p. 29; and Dange, "Prajāpati and His Daughter," *Purāṇa,* V, 40.

[139] Agrawala, *Matsya Purāṇa,* p. 29.

[140] See Dange, "Prajāpati and His Daughter," *Purāṇa,* V, 46.

[141] For Purāṇic references, see *ibid.,* V, 41–42.

explanation of Brahmā's behaviour is that he has been blinded by Kāma, pierced by the shafts of love.[142]

The long association of the androgyny with the incest motif had some influence on the relationship of Rādhā and Kṛṣṇa. Thus in the NārPR (II.3.23 ff.), in an account based on the PKh, we find that after Kṛṣṇa has become twofold as Rādhā and Kṛṣṇa, he is prepared to unite with her, but she runs away, afraid to speak, trembling in her heart. Kṛṣṇa then catches her, who is utterly abashed, and mounts her on his breast.[143] The fear motif, however, does not really suit Rādhā, and is not connected with her in the PKh. Rādhā traditionally is regarded first and foremost as Kṛṣṇa's beloved, not as his daughter. This means that the theme of incest could only be an inorganic addition, and more importantly, Rādhā's all-consuming desire for Kṛṣṇa is the essence of her feelings towards him. This is reflected in an etymology of Rādhā's name which appears in several places in our text. In PKh 48.37, following a reference to Rādhā's emanation from Kṛṣṇa's left side, it is said:

> She, seeing her beloved desirous of union, ran (*dadhāva*) to Hari;
> Therefore she is called Rādhā by those knowledgeable of the past. . . .[144]

In the PKh, Rādhā's reaction upon seeing the carnal intention of Kṛṣṇa is to run—but towards him, not away.

The importance of the primordial androgyny goes beyond purely cosmogonical considerations, reflecting a basic orientation or world view that sees sexual duality as a primary ontological feature of the universe. In this connection we may recall Wilson's statement that the BVP is "evidently a clumsy attempt to graft the

142 E.g., MatP III.33.

143 *sā dadhāva na covāca bhītā manasi kampitā/*
tāṃ dhṛtvorasi saṃsthāpya sa uvācātilajjitām//
(NārPR II.3.26)

144 *dṛṣṭvā riraṃsuṃ kāntañ ca sā dadhāva hareḥ puraḥ/*
tena rādhā samākhyātā purāvidbhir maheśvarī//
(Vaṅg reading.) The Ānand and Veṅk read "dadhāra" for "dadhāva." "Dadhāva" gives the better meaning in the context, and appears in parallel instances of this etymology of Rādhā. Thus in BKh 5.26, it is stated:
rāse sambhūya goloke sā dadhāva hareḥ puraḥ/
tena rādhā samākhyātā purāvidbhir dvijottama//
(Veṅk and Ānand)
Here, however, Rādhā runs to Kṛṣṇa to offer flowers and water for his feet (cf. BKh 5.25), the sexual aspect being neglected for the most part.

distinction of the sexes as prevailing in earth, hell, and heaven, upon a metaphysical theory of the origin of the universe."[145] What is involved here is one form or version of the old "anthropomorphism-question." In Western traditions, theologians have answered the charge of superimposing human attributes on God by countering that God made man in His own image. The compilers of our Purāṇa might well have responded to Wilson in a somewhat similar fashion by insisting that man and woman have been made in the image, or rather, are a microcosmic manifestation, of the primordial androgyny.

ii) The cosmic egg. Let us first examine the mythological accounts of the origin of the egg. The earliest references to the egg are in the RV. In X.121.1 ff., it is said that in the beginning, *hiraṇyagarbha* (the golden germ), possibly identified with Prajāpati,[146] came into being and rested upon the waters. In ŚB VI.1.1, Prajāpati, having created the primeval waters, enters them as an egg.[147] A similar account is found in *Manu* I.8–13, where Svayambhu creates the waters and places his seed (*bīja*) in them. The seed then becomes a golden egg (*aṇḍaṃ haimam*). A somewhat different version is given in ŚB XI.1.6.1, where the waters, desirous to create, practice austerities (*tapas*), and when heated, give birth to the egg.[148] According to CU III.19, the world in the beginning was *asat* (non-existent); it became *sat* and grew into an egg. In the Purāṇic accounts, we find the synthesis of the egg story with the Sāṃkhyan theory of creation.[149] For instance, in

[145] Wilson, "Analysis of the Puráńas," p. 101. See above, p. 119.

[146] See Deussen, *The Philosophy of the Upanishads*, p. 182; Agrawala, "Hiraṇyagarbha," *Purāṇa*, II, 287. Griffith, however, regards the identification of the golden germ with Prajāpati as reading too much into the text (*The Hymns of the Rigveda*, commentary on X.121.1).

[147] See Deussen, *The Philosophy of the Upanishads*, p. 183.

[148] See Datta, *The Story of Creation as Seen by the Seers*, p. 106.

[149] For the text history of the cosmogonic sections of the Purāṇas, Kirfel's *Das Purāṇa Pañcalakṣaṇa* is the main source. In the section on "Sarga und Pratisarga" (creation and secondary creation), Textgruppe (TG) I (based on AgniP 6b–17; BrahmaP 1.31–56; HV 27–53; ŚivaP 51.3–28), verses 10–14 give the oldest Purāṇic account of the golden egg. It is similar to the account in *Manu* I.8–13. It is interesting that, though Sāṃkhyan influence is evident in TG I (see verse 5), it has not yet affected the story of the cosmic egg. Kirfel, in the Einleitung, p. XXVIII, points out that the world-egg theory appearing in TG I (verses 12–14) is replaced in TG II A and II B by the Sāṃkhyan theory. In chapter one of TG II A (based on two similar versions of the PadP and on ViP I.2.10–66), we find the Sāṃkhyan principles introduced into the egg legend (see chapter 1, verse 23). The identical verse is found in TG II B, chapter 1 (based on BAP I.3.1–38; KūrP

ViP I.2, the egg arises from the aggregation of the Sāṃkhyan principles, *mahat* and so forth, the process implicitly being presided over by Viṣṇu. The BhP gives a similar account, but with Viṣṇu's (Bhagavat's) directing role made more explicit.[150]

In all the above accounts, we find that the origin of the egg is conceived either in non-sexual or in uni-sexual terms. In our text, as already seen, the golden egg (*aṇḍam survarṇābham*) is the product of Kṛṣṇa's seed (*garbha*), which was placed not in the waters, but in the womb (*yoni*) of Rādhā, where after a hundred *manvantaras* it is born as the egg and then cast into the waters. The PKh, in viewing the egg as the fruit of this cosmic copulative act, made a significant innovation in the development of feminine theology, the implications of which will be discussed below.

Returning for a moment to historical considerations, regarding the contents or outcome of the egg, two general schemes may be noted. First, the egg is often seen as giving birth to a creator being, such as Prajāpati, Puruṣa, or Virāṭ. But it is also said that the egg, splitting in two, forms the parts of the physical universe, either from the two halves of its shell, or from its inner contents.[151] In many cases, these two general schemes are combined.[152] In the PKh, though, the Mahāvirāṭ, identified with Mahāviṣṇu, is the first offspring of the egg, from whom emerges Brahmā, who then creates the universe.

One last point on the cosmic egg concerns the notions of *tapas* and *kāma* as the motivating forces behind the creation or development of the egg. These two might at first appear to be exclusive opposites, but both are associated with creative power. In ŚB XI.1.6.1–2, referred to above, the waters, desirous to create (*akāmayanta*), practiced *tapas,* and when heated, they produced the egg.[153] In the BVP, *tapas* is wholly supplanted by *kāma.*

iii) The cosmic wind and water. The importance of the waters for cosmogony has already become evident in the discussion of

---

4.6–66; LiṅgaP 70.3–66, MārkP 45.29–73; VāyuP 4.5–92), verse 55. TG III (MatP 2.22–4.32) retains traces of the TG I framework (v. 28), and also connects the egg with Prajāpati (v. 35). MatP 248.1 also connects the egg with Prajāpati (see Agrawala, *Matsya Purāṇa,* p. 15).

[150] See BhP III.6.1 ff. Cf. II.5.34 ff.

[151] E.g., CU III.19.

[152] E.g., *Manu* I.8–13; *Purāṇa Pañcalakṣaṇa,* "Sarga and Pratisarga," TG I.10–14.

[153] See Datta, *The Story of Creation as Seen by the Seers,* p. 106. Cf. *Aitareya Upaniṣad* I.1–4.

the cosmic egg, which floats upon them. The waters thus are often conceived as the support of the entire universe. Wind as a cosmic element is closely associated with breath (*prāṇa*). In AV XI.4.15 *prāṇa* is called *vātas* (wind), and XI.4 as a whole praises *prāṇa* as the controller of all, Lord of all, and upon whom all things are established.[154] In the BVP, the identification of wind with the vital breaths has previously been indicated. In our text, wind is also conceived as the ultimate physical support of the universe, including the waters.[155] Wind itself has no support, remaining in place only by Kṛṣṇa's command.

An interesting aspect of the cosmic elements concerns their origin. Often they are seen as pre-existent. But they could also be regarded as the product of some animate activity of a creator god. Thus in *Gopatha Brāhmaṇa* I.1.2–3, Brahmā heats himself, and from his pores perspiration flows forth, forming the cosmic waters, by which Brahmā supports the universe, and into which his seed (*retas*) falls. Our cosmogony derives the waters and wind from Rādhā's perspiration and breath.

iv) Brahmā's creative activity. Brahmā by early Christian times was connected with the notion of the primordial androgyny and with the cosmic egg.[156] But his birth from the cosmic egg, as well as from the navel or lotus of Viṣṇu, is not mentioned in the earliest accounts of his origin, in which he is simply born out of the waters.[157] In a late passage of the Rāmāyana (VII.104.7), we find him produced from Viṣṇu's navel and ordered to create the worlds.[158] This of course is an implicit subordination of Brahmā to Viṣṇu, and points to one of the important functions of the cosmogonies in the Purāṇas: to reveal the true hierarchy of the gods by their respective roles in creation. Thus in the PKh, the birth of Brahmā from the Virāṭ, himself arisen from the golden egg, clearly illustrates the superiority of Rādhā and Kṛṣṇa to Brahmā.

[154] Cf. Deussen, *The Philosophy of the Upanishads*, p. 183.

[155] Our text does not give a fully consistent cosmographic scheme. In PKh 34.51–52, by Kṛṣṇa's command, wind (*vāyu*) supports the water (*toya*), which supports the world-tortoise (Kūrma), who holds the cosmic serpent (Ananta), upon whom the earth rests. In KJKh 73.13–14, through fear of Kṛṣṇa, the wind (*vāyu*) supports the world-tortoise (*kacchapa*), holding the cosmic serpent (Śeṣa), who supports the mountains, upholding the nether regions, upon which rest the waters (*jala*) supporting the earth.

[156] See *Manu* I.9 and I.32.

[157] See Hopkins, *Epic Mythology*, p. 189.

[158] See *ibid.*, pp. 191–2.

In view of the original Brahmāite nature of the BVP and the rather complete recast by later Vaiṣṇavas, the subordination of Brahmā to Kṛṣṇa has special significance for our text. One stage in the process of subordination is found in the cosmogony of BKh 4. This passage is also important for the copulative cosmogony, for PKh 2–3 is modelled on BKh 4. Incidentally, therefore, just as with the doctrine of Prakṛti's divisional manifestation, the dependence of the three introductory chapters of the PKh upon the early chapters of the BKh is further demonstrated.[159] Yet in the case of the copulative cosmogony, the adaptation was less imitative and potentially, at least, far more significant. In order to show both how Brahmā became subordinated to Kṛṣṇa and the way in which PKh 2–3 utilized BKh 4, let us first summarize the latter.

Following the emanation of the other gods and goddesses from Kṛṣṇa's body, Kāma emerged from his heart, armed with five arrows. From his left side came out the beautiful Rati. Kāma, to test his arrows, shot them at the gods. They at once were filled with desire, and Brahmā, who was looking at Rati, discharged his seed. He was ashamed and covered it with his garment, but the cloth burst into flame, and thus Agni was born. Kṛṣṇa, seeing the fire increasing, produced a drop of water from his mouth (*mukhabindu*), along with the wind of his breath. The drop, inundating the universe, calmed or reduced the fire. Then from the waters arose the god Varuṇa and from his left side his wife Vāruṇī. Svāhā also was born from the left side of Fire, and Vāyavī from the left side of Wind. Meanwhile, Kṛṣṇa also had been pierced by Kāma's arrows and emitted his seed. Through shame, he threw it into the water. After a thousand years it formed an egg (*ḍimbha*), from which was born the Mahāvirāṭ, in each of whose hair-pores exists a universe. He is also known as Mahāviṣṇu and is a sixteenth part of Kṛṣṇa. While he was lying on the waters, two demons arose from the secretions of his ears and attempted to slay Brahmā, whereupon they were killed by Nārāyaṇa. From the marrow of the demons, the earth was made.

159 Haraprasada Shastri has stated that the whole of the BKh was merely an introduction to the Purāṇa proper, which he felt "really begins in earnest from the beginning of the Prakṛti-khaṇḍa, and ends with the 130th chapter [of the KJKh] . . ." (*Catalogue*, V, clvii). Shastri thus sees the BKh, and the final chapters of the KJKh, as late additions to the main text. My study has indicated, however, that the BKh is probably one of the oldest parts of the BVP, and in any case is almost certainly older than PKh 1–3.

In this account, the derivation of the egg from Kṛṣṇa's seed, I propose, represents the revision of an earlier story in which the egg was produced from Brahmā. This is suggested not only by Brahmā's long association with the egg, but also by the repetition of the seed emission, first from Brahmā and then from Kṛṣṇa.[160]

To illustrate the relationship of BKh 4 and PKh 2–3, let us schematize the two accounts:

BKh 4:

Kāma shoots Brahmā → seed, covered by cloth → fire
↓
Svāhā

Kṛṣṇa, to calm the fire, emits from his mouth → breath & water
↓ ↓
Vāyu Varuṇa
↓ ↓
Vāyavī Vāruṇī

Kāma shoots Kṛṣṇa → seed → egg, thrown into water → Mahāvirāṭ
↓
2 demons
↓
earth

PKh 2–3:

Female
Kṛṣṇa egg, thrown into water → Mahāviraṭ
Male
↓
Brahmā, who creates the universe

(from the exertion of the sex act)

perspiration → waters → Varuṇa → Varuṇānī

breath → Vāyu → Vāyavī (not actually named)

[160] Cf. BhP III.10.5–6, where Brahmā is associated with wind and water.

The above diagrams show how the PKh has taken over many of the older cosmogonic notions and resynthesized them according to the love-making of Rādhā and Kṛṣṇa.

PKh 2–3, however, is not the earliest account of this copulative cosmogony. Traces of an earlier version, retaining certain features closer to that of the BKh, are found in GKh 42.43 ff. Here, for instance, the egg is referred to as *ḍimbha* (as in BKh), rather than as *aṇḍa* (as in PKh). The wind and water (in GKh 42.44–45) apparently derive from Kṛṣṇa, and in any case are not specifically ascribed to the female. Further, the water is not perspiration but a "mouth-drop" (*mukhabindu*), clearly reflecting the BKh account (cf. BKh 4.15: *mukhabindu*). Another version, closer to PKh 2–3, appears in GKh 45.22 ff. This passage explicitly identifies Rādhā with the female. The egg is called *ḍimbha,* but the wind is derived from Rādhā, and the water is referred to as "perspiration from fear" (*bhayagharmajala,* GKh 45.26; cf. PKh 2.46: *gharmatoya*). It is interesting that both versions of the copulative cosmogony in the GKh conclude with an account of the five forms of Prakṛti.[161] In KJKh 41.68 ff., another account of the copulative cosmogony also concludes with reference to the principle forms of Prakṛti. The whole cosmogony, in this last instance, has been inserted into a Śaivite story. The NārPR gives additional evidence regarding the transition from BKh 4 to PKh 2–3. In NārPR II.3.23 ff., referred to above, the water derives from perspiration, but of Kṛṣṇa, not Rādhā,[162] and the egg is referred to as *ḍimbha.*[163] This account in addition makes reference to the five forms of Prakṛti.[164] The above passages from the GKh, KJKh, and NārPR all wish to express the complementary nature of the two doctrines of the divisional manifestation and the cosmogonic copulation.

A brief reference to the latter cosmogony is found in the story of Paraśurāma and Gaṇeśa in BAP III.21–58. This section, as we have seen, is a late addition to the Purāṇa, and seems to have been based in part on the GKh.[165] It is almost certain that the

[161] GKh 42.56 and 45.27 ff.
[162] *bhūriśrameṇa kṛṣṇasya gātre gharmo babhūva ha/*
(NārPR II.3.34)
[163] The NārPR also refers to this cosmogony in II.2.37 ff.
[164] See above, pp. 164–165.
[165] See above, pp. 35–36.

BAP has assimilated its notions about Rādhā's cosmogonic role from the GKh. Thus in BAP III.43.9, it is said.

> From her [Rādhā's] womb has arisen the higher Virāṭ; from a portion of him has arisen the [lower] Virāṭ, from whose navel-lotus has arisen the creator, solely engaged in arranging [the world],
> By whom all this universe animate and inanimate was created. She [Rādhā] is the mother of him, in whose hair-pores appear the Brahmāṇḍas; may she be ever pleased.[166]

c) *Implications of the copulative cosmogony*

In considering some of the broader implications of the copulative cosmogony, let us begin with a remark of Banikanta Kakati, who compares the BVP with the DBhP. This latter, we may recall, glorifies the goddess Durgā, and its ninth book is only a slightly recast version of the PKh.[167] Kakati writes:

> The *Devī Bhāgavata* and the *Brahma Vaivarta* are parallel compositions; both idolising the female principle in nature and in human society. But while the *Devī Bhāgavata* deifies the motherhood aspect in the female principle, the *Brahma Vaivarta* stresses the sexual side of it. The *Devī Bhāgavata* built up the Mother Goddess while the *Brahma Vaivarta* created the eternal feminine in Rādhā, the goddess of amour and all that amour stands for in metaphysical sublimations.[168]

Kakati's analysis, as a general statement, is not without justification. But regarding the BVP, it overlooks the significance of the copulative cosmogony. This cosmogony, of course, does stress the sexual or amorous aspects of Rādhā. Her love-making with Kṛṣṇa,

[166] *yasyā garbhasamudbhavo hy ativirāḍ yasyāṃśabhūto*
virāṭ yannābhyamburuhodbhavena vidhinaikānto-
padiṣṭena vai/
sṛṣṭaṃ sarvam idaṃ carācaram ayaṃ viśvam ca
yadromasu brahmāṇḍāni vibhānti tasya jananī
śaśvat prasannā 'stu sā//

[167] Kakati supposes the BVP to have been written in imitation of the DBhP (*Viṣṇuite Myths and Legends in Folklore Setting*, p. 86), but Hazra's view that the DBhP depends on the BVP is surely correct, as we have also shown in Appendix A.

[168] *Viṣṇuite Myths and Legends*, pp. 85–86.

as has been shown, is the guiding principle synthesizing the older cosmogonic elements. But with the breaking of the egg and the emergence from it of Mahāvirāṭ and eventually the worlds, a new dimension in the theology of Rādhā arises. Rādhā clearly has become a mother, both of Mahāviṣṇu (Mahāvirāṭ) and of the universe. Thus Kṛṣṇa, in consoling his newborn son, weeping from hunger, says:

> In meditation you shall surely see my pleasing form constantly,
> And your charming mother resting on my breast.[169]

Here, then, is the acknowledgement of Rādhā's new maternal role, along with reference to her older amorous aspect.

Throughout our Purāṇa, we find frequent recognition of Rādhā's new status. As the mother of Mahāviṣṇu, she is referred to as *mahāviṣṇor mātṛ*,[170] *mahāviṣṇoḥ prasū*,[171] *mahāviṣṇuvidhātrī*,[172] and *mahāviṣṇor jananī*.[173] As mother of the universe, she is called *sarvamātṛ*,[174] *jaganmātṛ*,[175] *jagatām mātṛ*,[176] *jagadambikā*,[177] *jagatprasū*,[178] *trijagatprasū*,[179] and *trailokyamātṛ*.[180] Rādhā, in explaining the etmyology of her own name, refers to the two aspects of her motherhood:

> The syllable "rā" signifies Mahāviṣṇu, in whose hair [-pores] the worlds exist;
> [The syllable] "dhā" [means] creatrix or wet nurse (*dhātrī*), in the sense of mother, in the worlds containing all creatures.

169 *dhyānena kamanīyaṃ māṃ nityaṃ drakṣyasi niścitam//*
mātaraṃ kamanīyāṃ ca mama vakṣaḥsthalastitām/
(PKh 3.46–47)

170 PKh 55.77; KJKh 92.71 and 124.83.

171 PKh 48.51; 54.88; 54.104.

172 PKh 55.18.

173 PKh 56.43. Cf. KJKh 124.7: *vasoḥ sarvanivāsasya prasūḥ*. The epithet *mahāviṣṇor jananī* is also applied to Durgā, in PKh 64.12, where she is identified with Rādhā.

174 PKh 1.47; KJKh 92.85.

175 KJKh 124.3.

176 PKh 55.44; KJKh 124.11.

177 PKh 55.74.

178 PKh 54.176.

179 KJKh 96.4.

180 KJKh 124.2.

> I am the wet nurse, the mother of all these; I am the goddess Mūlaprakṛti.[181]

We see here also the close association of Rādhā as mother with Mūlaprakṛti. This appears in many of the other cases cited above.[182] Her claim, then, to the status of Primordial Nature largely depends upon her maternal role, whose main support is the copulative cosmogony.

The view of Rādhā as mother in many ways constitutes a radical break with tradition. In the earlier accounts of Rādhā, as the mistress of Kṛṣṇa, she had had little to do with a maternal role. Even when she was portrayed as Kṛṣṇa's wife, the emphasis on her longing in separation from Kṛṣṇa, after his departure for Mathurā, precluded any real possibility of a settled married life. Accordingly, Rādhā remained childless.[183] The strength of the traditional view is reflected by the fact that, in the PKh 2–3 account describing Rādhā's cosmic motherhood, she is also cursed by Kṛṣṇa to be forevermore barren for having thrown away the world-egg in anger. It is of interest that all reference to Rādhā's act of renunciation of her motherhood and her being cursed by Kṛṣṇa has been left out in the copulative cosmogonies of GKh 42.43 ff. and 45.22 ff.

To summarize, the copulative cosmogony took over the ancient themes of the androgyny, the egg, the cosmic elements, and Brahmā's creative activity, and restructured them according to the principle of Rādhā and Kṛṣṇa's love-making. In the process, a new dimension was added to the theology of Rādhā. This development was a significant experiment in feminine theology, combining the amorous and the maternal, and was to have important consequences for devotional and soteriological views.

[181] *rāśabdaś ca mahāviṣṇur viśvāni yasya lomasu/*
viśvaprāṇiṣu viṣveṣu dhā dhātrī mātṛvacakaḥ//
dhātrī mātā 'ham eteṣaṃ mūlaprakṛtir īśvarī/
(KJKh 111.57–58a)

For the two aspects of her motherhood combined, see also KJKh 124.98: *jagatāṃ mātaraṃ vedhasām api.* Other references to Rādhā as mother occur in PKh 49.32, KJKh 3.103; 15.105; 15.106; 96.12; 124.8.

[182] PKh 48.51; 54.104; 55.18; 55.77; 56.41 and 43; KJKh 124.7.

[183] Cf. S. M. Pandey and Norman Zide, "Sūrdās and His Krishna-*bhakti*," *Krishna: Myths, Rites, and Attitudes* (Milton Singer, ed.), pp. 184–186.

10

Prakṛti: Her Redemptive Role

Prakṛti is the female principle of the universe and all women are sprung from her parts. Accordingly, an insult to a woman is an offense against the goddess Nature herself. So at least PKh 1.143 declares.[1] But elsewhere in the PKh, and throughout the BVP as a whole, there are caustic condemnations of women as one of the greatest obstacles to salvation. This ambivalent attitude towards women extends to Prakṛti and has significant implications for her redemptive role. Therefore let us begin our analysis of Prakṛti's redemptive activity by examining in some detail the various views of women expressed in our text.

1. On Women

Following are some typical condemnations of women as impediments to redemption:

> . . . the beauty of a woman is the cause of infatuation (*moha*),
> The receptacle of all delusion (*māyā*), causing the increase of desire (*kāma*).

[1] *kalāṃśāṃśasamudbhūtāḥ prativiśveṣu yoṣitaḥ/*
yoṣitām apamānena prakṛteś ca parābhavaḥ//
Cf. BKh 30.16:
sā [prakṛti] ca yoṣitsvarūpā ca prativiśveṣu māyayā/
yoṣitām apamānena parābhūtā ca sā bhavet//
See also KJKh 33.50cd–51ab.

. . . .

It is a barrier on the way to liberation (*mokṣa*), hindering devotion to Hari.
It is an unbreakable cord binding men to the world.
It destroys indifference (*vairāgya*) and constantly nurtures passion (*rāga*).

. . . .

It is the abode of mistrust, deceit,
And pride. It is a jar of poison with honey at the mouth.[2]
A woman's beauty obstructs the path to liberation in the three worlds,
Hinders religious austerity (*tapasyā*), and is the eternal cause of delusion (*moha*).
It is a heavy chain binding men to the prison of the world,
Which cannot be sundered even by the sword of knowledge of Śaṃkara and other great beings.[3]
[This sea of *saṃsāra,*] with waves in the forms of births, teeming with multitudes of alligators in the shape of women,
With currents consisting of copulation, is deep and treacherous.[4]
The radiant face, buttocks and breasts of a woman
Are the abode of desire (*kāma*), the seed of destruction and the residence of vice (*adharma*).
Her vagina is a hell-pit, filled with mucus and urine,
Stinking and evil, bringing about the punishment of Yama.
When a man enters his organ into that vile vagina of women,
He himself enters the Raurava Hell in age after age.[5]

And finally, the goddess Tulsi delivers the following diatribe against her own sex:

Only a libertine, of bad family, untutored in *dharmaśāstra,*
Ignorant of *śruti,* filled with lust, desires a woman.
At first, she is like honey, but in the end is the death of a man,
Ever like a jar of poison with nectar at the mouth.
She speaks sweetly, but her heart is always sharp as a razor.

[2] GKh 6.55, 57–58ab, 59.
[3] KJKh 24.17–18. Regarding the name Śaṃkara, see above, p. 21, note 1.
[4] KJKh 32.75.
[5] KJKh 86.92–94.

She is constantly intent on her own desires,
And for this purpose alone is obedient to her husband.
Inside she is impure, though her face is bright.

. . . .

Seeing a well-dressed man, she desires [him] always in her heart,
Carefully displaying chastity on the outside,
[Yet seeking] desires and pleasure always, being the abode of desire and deluding the mind,
Pretending to be modest but inwardly desirous of intercourse.

. . . .

She is a constant impediment on the path of asceticism (*tapas*), a barrier on the way to salvation,
Interrupting devotion to Hari, and the source of all delusion (*māyā*).
She is an iron fetter in this prison of the world.

. . . .

She is beautiful on the outside, vile on the inside:
The receptacle of urine, pus, feces;
She is evil smelling, noxious, smeared with menstrual flow, and unpurified.
By the creator she was made in the form of the deceit of deceivers (*māyārūpaṃ māyinām*);
She is poison to seekers of salvation and never should be gazed upon.[6]

These examples clearly emphasize sexual allurement as the great danger of women. This attitude is rooted in an ancient ethic of asceticism, in which detachment of the mind from all worldly desires was regarded as the prerequisite for, and in part an actual participation in, the final state of liberation. Austerities (*tapas*) were regarded as the chief means to mental detachment, and thus our text repeatedly censures women, with their power to arouse desire, as impediments to *tapas*.

The power to arouse desire is also the power to delude. Thus we find that women are frequently regarded as the cause not only of *kāma* or *rāga*, but of *moha* or *māyā* as well. This delusion, or deception, causes mankind to turn his mind and heart away from the proper object of all thoughts and feelings, Hari or Kṛṣṇa.

[6] PKh 16.43–46, 48cd–50ab, 57cd–58, 59cd–61.

Women are thus an obstacle both to asceticism and to devotion.

On the other hand, Kṛṣṇa, in speaking of the duties of a wife, declares:

> A beautiful woman, gazing upon her good husband, regards him as equal to nectar,
> Greeting him eagerly with a smile and affectionate devotion,
> [Such a] chaste woman redeems a thousand ancestors.
> The husband of a devoted wife is freed from all sins.
> The spouses of chaste women have not to endure the suffering of *karma*,
> And with their wives, free of *karma*, they rejoice in the abode of Hari.
>
> ....
>
> By the dust of the feet of chaste women, the earth is at once purified.
> A man, bowing to a loyal wife, is released from sin.[7]

In PKh 59.15, it is stated:

> A man without a wife is impure to perform rites for the gods or manes,
> And his daily rites are fruitless.

And in PKh 6.66–67ab:

> A man whose wife is easily controlled, well-behaved, and chaste,
> Attains the happiness of heaven in this world and *dharma* and *mokṣa* in the next.
> He whose wife is chaste is liberated, pure, and content.[8]

The next half verse, however, asserts that the husband of an unchaste wife is wretched and impure, and though seemingly alive, is really dead. Kṛṣṇa's praise above, we may note, was reserved for the chaste woman. There thus appears to be a general division of women into two types. This is made quite explicit in several places in our Purāṇa. Following the diatribe of Tulsi quoted above, Śaṅkhacūḍa, her husband-to-be, replies:

> Your words [condemning women], O goddess, are but a half-truth.

[7] KJKh 83.120–122, 126.
[8] Cf. GKh 28.5.

Some [of what you say] is true, some is false, now listen to me.
The creator made the form of women, deluding all, of two kinds,
The true (*vāstava*) and the treacherous (*kṛtyārūpa*), the praiseworthy and the contemptible.
Lakṣmī, Sarasvatī, Durgā, Sāvitrī, and Rādhikā, to begin with,
Who constitute in essence the thread of creation, were constructed most excellently by the creator.
Whoever is a portion of them, bearing the form of a woman, is regarded as true,
Praiseworthy, honorable, and the cause of all good.

. . . .

The heavenly whores and so forth are the treacherous ones,
Contemptible, having the form of prostitutes in the worlds.
[Those women] endowed with *sattva* and pure by nature,
The best in the worlds, virtuous and praiseworthy.
They are to be considered as true according to the wise.
Among the treacherous, there are two sorts: those endowed with *rajas,* and those endowed with *tamas.*[9]

This passage apparently is based on PKh 1.146–149, where the following account is given:

All women are sprung from Parkṛti, the best, the worst, and the intermediate.
The best are derived from the *sattva* portion; they are well-mannered and chaste.
The intermediate are parts of *rajas,*
Seeking pleasure and ever intent on their own ends.
The worst are parts of *tamas,* of unknown ancestry,
Bad-mouthed, unchaste, licentious, independent, fond of quarrel.
Unchaste women on earth and the heavenly nymphs
Are known as prostitutes, and are parts of *tamas.*[10]

[9] PKh 16.63–66, 73–75.

[10] The division of women into these two or three types is found throughout the BVP: BKh 6.36cd–41; 9.69–70; 15.16–17; 23.21–28 (where all three types are condemned as seeking their own purposes); 24.10–13; KJKh 32.31cd–32ab; 84.10–17; 84.23cd–41ab.

Here we see that the three basic types of women are derived from the *guṇas* of Prakṛti. It is the *rājasī* and especially the *tāmasī* women who hinder men from attaining peace in the world and salvation hereafter. The *sāttvikī* women, on the other hand, help their husbands perform religious rites, free them from sin and *karma,* and even lead them to liberation and the land of Hari.

2. The two powers of Prakṛti: *vivecikā* and *āvaraṇi*

When Śiva was asked by Kṛṣṇa to accept the hand of Pārvatī, he protested:

> I will not marry Parkṛti now . . .
> For she obstructs devotion to you and blocks the path of service (*dāsyamārga*).
> She obscures knowledge of reality and impedes yoga.
> She removes the desire for liberation; herself full of lust, she increases the passion (*kāma*) of others.
> She hinders austerities and is the source of great delusion (*mahāmoha*).
> She is an iron fetter to this terrible prison that is the world.[11]

Prakṛti thus is scorned in the same manner as mortal women. Throughout the BVP, emphasis is given to Prakṛti's or Māyā's deluding power. She deludes not just the worlds but the gods as well, including Brahmā, Viṣṇu, and Śiva.[12] But as with women, Prakṛti has another aspect. For instance, even as Viṣṇumāyā, she is said to bestow devotion to Viṣṇu (*viṣṇubhaktipradā*).[13] In order to understand better these two sides of Prakṛti, let us examine certain historical aspects related to her soteriological role.

In the older Sāṃkhyan view, salvation involves the complete separation or isolation of the sentient *puruṣa* from the inanimate *prakṛti.* It is lack of discrimination (*aviveka*) between these two principles that binds men to the world of experience.[14] Though involvement with *prakṛti* constitutes bondage,[15] the SK states

[11] BKh 6.6–8.
[12] PKh 54.88–90.
[13] PKh 30.160.
[14] See SK 55. Cf. Hiriyanna, *Outlines,* pp. 289–290.
[15] To be sure, the *puruṣa* itself is only apparently and never actually bound. See SK 62–63.

that *prakṛti* works solely for the emancipation of *puruṣa*.[16] Prakṛti thus binds, but also liberates.

Prakṛti, in her binding or deluding aspect, is usually associated with *māyā*. The connection of *prakṛti* with *māyā* is found as early as the BhG.[17] Yet in the BhG, *māyā* is not only a world-deluding power,[18] but also the means by which Kṛṣṇa comes into the world for the welfare of mankind.[19] *Māyā,* then, as well as *prakṛti,* has a dual function, hindering or deluding man, yet also working for his benefit.

When *prakṛti,* with *māyā,* became personified, this dual character was to persist. One of the earliest and clearest examples of this is found in the frame story of the MārkP *Devīmāhātmya.* A king, Suratha by name, deprived of his sovereignty, meets a destitute merchant, called Samādhi, who has been turned out by his family. Both men, pondering their respective misfortunes, go to the sage Medhas. He explains to them that all the world is deluded by Mahāmāyā, the illusion of Hari. This goddess, Mahāmāyā, also is responsible for the creation of the whole world, and even grants emancipation. Medhas says:

> She is supreme knowledge, the eternal cause of redemption. She is the cause of bondage to the world; she is the ruler of all lords.[20]

The king and merchant then inquire about the nature and deeds of this goddess. At this point, Medhas narrates the greatness (*māhātmya*) of the Devī. At the conclusion, the sage urges Suratha and Samādhi to propitiate the goddess, who grants to men pleasure, heaven, and redemption.[21] They proceed to worship her, and she appears before them. Suratha asks for such things as the recovery of his own kingdom, while Samādhi asks for the knowledge that cuts all the bonds of worldly attachment. She grants both requests.

This same story appears in PKh 62–65, with elaborations and

[16] See SK 56–60.
[17] See BhG IV.6.
[18] See BhG VII.13–14.
[19] See BhG IV.6. Cf. KJKh 13.48.
[20] *sā vidyā paramā mukter hetubhūtā sanātanī/*
saṃsārabandhahetuś ca saiva sarveśvareśvarī//
(MārkP LXXXI.44)
[21] *ārādhitā saiva nṛṇāṃ bhogasvargāpavargadā/* (MārkP XCIII.3)

revisions.[22] The goddess's deluding and saving roles are more clearly defined and systemized. Her deluding aspect is explicitly related to Suratha's request for his kingdom, her saving aspect to Samādhi's request for knowledge. Further, this knowledge is interpreted in terms of *kṛṣṇabhakti.* All these features are brought out in the following passage, in which Medhas is speaking to Suratha and Samādhi:

> Viṣṇumāyā, hard to overcome, consisting of the three *guṇas,*
> Obscures the world by *māyā* through the command of Kṛṣṇa who is without *guṇas.*
> She is filled with compassion (*kṛpāmayī*), O King, and shows mercy (*kṛpā*) to the righteous,
> Granting them devotion to Kṛṣṇa, hard to attain, through her mercy.
> To those who are deluded, Māyā does not show compassion, O King.
> With *māyā* she binds these unfortunate ones with the snare of delusion (*moha*).
> These fools constantly wander in the transient, impermanent *saṃsāra,*
> Thinking it eternal, abandoning the supreme Lord.
>
> . . . .
>
> In this terrible ocean of the world, she is a pilot,
> Ever helping the distressed to cross over by means of the boat of *kṛṣṇabhakti.*
> Vaiṣṇavī cuts the bonds of *karma* of the Vaiṣṇavas,
> For she is the sharp sword of Kṛṣṇa, the Supreme.
> Discrimination (*vivecikā*) and obscuration (*āvaraṇi*) constitute the twofold power of Śakti, O King.
> The former she gives to a *bhakta,* the latter to others.[23]
> Discrimination, given to Vaiṣṇavas and the virtuous, consists in the realization:

[22] This story also appears in DBhP V.32–35. For a comparison of the *Devīmāhātmya* and the DBhP accounts, see Sharma, "Verbal Similarities between the Durgā-Sapta-Śapti and the Devī-Bhāgavata-Purāṇa and Other Considerations Bearing on Their Date," *Purāṇa,* V, 91–97, 109–110.

[23] Veṅk and Ānand read:

pūrvaṃ dadāti bhaktāya cetarāya parātparā// (PKh 62.34)

Vaṅg, however, seems to make better sense, and was used in my translation:

pūrvāṃ dadāti bhaktāya cetarāya parāṃ parā//

"Śrī Kṛṣṇa in essence is the true (or real); all else is transient."
Obscuration, consisting in the thought: "This wealth of mine is eternal,"
Is given to non-Vaiṣṇavas and the unvirtuous who are subject to the suffering of *karma*.

. . . .

O King, go to the riverbank and worship the eternal Durgā.
To you, filled with desire, the Goddess will give an intellect [subject to] obscuration.
To the merchant, a Vaiṣṇava free of desire, Vaiṣṇavī,
Full of compassion, will give a pure intellect [endowed with] discrimination.[24]

The following points may be noted in regard to the metaphors used in this passage. We may recall that Śiva had refused to marry Prakṛti on the grounds that she was an iron fetter to the world-prison, and that women have often been likened in our text to an uncuttable chain or cord that not even the sword of knowledge of Śaṃkara can break.[25] But here, we see that Viṣṇumāyā herself is the "sharp sword of Kṛṣṇa," cutting worldly bonds. The analogy of the boat and pilot is also instructive. In KJKh 110.4, it is said:

[The goddess] Prakṛti, consisting of *māyā*, is a boat for crossing the ocean of the world.
You [Kṛṣṇa], full of compassion, are the pilot for guiding across your devotees.[26]

The substitution of Viṣṇumāyā for Kṛṣṇa as the pilot in the speech of Medhas seems to reflect a tendency to place Prakṛti in the pre-eminent soteriological role, even though Kṛṣṇa remains the ontological Supreme and the ultimate object of devotion.

In this connection, we may note the emphasis placed on the mercy of Viṣṇumāyā. *Kṛpā* (compassion, mercy) appears in the

[24] PKh 62.18–21, 32–36, 38–39. Cf. GKh 24.36cd–38ab:
māyā dadāti tāṃ bhaktiṃ pratijanmani sevitā//
parituṣṭā jagaddhātrī bhaktebhyo buddhidāyinī/
parā paramabhaktāya māyā yasmai dadāti ca//
māyāṃ tasmai mohayituṃ na vivekaṃ kadā cana/

[25] See p. 182, above.

[26] *māyāmayī sā prakṛtir bhavābdhitaraṇe tariḥ/*
tvam eva karṇadhāraś ca bhaktottirṇe kṛpāmaya// (KJKh 110.4)
Cf. PKh 62.32; KJKh 96.10; 43.75.

long passage quoted above. Elsewhere, we also find *prasāda* (grace) and *anugraha* (favor):

> By the grace (*prasādena*) of the goddess, he [Samādhi] became the servant of Kṛṣṇa.[27]
> Whom I [Durgā] favor (*anugṛhṇāmi*), to him I give pure,
> Unwavering and steadfast devotion to Śrī Kṛṣṇa, the Supreme Self.
> Whom I delude, to him I give wealth,
> False and deluding like a daydream.[28]

Kṛpā, prasāda, and *anugraha,* we have seen, are frequently associated with Kṛṣṇa throughout our text. In this regard, then, Prakṛti is fully as compassionate and full of grace as Kṛṣṇa.

The notion of grace also appears in the MārkP *Devīmāhātmya,* but there grace may result in material prosperity. Caṇḍikā says:

> Having heard my glorification, then [in the great autumnal festival], a man who is filled with devotion,
> Will be freed from all suffering, and endowed with wealth, grain and children,
> Through my grace (*prasādena*), without doubt.[29]

The PKh version associates grace solely with devotion to Kṛṣṇa, and wealth with delusion.

In the story of Suratha and Samādhi, Prakṛti is identified with Durgā rather than Rādhā. But as we have seen, our text often identifies Rādhā with Durgā, and it is not surprising, then, that Durgā's dual function is "transferred" to Rādhā. For instance, in one story, the sage Sutapas, advising the distressed king Suyajña, says with reference to Rādhā:

> The eternal Viṣṇumāyā bestows devotion to Hari.
> Whom she favors, to them she gives *bhakti.*
> And whom Māyā deludes, to them she does not give it.

[27] *bhagavatyāḥ prasādena kṛṣṇadāso babhūva saḥ//* (PKh 63.44)

[28] *ahaṃ yam anugṛhṇāmi tasmai dāsyāmi nirmalām/*
niścalāṃ sudṛḍhāṃ bhaktiṃ śrikṛṣṇe paramātmani//
karomi vañcanāṃ yaṃ yaṃ tebhyo dāsyāmi sampadam/
prātaḥ svapnasvarūpāṃ ca mithyeti bhramarūpiṇīm//
(PKh 65.40–41)

[29] *tasyāṃ mamaitan māhātmyaṃ śrutvā bhaktisamanvitaḥ//*
sarvābadhāvinirmukto dhanadhānyasutānvitaḥ/
manuṣyo matprasādena bhaviṣyati na saṃśayaḥ//
(MārkP XCII.11–12)

She deceives them with transient wealth.
She is constituted of love (*preman*) for Kṛṣṇa, is his *śakti* and the presiding deity of his life.
Worship that Rādhā, without qualities, the bestower of all wealth.
Quickly you shall go to Goloka, through her favor and service.
She has been served and worshipped by Kṛṣṇa, who is propitiated by all.
Bhaktas, by serving him, unattainable by meditation,[30] hard to be propitiated, without qualities,
In a long time, after many births, go to Goloka.
By serving her, full of compassion, devotees go there in a short time.
She is the mother of Mahāviṣṇu, representing all welfare.[31]

This passage not only indicates Rādhā's dual function, but also her pre-eminence in a redemptive capacity. The worship of Kṛṣṇa is a difficult path, leading to the ultimate goal (Goloka) only after several lifetimes. Devotion to Rādhā, on the other hand, has immediate results. This same notion is repeated in PKh 55.4cd–5:

By service to him [Kṛṣṇa], you shall obtain his world after many births.
Worship the Supreme Rādhā, the presiding deity of his life.
By the grace [of Rādhā], full of compassion, you will quickly attain his abode.[32]

The importance of Rādhā in a soteriological role is also brought out in connection with the universality or impartiality of Kṛṣṇa's mercy. Rādhā herself says to Kṛṣṇa that his mercy is equal to the

[30] Veṅk and Ānand have *dhyānasādhyam* (attainable by meditation). Vaṅg, however, has *dhyānāsādhyam*, which seems the better reading in this context.

[31] PKh 54.126–131.

[32] *tatsevayā ca tallokaṃ prāpsyase bahujanmataḥ//*
tatprāṇādhiṣṭhātṛdevīm bhaja rādhāṃ parātparām/
kṛpāmayīprasādena śīghraṃ prāpnoti tatpadam//
(PKh 55.4–5)

Cf. NārPR II.6.31, 32cd–33ab [text has confused numbering]:
ārādhya suciraṃ kṛṣṇaṃ yad yat kāryam bhaven nṛṇām/
rādhopāsanayā tac ca bhavet svalpena kālataḥ// (31)
viṣṇumāyā bhāgavatī kṛpāṃ yaṃ yaṃ karoti ca// (32)
sa ca prāpnoti kṛṣṇaṃ ca tadbhaktidāsyam īpsitam/ (33ab?)

fit and the unfit.[33] But Rādhā first qualifies this statement as follows:

> Some [men] are not dear to the lord, others are dear.
> Those who do not remember me do not receive your [Kṛṣṇa's] mercy.[34]

The etymology of Rādhā's name, as given in our Purāṇa, further reveals her redemptive role:

> [The letter] "r" [destroys] the sins of a crore of births and the consequences of *karma* good and bad.
> The letter "ā" dispenses with dwelling in a womb, death, and disease.
> "Dh" [destroys] the decrease of life; "ā" [destroys] the bonds of the world.
> By hearing (*śravaṇa*), remembering (*smaraṇa*), or pronouncing (*ukti*) [these letters, these evils] perish without doubt.
> For "r" represents unswerving devotion and service to Kṛṣṇa's lotus-feet,
> ....
> "Dh" represents dwelling together (*sahavāsa*) [with Kṛṣṇa] for eternity;[35]
> It gives *sārṣṭi, sārūpya,* and knowledge of reality equal to Hari's.[36]

This etymology is similar to that of Kṛṣṇa's referred to earlier.[37] It reveals that the devotional acts such as *śravaṇa* and *smaraṇa* have been introduced into the worship of Rādhā.[38] And her worship is here connected with the traditional states of *mukti*.[39] It should be noted in the above passage that Kṛṣṇa, apparently,

[33] KJKh 15.80. Cf. pp. 193–194 above.
[34] KJKh 15.79.
[35] I have translated *tattulyakāla,* literally, "the same time as his," by "eternity."
[36] KJKh 13.105cd–107, 108cd–109ab. For another etymology of Rādhā's name, cf. NārPR II.3.38;
rāśabdoccāraṇād bhakto bhaktiṃ muktiṃ ca rāti saḥ/
dhāśabdoccāraṇenaiva dhāvaty eva hareḥ padam//
[37] See p. 86 above.
[38] Cf. pp. 80 ff. above. In DBhP VII.37.14 ff., we find that supreme *bhakti* is defined, in large part, in terms of the various *bhakti*-marks, such as hearing, and meditating upon the names and deeds *of the Devī.*
[39] Cf. pp. 109 ff.

remains as the ultimate and highest goal. Let us look, though, at the following statement, by Kṛṣṇa himself:

> To someone making the sound "rā," I, trembling, grant him the highest devotion.
> Through [my] desire to listen, I go after him, who makes the sound "dhā."
> Those who serve me, offering the sixteen ingredients of worship
> For a lifetime, arouse delight in me.
> Greater is my delight in hearing the sound "rādhā,"
> And dearer to me [than those who offer the sixteen ingredients], O Rādhā, is he who utters "rādhā."[40]

Kṛṣṇa thus extols the worship of Rādhā above the worship of himself. Let us also look at KJKh 15.31–35, where Rādhā offers to Nanda a boon:

> "Choose a boon, O Lord of Vraja [Nanda], which is desired in your heart.
> I shall give it to you easily, though it may be rarely attained by the gods."
> Having heard the words of Rādhā, the Lord of Vraja said to her:
> "Give me devotion to the feet of both of you [Rādhā and Kṛṣṇa]; I have no other desire.
> You may grant dwelling in the presence of both of you, difficult to attain.
> Give that to us [Nanda and Yaśodā], O Mother of the worlds, supreme Goddess."
> Having heard the words of Nanda, the supreme Goddess said:
> "I shall give to you unequalled *dāsya;* now you shall have devotion.
> May both of you [Nanda and Yaśodā], day and night, constantly remember
> Our lotus-feet, hard to attain, in your cheerful heart."

Here, Rādhā and Kṛṣṇa appear together as the ultimate object of devotion and the final goal. It is of interest that Nanda refers

[40] KJKh 15.70cd–72.

to Rādhā as "Mother of the worlds," thus suggesting that there is some connection between her maternal and redemptive functions.[41] Let us then turn to the larger question of the relationship of Prakṛti's cosmogonic and redemptive roles.

3. Cosmogony and redemption

It was mentioned above that the cosmogonic accounts in the Purāṇas serve to reveal the hierarchy of the gods, and thus the nature of ultimate reality in general. More importantly, cosmogonic myths show the specific kind of relationship that exists between the created world, including man, and ultimate reality. These myths, therefore, have a direct bearing on soteriology. We have already seen that the BVP contains two general notions regarding redemption: that of mergence with the Supreme, and that of becoming an attendant of the Lord. The two cosmogonic schemes of Prakṛti's divisional manifestation and her copulative act of creation correspond in large part to these two notions of redemption.

The doctrine of Prakṛti's divisional manifestation is closely related to the theory of cosmic cycles. At the beginning of a cosmic age, after Prakṛti's emergence from Kṛṣṇa's left side, all female entities become manifest or emanate from her. At the dissolution, the process is reversed. We have already quoted one passage in which the goddesses merge back into Kṛṣṇa's body in the universal destruction.[42] This passage, it was seen, represented an early stage in the development of the doctrine of Prakṛti's five forms, in which the goddesses were still derived directly from Kṛṣṇa rather than Prakṛti. In PKh 53.45–46, it is stated:

> The goddess Mūlaprakṛti, the seed of all,
> In time dissolves into the Lord of time, Kṛṣṇa, and meditates upon him.
> Thus all are afraid of time, both Prakṛti and those derived from Prakṛti [*prākṛta*].

[41] Cf. KJKh 30.160, where Prakṛti or Viṣṇumāyā is called both *viṣṇubhaktipradā* and *sarvamātṛ*.

[42] PKh 34.62 ff. See p. 155 above. See also Appendix A, section 4, for the DBhP parallel text, which adds a few lines (IX.67cd ff.), in which Kṛṣṇa is said to dissolve into Prakṛti.

They become manifest and disappear in time into the Supreme Self.[43]

Occasionally, our text derives only female beings from Prakṛti, male beings arising from Kṛṣṇa. Thus in KJKh 15.104cd, it is said that "Men are *aṃśas* of Hari; women are *aṃśas* of you [Rādhā]."[44] But there is also a tendency in the BVP to derive all beings, male and female, from Prakṛti. PKh 12.14cd, for instance, states: "All men are derived from Nature (*prākṛta*); women are portions (*kalās*) of Nature."[45] Accordingly, when our text says that all beings derived from Nature perish or dissolve back into her in the dissolution, this includes all mankind.[46]

The doctrine of Prakṛti's divisional manifestation and reabsorption points to the dependence of man upon Prakṛti and his essential identity with her, and ultimately with Kṛṣṇa. But we have seen that the idea of *mukti* as mergence or identity is ultimately discarded by our Purāṇa, not only because of the soteriological problems raised by the association of mergence with dissolution (and the endless cycle of *pralayas*), but also because of the monistic presuppositions that run counter to the idea of *mukti* as service. It is not surprising, then, that the soteriological implica-

[43] *sā sarvabījarūpā ca mūlaprakṛtir īśvarī/*
kāle līnā ca kāleśe kṛṣṇe taṃ dhyāyati sma sā//
evaṃ sarve kālabhītāḥ prakṛtiḥ prākṛtās tathā/
āvirbhūtās tirobhūtāḥ kālena paramātmani//

[44] *puruṣāś ca harer aṃśās tvadaṃśā nikhilāḥ striyaḥ//*
Cf. KJKh 67.67ab:
yā yoṣit sā ca bhavatī [Rādhā] *yaḥ pumān so 'ham eva ca/*

[45] *sarve prākṛtikāḥ puṃsaḥ kāminyaḥ prakṛteḥ kalāḥ//*

[46] See KJKh 67.53:
ye ye prākṛtikā rādhe te naṣṭāḥ prākṛte laye//
The idea of a *prākṛta laya* or natural dissolution goes back at least to the ViP. In ViP I.2.25, the natural dissolution is defined as follows:
prakṛtau saṃsthitaṃ vyaktam atītapralaye tu yat/
tasmāt prākṛtasañjñeyam ucyate pratisañcaraḥ//
In ViP I.7.38–40, four kinds of dissolution are mentioned: *naimittika* (occasional), *prākṛta* (natural), *ātyantika* (absolute), and *nitya* (perpetual). The natural dissolution is here defined as:
prayāti prākṛte caiva brahmāṇḍaṃ prakṛtau layam// (I.7.39)
Cf. ViP VI.3.1–2, where three dissolutions are defined (the four above, minus *nitya*). The BVP, however, defines the *prākṛta laya* differently from the ViP:
tatraiva [= in Kṛṣṇa] *prakṛtir līnā tena prākṛtiko layaḥ//* (PKh 7.77)
According to the ViP, the dissolution is called *prākṛta* because all the manifest world dissolves into Nature; according to the BVP, it is because Nature herself dissolves into Kṛṣṇa.

tions of the doctrine of divisional manifestation have not been emphasized or elaborated in our text.

In turning to the copulative cosmogony, we find a different kind of relationship between man and the Ultimate. Prakṛti and Puruṣa, or Rādhā and Kṛṣṇa, are the parents of the world, and by extension of mankind. Above we saw the various epithets of Rādhā in her maternal capacity.[47] Kṛṣṇa accordingly is called the father of the world (*jagatpitṛ*).[48] Kṛṣṇa himself declares to Śiva:

> Puruṣa ever is eternal; eternal is the goddess Prakṛti.
> Always these two, embracing, are the parents of the world, O Śiva.[49]

This view of the relation of Rādhā and Kṛṣṇa to the world easily harmonizes with the notion of *mukti* as service. In the first place, the relationship of parents to children is fundamentally dualistic. The idea of reabsorption or mergence would appear to be foreign to it. Secondly, the proper attitude towards one's parents is that of respect, and service. Thus of the four traditional personal attitudes (*sākhya, vātsalya, mādhurya,* and *dāsya*) that a devotee may adopt towards the deity, *dāsya* is the most appropriate for filial respect and devotion.

We find, then, that Rādhā's amorous aspect has been wholly "transcendentalized." She is no longer a symbol of the human soul longing for the Supreme. Rather, she is the Divine Mother, and thus her love relation to Kṛṣṇa does not serve as the model for man's attitude towards God, but testifies to her qualification as redemptress. As Kṛṣṇa's beloved, she is favored with his grace, and thus is able to bestow that grace upon her devotees, who are her children. In part, she may still be a model for man, for as Kṛṣṇa's wife, she renders *sevā* to him. In fact, it was by *sevā* that she attained her status as his beloved. However, it is primarily her maternal aspect, as mediatrix between father and children, that is of direct importance to man, providing him with the necessary grace to become a servant of Kṛṣṇa. Thus in KJKh 124.97, it is said:

47 See p. 179 above.
48 PKh 2.40.
49 *puruṣaś ca sadā nityo nityā prakṛtir īśvarī*
sadā tau dvau ca saṃśliṣṭau sarveṣaṃ pitarau śiva// (KJKh 43.63)
Cf. *Kumārasambhava* II.7, quoted in chapter 9, note 21.

Those intent on meditation reflect upon Rādhā. . . .
Here in this world they [become] *jīvanmuktas*; and in the next, *pārṣadas* of Kṛṣṇa.[50]

And in PKh 1.54, Rādhā is called "the sole bestower of *dāsya* to the devotees of Śrī Kṛṣṇa."[51]

Let us examine more fully the relation of Prakṛti's maternal and mediating roles. As a mother, she appears to be closer and more accessible to her children than is their father. Particularly is she willing to forgive their faults. Paraśurāma, for instance, says to Durgā:

Protect me, protect me, O Mother of the world; forgive my faults.
Where is the mother who is angered with the faults of her children!?[52]

For such reasons, it seems, the worship of Prakṛti (as Rādhā), is easier and bears fruit sooner than the worship of Kṛṣṇa. In this connection, we may note that our text frequently refers to the greater venerability of the mother than of the father. In KJKh 52.34cd–35ab, there is an explanation of why the sages always pronounce the name of Rādhā before that of Kṛṣṇa:

Prakṛti is the mother of the world, and Puruṣa the father of the world.
The mother of the three worlds is a hundred times more venerable than the father.[53]

The notion of the mother's greater venerability apparently goes back at least to *Manu* II.145: "The teacher is ten times more venerable than a sub-teacher, the father a hundred times more than a teacher, but the mother a thousand times more than the father."[54] In the BVP, the mother's hundredfold superiority often is found in a series of such comparisons, leading up to the ultimate superiority of the *guru*, who is a hundred times more

50 The Veṅk reading is a bit confused. Ānand gives the better reading:
dhyāne dhyānena rādhāyā dhyāyante dhyānatatparaḥ/
ihaiva jīvanmuktās te paratra kṛṣṇapārṣadāḥ//

51 *śrīkṛṣṇabhaktadāsyaikadāyinī*

52 *rakṣa rakṣa jaganmātar aparādhaṃ kṣamasva me/*
śiśūnām aparādhena kuto mātā hi kupyati// (GKh 45.57)

53 *jaganmātā ca prakṛtiḥ puruṣaś ca jagatpitā//*
garīyasī trijagatāṃ mātā śataguṇaiḥ pituḥ/

54 Bühler's translation.

venerable than the mother.[55] But in one case, the mother is identified with the *guru*. The example appears again in the context of explaining the proper order of the names of Rādhā and Kṛṣṇa:

> [Whoever] first pronounces "Rādhā" and afterwards "Kṛṣṇa, the Supreme,"
> He indeed is a learned yogin and goes easily to Goloka.
> A great sinner, in reversing the order, commits [as it were] the murder of a Brahman.
> You [Rādhā] are the mother of the world; the Supreme Self Hari is the father.
> The *guru* of the father is the mother, to be worshipped and honored [as] supreme.[56]

It is in her role as maternal mediatrix that Rādhā comes closest to attaining supremacy over Kṛṣṇa in our Purāṇa.

[55] E.g., PKh 34.7:
pituḥ śataguṇā mātā gauraveṇātiricyate/
mātuḥ śataguṇaiḥ pūjyo jñānadātā guruḥ prabho//
Cf. PKh 30.189.

[56] *ādau rādhāṃ samuccārya paścāt kṛṣṇaṃ parātparam//*
sa eva paṇḍito yogī golokaṃ yāti līlayā/
vyatikrame mahāpāpī brahmahatyāṃ labhed dhruvam//
jagatāṃ bhavatī mātā paramātmā pitā hariḥ/
pitur eva gurur mātā pūjyā vandyā parātparā// (KJKh 124.9–11)
Cf. NārPR II.6.6–7:
ādau samuccared rādhāṃ paścāt kṛṣṇaṃ ca mādhavam/
viparītaṃ yadi paṭhet brahmahatyāṃ labhed dhruvam//
śrīkṛṣṇo jagatām tāto jaganmātā ca rādhikā/
pituḥ śataguṇe mātā vandyā pūjyā garīyasī//

PART D

CONCLUSION

11

Some Final Considerations on the *Brahmavaivarta Purāṇa*

The development of Rādhāism in North India may be said to have followed two general paths: one in which Rādhā is regarded not as Kṛṣṇa's wife but as *parakīyā* (unmarried, or wed to another), the other in which she is regarded as *svakīyā* (Kṛṣṇa's own wife). For those who espoused the *parakīyā* ideal, *svakīyā* or conjugal love was not intense enough, for long familiarity with a spouse erodes the mystery of love, taking with it the unrestrained passion for the beloved. Further, it was felt that *parakīyā* love alone can be free of consideration for worldly ties and conventions, and thus is the highest and purest love.[1] The *parakīyā* interpretation of Rādhā's and Kṛṣṇa's love predominated in late Bengal Vaiṣṇavism. It was accepted by some "orthodox" Vaiṣṇavas, and especially by the Tāntric Vaiṣṇavas or Sahajiyās. The Tāntrics tended to view social-moral laws as restrictive, binding man to the mundane level, and thus it was natural for the Sahajiyās to propound the ideal of illicit love. For those who favored the *svakīyā* ideal, *parakīyā* love was seen as *kāma* (selfish desire), rather than as *preman* (self-surrendering love).[2]

When Rādhā is conceived as a symbol of the human soul longing for God, the question of her marital status is significant, for

[1] Cf. Dimock, "Doctrine and Practice among the Vaiṣṇavas of Bengal," *Krishna: Myths, Rites, and Attitudes*, pp. 56–63; Sh. Dasgupta, *Obscure Religious Cults*, pp. 124–125. Dasgupta makes the mystifying statement that Rādhā is never depicted as Kṛṣṇa's wife in any legend. He apparently was not very familiar with the BVP.

[2] Cf. Vaudeville, "Evolution of Love-symbolism in Bhagavatism," JAOS, LXXXII, 31–40.

her own love serves as a model for all men. When she is regarded as a goddess, this question in some ways becomes less crucial, especially when man's relation to her is conceived in terms of *dāsya*. In this instance, her relationship to Kṛṣṇa no longer directly affects man. Yet in Tāntric views, Rādhā as the Divine Feminine is manifest in all female beings and Kṛṣṇa in all male beings. Here the relationship of the supreme pair again directly affects man's devotional attitudes and conduct.

The BVP, as we have seen, clearly portrays Rādhā as *svakīyā*, as in KJKh 15, where her marriage to Kṛṣṇa is described.[3] Two points may be made with regard to Rādhā's *svakīyā* status in the BVP. First, our Purāṇa, though taking over many Tāntric notions, as in the view that every woman is an *aṃśa* of Rādhā and every man of Kṛṣṇa, holds in high respect social-moral law and condemns the path of the Vāmācārins, thereby rejecting the ideal of adulterine love. Second, even the BVP's acceptance of the Tāntric idea of a "human-divine unity" is qualified by a dualistic view of man and the Absolute. This dualism is conceived in terms of a parent-child relationship, Rādhā and Kṛṣṇa being the mother and father of all creatures. It would seem that Rādhā's maternal role more easily harmonizes with a *svakīyā* than a *parakīyā* status.

Regarding the significance of the BVP for later religious movements, little can be said with certainty. It seems unlikely that the Purāṇa, despite its Tāntric legacy, would have been favorably received by the Vaiṣṇava Sahajiyās, with their espousal of the *parakīyā* ideal. The influence of the BVP was probably much greater in those Vaiṣṇava circles which adhered to the *svakīyā* ideal, as in the Vallabha school.

We have already remarked that Rādhā occupied no place in the teachings of Vallabha himself.[4] Von Glasenapp writes:

> Die Gestalt der Rādhā . . . spielt in Vallabhas philosophischem System keine Rolle, im Gegensatz zu denjenigen der Schule des Caitanya und anderer Meister. . . . Vallabhas Sohn Viṭṭhaleśvara feiert Rādhā hingegen als die svāminī in einer Anzahl von Werken; es ist möglich, dass sein Rādhākult unter dem Einfluss der Anhänger Caitanyas entstanden ist,

[3] Further, the BVP discounts the view that Rādhā belongs to another, i.e. Rāyāṇa. On the one hand, it is held that Rāyāṇa is not really other than Kṛṣṇa but an *aṃśa* of him; on the other, it is said that only a *chāyā* (illusory image) of Rādhā is married to Rāyāṇa. See above, p. 22, note 10.

[4] See above, p. 28.

mit denen er während seines Aufenthalts in Purī zusammentraf.[5]

It is possible that Viṭṭhaleśvara and other Vallabhācārins were influenced not only by the followers of Caitanya, but also by the BVP. Farquhar says that according to the theology of the sect, "From Kṛishṇa's side springs Rādhā, and from the pores of the skin of Kṛishṇa and Rādhā come millions of gopās and gopīs and also cattle. . . ."[6] Farquhar's source was apparently a modern follower of Vallabha. In any case, the above notions are almost identical with those of the BVP. We may also mention the poetry of Sūr Dās, the greatest of the *aṣṭchāp,* or "eight seals" of the sect. Sūr Dās writes:

> Kṛṣṇa said to Rādhā—"By living in Braj you have forgotten yourself. Know that Prakṛti and Puruṣa are the same; there is a difference only in words. . . . We have two bodies but the soul is the same. I created you for the sake of joy."[7]

And similarly (Rādhā speaking):

> Why did I forget that we are Prakṛti and Puruṣa, and that I am the wife and he is the husband. . . . It is only a new acquaintance . . . this sport goes on birth after birth and age after age.[8]

The identification of Puruṣa and Prakṛti with Kṛṣṇa and Rādhā in the poems of Sūr Dās reflects the same basic view as the BVP.

There is, of course, the question as to whether there was any direct connection between the Vallabha school and the BVP, for both may have drawn upon a common store of legends and ideas concerning Rādhā and Kṛṣṇa. Further, it is still unclear whether the BVP is older than the school of Vallabha. My feeling is that it is. In any event, it seems very doubtful that the BVP was the work of the followers of Vallabha. The BVP lacks much of the technical terminology of Vallabha's school. The term "*puṣṭi*" in the sense of "grace," for instance, so far as I know, does not occur in the Purāṇa. There are also differences on various theological-devotional matters, such as the role of the nine marks of *bhakti.*[9]

The Caitanya school in its early period, it seems, also favored

[5] *Von Buddha zu Gandhi,* pp. 238–239.
[6] *Outline,* p. 314.
[7] Quoted by Misra in *The Religious Poetry of Sūrdās,* pp. 87–88.
[8] Quoted in *ibid.,* p. 88.
[9] See above, p. 83.

the *svakīyā* ideal. This is the view, apparently, of the two great Gosvāmins, Rūpa and Jīva.[10] Yet regarding the relation of the Caitanya school and the BVP, De writes: "The Caitanya movement in Bengal . . . does not appear to have accepted the *Brahmavaivarta* Purāṇa as canonical. Its chief scripture was the *Śrīmad-bhāgavata*. . . . Its glorification of the Rādhā-legend need not of itself connect it with the *Brahmavaivarta*, to which it seldom refers."[11] It would seem that when the Caitanya followers do refer to the BVP, it is to the earlier rather than the extant Purāṇa. In the course of this study, we have seen significant differences between the BVP and the doctrines of the Caitanya school, but also many similarities. In general, the BVP seems closer to the Caitanya school than to the Vallabhas.

Two final sects that should be mentioned in connection with the BVP are the Rādhāvallabhins and the Sakhībhavas. The Rādhāvallabhins are worshippers of Rādhāvallabha, the beloved of Rādhā or Kṛṣṇa. In their actual devotions, Rādhā plays the more important role. Wilson, in explaining the doctrines of the Rādhāvallabhins, resorted mainly to accounts of Rādhā and Kṛṣṇa from the BVP.[12] Wilson seems to suggest that the doctrines of the sect are based upon the Purāṇa, though this is not explicitly stated. Farquhar quotes a modern follower of the sect who says: "Kṛishṇa is the servant of Rādhā. He may do the coolie-work of building the world, but Rādhā sits as Queen. He is at best her Secretary of State. We win the favour of Kṛishṇa by worshipping Rādhā."[13] The last statement in particular reflects the attitude of the BVP. The sect was founded by Hari Vaṃśa at Vṛndāvana in 1585. It seems almost certain that the BVP was compiled before this time, so that it is certainly reasonable to suppose that the BVP had some influence on the sect.[14]

The Sakhībhavas, an offshoot of the Rādhāvallabhins, held as the supreme goal becoming a *sakhī* or companion of Rādhā.[15]

[10] Cf. De, VFM, pp. 154–155, 264–266, 310–312; Dimock, *The Place of the Hidden Moon,* pp. 201–202, and "Doctrine and Practice among the Vaiṣṇavas of Bengal," *Krishna: Myths, Rites, and Attitudes,* pp. 55–56.

[11] VFM, p. 10.

[12] *Sects,* pp. 173–177. Cf. Grierson, "Rādhāvallabhīs," ERE, X, 559–560.

[13] *Outline,* p. 318.

[14] Little has been written on the Rādhāvallabhīs. Aside from works already mentioned, one important contribution is Growse's *Mathurá,* pp. 199–216, which includes translations of Hari Vaṃśa's own writings.

[15] Cf. Wilson, *Sects,* pp. 177–178; Bhandarkar, *Vaiṣṇavism, Śaivism,* p. 86.

Accordingly, members assumed female dress and manners and affected to experience the monthly cycle. Bhandarkar concludes his brief consideration of the Sakhībhavas by saying: "They deserve notice here only to show that, when the female element is idolised and made the object of special worship, such disgusting corruptions must ensue. The worship of Durgā in the form of Tripurasundarī has led to the same result."[16] One might ponder, however, whether "idolisation" of the male element has not also led to what Bhandarkar would regard as "disgusting corruptions." In any case, it is certainly questionable whether such "corruptions" are an inevitable result of worshipping the female element. The BVP, at least, gives no support to the notion of men adopting the manners of women. The Sakhībhavas may well owe more to the PadP, which states that one should consider oneself to be a young, beautiful woman, a companion of Rādhā, intent on her service, holding her in greater affection than Kṛṣṇa.[17]

In summary, it seems that the role of the BVP in later devotional movements, despite its possible influence on the Vallabhas and other sects, is rather limited, especially when compared to that of the BhP. We may recall, though, that the BVP did exert significant influence on some late Sanskrit works, such as the DBhP. It nonetheless appears that the BVP, historically, is more important as a reflection of particular developments in North India in the fifteenth and sixteenth centuries than as a molder of religious attitudes in its own right.[18]

[16] *Vaiṣṇavism, Śaivism,* p. 86.

[17] *ātmānaṃ cintayet tatra tāsāṃ madhye manoramām/*
rūpayauvanasampannāṃ kśoriṃ pramadākṛtim//
. . . .
rādhikānucarīṃ nityaṃ tat sevanaparāyanām/
kṛṣṇād apy adhikaṃ prema rādhikāyāṃ prakurvatīm//
(PadP V.83.7 and 9)

[18] The relative neglect of the BVP by the Hindu community is perhaps indicated by the apparent scarcity of translations of the Purāṇa into the Prakrits. V. Raghavan, in an article, "Tamil Versions of the Purāṇas," surveys the main Purāṇas rendered into Tamil. The BVP is not included in his survey. (*Purāṇa,* II, 225–242. Cf. Dikshitar, "The Purāṇas: A Study," IHQ, VIII, 765.) Similarly, in an article on "Telugu Versions of the Purāṇas," K. V. Ramakoti lists Telugu translations of all major Purāṇas (in part or whole), except for the BVP. (*Purāṇa,* IV, 384–407.) Ramakoti, though, apparently was unaware of the Telugu version of the first three *khaṇḍas* of the BVP, listed in L. D. Barnett's *A Supplementary Catalogue of the Sanskrit, Pali, and Prakrit Books in the Library of the British Museum,* p. 795. The date of the translation, according to the *Catalogue,* is 1905.

APPENDIX A

PARALLEL PASSAGES FROM THE PKh AND DBhP IX

In Chapter 2 on the history of the BVP, we stated that the DBhP in its ninth *skandha* has borrowed from the PKh and not vice versa. To confirm this view and to show the nature of the changes made by the DBhP, we have placed in parallel a few selected passages from each text. It will be seen that the DBhP in many cases has emphasized and further elaborated the feminine aspects of the theology of the PKh, raising the Goddess not only to soteriological and cosmological, but to ontological supremacy as well.

Before beginning with the text parallels, we may note another kind of evidence strongly suggesting that the DBhP has borrowed from the PKh. In the PKh, the main interlocutors of the account are Nārāyaṇa and Nārada. The BVP as a whole, though, is narrated to Śaunaka by Sauti (or Sūta), who had learned the Purāṇa from Vyāsa, the pupil of Nārada, the pupil of Nārāyaṇa. In the PKh, then, it is actually Sauti who narrates to Śaunaka the conversation of Nārada and Nārāyaṇa. Occasionally, the PKh refers to Sauti and Śaunaka as the final interlocutors, as in PKh 6.11. These references to Sauti (or Sūta) and Śaunaka also appear in the DBhP, as in IX.6.11. Yet the chain of interlocutors in the DBhP is somewhat different from that of the BVP. To be sure, in the DBhP, Sūta and Śaunaka (or his fellow sages) are the final interlocutors, as seen in I.1.2. In DBhP II. 12.1 ff., Sūta begins to narrate the conversation of Vyāsa and Janamejaya. In VIII.1.5 ff., Vyāsa begins to narrate the conversation of Nārada and Nārāyaṇa, who are the main speakers in *skandhas* VIII and IX. The chain of interlocutors in the two Purāṇas, then, may be schematized as follows:

BVP		DBhP			
Nārāyaṇa	Nārada		Nārāyaṇa	Nārada	
	Sauti	Śaunaka		Vyāsa	Janamejaya
				Sūta	Śaunaka

In DBhP IX, the middle pair of interlocutors, Vyāsa and Janamejaya, has been completely forgotten. Accordingly, it appears as though Sūta were directly relating to Śaunaka the conversation of Nārāyaṇa and Nārada. The apparent disregard of Vyāsa and Janamejaya seems to be most easily explained on the supposition that the DBhP has borrowed from the PKh, and in the process took over the latter's interlocutory framework.

Let us now turn to the text parallels. Italics indicate interesting or significant differences between the two texts.

1. On the Supreme Reality

Both passages below relate that the various goddesses attained their exalted positions by devotion to and knowledge of the Supreme Reality. The two passages thus begin with a description of that Reality, as *paramātman, paraṃ brahman,* and so forth. In PKh 7.83cd, this Reality is specifically identified with Kṛṣṇa. In the DBhP parallel, Kṛṣṇa is not mentioned; rather, the *paramātman* is said to bear the form of *sat, cit,* and *ānanda.* In DBhP 8.88ab, we see that Mahāmāyā, or Prakṛti, is identified with *sat, cit,* and *ānanda,* i.e., with *paraṃ brahman.* This verse is missing in the PKh. The DBhP has almost certainly added 88ab, for the surrounding verses, 87cd and 88cd, nearly identical with the PKh, subordinate Prakṛti to Brahman. Later, the DBhP derives the status and privileges of the goddesses from their worship of Śakti or Devī, in contrast to the PKh, which derives them ultimately from Kṛṣṇa. The DBhP, therefore, seems to retain much of the PKh framework, but with alterations to fit its own, more extreme feminine theological viewpoint.

PKh 7.83cd ff.	DBhP IX.8.79 ff.
sarveṣāṃ paramātmā ca *śrīkṛṣṇaḥ prakṛteḥ paraḥ*//83	id.* *saccidānandarūpadhṛk*/79
. . . .	. . . .
svecchāmayaṃ paraṃ brahma nirliptaṃ nirguṇaṃ param//87	id. nirguṇaṃ prakṛteḥ param//83

* DBhP lines that are identical to the PKh parallel will be indicated by "id."

mahāmāyā ca prakṛtiḥ sarvaśaktimatīśvarī/	id. sarvaśaktimayīśvarī//87 *saiva proktā bhagavatī* *saccidānandarūpiṇī/*
yaj-[parabrahma-] jñānād yasya tapasā yadbhaktyā yasya sevayā//93	id. id. id. //88
yeṣāṃ yā yāś ca devyo vai pūjitās *tasya* [kṛṣṇasya] *sevayā*/107	anyā yā yāś ca tā devyaḥ pūjitaḥ *śaktisevayā*//100
durgā ca *tat*-[kṛṣṇa-]*padaṃ* *dhyātvā* sarvapūjyā babhūva ha//108	durgā ca *tat*-[śakti-]*padaṃ* *dhyātvā* id. /102
lakṣmīr yugaśataṃ divyaṃ tapas taptvā ca puṣkare/ sarvasampatpradātrī sā *cābhavat tasya* [kṛṣṇasya] *sevayā*//110	id. id. //103 sarvasampatpradātrī ca *jātā devīniṣevaṇāt*/104

2. On types of devotees and their rewards after death

In the following parallels, we see that the DBhP has tended to delete mention of Viṣṇu and Vaiṣṇavas. Thus the DBhP, in 29.26b, does not specify as Viṣṇu's the supreme heaven, from which there is no return. The DBhP adds a new verse (34), in which the land of no return is identified with Maṇidvīpa, the heaven of Mūlaprakṛti. That this is an addition on the part of the DBhP and not a deletion on the part of the PKh is indicated by the fact that the DBhP knows of both Goloka and Maṇidvīpa, while the PKh knows only of Goloka. Had the PKh compiler borrowed from the DBhP, it seems unlikely that he would never mention Maṇidvīpa. He would, I think, have been inclined to include, and if necessary to subordinate, but not to disregard entirely, the heaven of the Devī. Further, in the DBhP passage itself, the present position of verse 34 seems not entirely appropriate, since the surrounding verses are dealing with the various heavens from which there is return.

We may also note the differences in verses 37 and 38 of each text. The PKh version may be translated as follows:

> Brahmans who are Haribhaktas and free of desire, [although] abandoning their own duties,

Even they go to Hari's world eventually, on the strength of their *bhakti!*
Brahmans who always serve other gods, [if] abandoning their own duties,
Have their good conduct destroyed, and such fools surely go to hell.

The DBhP has lost the "punch" of these verses by altering 37 to read:

> Brahmans who are Haribhaktas and free of desire, *and devoted to their own duties,*
> They go to Hari's world eventually, on the strength of their *bhakti!*

PKh 26.25cd ff.	DBhP IX.29.24cd ff.
niṣkāmaś ca sakāmaś ca	id.
vaiṣṇavo dvividhaḥ sati//25	*brahmaṇo* dvividhaḥ sati//24
sakāmaś ca pradhānaś ca	sakāmāc ca pradhānaś ca
niṣkāmo bhakta eva ca/	id. /
karmabhogī sakāmaś ca	id.
niṣkāmo nirupadravaḥ//26	id. //25
sa yāti dehaṃ tyaktvā ca	id.
padaṃ *viṣṇor* nirāmayam/	padaṃ *yat tan* nirāmayam/
punarāgamanaṃ nāsti	id.
teṣāṃ niṣkāmināṃ sati//27	id. //26
ye sevante ca dvibhujaṃ	sevante dvibhujaṃ kṛṣṇaṃ
kṛṣṇam ātmānam īśvaram/	paramātmānam īśvaram/
golokaṃ yānti te bhaktā	golokaṃ prati te bhaktā
divyarūpavidhāriṇaḥ//28	id. //27
....	....
svadharmaniratā viprāḥ	id.
sūryabhaktāś ca bhārate/	id. /
vrajanti sūryalokaṃ te	vrajanti te sūryalokaṃ
punar āyānti bhāratam//34	punar āyānti bharate//33
	mūlaprakṛtibhaktā ye
	niṣkāmā dharmacariṇaḥ/
	maṇidvīpaṃ prayānty eva
	punarāvṛttivarjitam//34
svadharmaniratā viprāḥ	svadharmaniratā bhaktāḥ
śaivāḥ śāktāś ca gāṇapāḥ/	id. /
te yānti śivalokaṃ ca	id.
punar āyānti bhāratam//35	punar āyānti bhārate//35
ye viprā anyadeveṣṭāḥ	ye viprā anyadevejyāḥ
svadharmaniratāḥ sati/	id. /

te gatvā śakralokaṃ ca	te yānti sarvalokaṃ ca
punar āyānti bhāratam//36	punar āyānti bhārate//36
haribhaktāś ca niṣkāmāḥ	id.
svadharmarahitā dvijāḥ/	*svadharmaniratā* dvijāḥ/
te 'pi yānti harer lokaṃ	*te ca* yānti harer lokaṃ
kramād bhaktibalād aho//37	id. //37
svadharmarahitā viprā	id.
devānyasevinaḥ sadā/	devānyasevanāḥ sadā/
bhraṣṭācārāś ca bālāś ca	bhraṣṭācārāś ca kāmāś ca
te yānti narakaṃ dhruvam//38	id. //38

3. On the two kinds of *mukti,* or *bhakti,* along with an identification of the Supreme

As we have seen in chapter 6, *bhakti* and *mukti* are in part identical. In the following parallel passages, the DBhP speaks of *bhakti,* the PKh of *mukti.* Yet in the context, the DBhP account is perhaps not wholly congruous, for it makes *nirvāṇa,* in which there is no duality, no master and servant, a form of *bhakti,* rather than of *mukti.* Further, in DBhP 29.19, the notion that *bhakti* is one of the two forms of *bhakti* seems a bit redundant. Of special interest in DBhP 28.11ab is the identification of *bhagavān* with *parātmā prakṛtiḥ parā,* instead of with *śrīkṛṣṇaḥ prakṛteḥ paraḥ.*

PKh 25.10 ff.	DBhP IX.28.8cd ff.
muktiś ca dvividhā sādhvi	*bhaktiś* ca dvividhā sādhvi
śrutyuktā sarvasammatā/	id. //8
nirvāṇapadadātrī ca	id.
haribhaktipradā nṛṇām//10	harirūpapradā nṛṇām/
haribhaktisvarūpāṃ ca	harirūpasvarūpāṃ ca
muktiṃ vañcchanti vaiṣṇavāḥ/	*bhaktiṃ* vañcchanti vaiṣṇavāḥ //9
anye nirvāṇarūpāṃ ca	anye nirvāṇam icchanti
muktim icchanti sādhavaḥ//11	yogino brahmavittamāḥ/
karmaṇo bījarūpaś ca	id.
santataṃ tatphalapradaḥ/	satataṃ tatphalapradaḥ//10
karmarūpaś ca bhagavāñ	karmarūpaś ca bhagavān
chrīkṛṣṇaḥ prakṛteḥ paraḥ//12	*parātmā prakṛtiḥ parā*/11

PKh 26.19cd-20ab	DBhP IX.29.19
karmanirmūlane *muktiḥ*	karmanirmūlane *bhaktiḥ*
sā coktā dvividhā matā//19	sā coktā dvividhā sati/
nirvāṇarūpā sevā ca	nirvāṇarūpā bhaktiś ca
kṛṣṇasya paramātmanaḥ/20	*brahmaṇaḥ prakṛter iha*//19

4. On cosmic manifestation and dissolution

In our chapter on Prakṛti's cosmogonic roles, we saw that according to the PKh, Kṛṣṇa, in the beginning, divides into two, becoming male (*puruṣa* or *puṃs*) and female (*prakṛti* or *strī*). Afterwards, Kṛṣṇa becomes two-armed and four-armed in Goloka and Vaikuṇṭha respectively. In DBhP IX.8.80, however, Kṛṣṇa, half man and half woman, is said to arise from the splendor of Prakṛti! Further, it is she, identified with Kṛṣṇa, who becomes twofold, in the two-armed and four-armed manifestations (8.81). According to the PKh, in dissolution, everything merges back into Kṛṣṇa, including Prakṛti. The various goddesses dissolve into the parts of Kṛṣṇa's body from which they arose, as Durgā into his *buddhi*. The DBhP still preserves something of this scheme (see 8.72cd–74ab and 38.55cd–56ab). But the DBhP, in *adhyāya* 38, has added verses 67cd-69, in which Kṛṣṇa is said to dissolve finally into Prakṛti! Finally, we may note that in PKh 7.78cd, dissolution is said to occur in an eye-wink of Kṛṣṇa, in DBhP 8.75ab, in an eye-wink of Devī.

PKh 7.76 ff.	DBhP IX.8.72cd ff.
pralayaḥ prākṛto jñeyas	id.
tatrādṛṣṭā vasundharā/	id. //72
jalaplutāni viśvāni	id.
brahmaviṣṇuśivādayaḥ//76	id. /
ṛṣayo jīvinaḥ sarve	ṛṣayo jñāninaḥ sarve
līnāḥ *kṛṣṇe parātpare*/	līnāḥ *satye cidātmani*//73
tatraiva prakṛtir līnā	id.
tena prākṛtiko layaḥ//77	tatra prākṛtiko layaḥ/
laye prākṛtike 'tīte	laye prākṛtike jate
pāte ca brahmaṇo mune/	id. //74
nimeṣamātraḥ kālaś ca	nimeṣamātraṃ kālaś ca
kṛṣṇasya paramātmanaḥ//78	*śrīdevyāḥ procyate mune*/
evaṃ naśyanti sarvāṇi	id.
brahmāṇḍāny akhilāni ca/	id. //75
sthitau golokavaikuṇṭhau	
śrīkṛṣṇaś ca sapārṣadaḥ//79	
nimeṣamātraḥ pralayo	
yatra viśvaṃ jalaplutam/	
nimeṣānantare kāle	nimeṣāntarakālena
punaḥ sṛṣṭiḥ krameṇa ca//80	punaḥ sṛṣṭikrameṇa ca/76
. . . .	. . . .
brahmāṇḍānāṃ ca sarveṣām	
īśvaraś caika eva saḥ/	
sarveṣāṃ paramātmā ca	id.
śrīkṛṣṇaḥ prakṛteḥ paraḥ//83	*saccidānandarūpadhṛk*/

brahmādayaś ca tasyāṃśas	id.
tasyāṃśaś ca mahāvirāṭ/	id. //79
tasyāṃśaś ca virāṭ kṣudras	tasyāṃśaś ca virāṭ kṣudraḥ
tasyāṃśā prakṛtiḥ smṛtā//84	*saiveyaṃ prakṛtiḥ parā*/
	tasyāḥ sa kāśāt saṃjāto
	'py ardhanārīśvaras[1]*tataḥ*//80
sa ca kṛṣṇo dvidhābhūto	*saiva* kṛṣṇo dvividhābhūto
dvibhujaś ca caturbhujaḥ/	id. /
caturbhujaś ca vaikuṇṭhe	id.
goloke dvibhujaḥ svayam//85	id. //81
	....
	mahāmāyā ca prakṛtiḥ
	sarvaśaktimayīśvarī//87

PKh 34.56cd ff.	DBhP IX.38.52 ff.
brahmaṇaś ca nipāte vai	brahmaṇaś ca nipāte ca
cakṣur unmīlanaṃ hareḥ//56	id. /
cakṣur nimīlane tasya	cakṣur unmīlane tasya
layaṃ prākṛtikaṃ viduḥ/	id. //52
pralaye prākṛtāḥ sarve	pralaye prākṛte sarve
devādyāś ca carācarāḥ//57	id. /
līnā dhātari dhātā ca	līnā dhātā vidhātā ca
śrīkṛṣṇe nābhipaṅkaje/	śrīkṛṣṇanābhipaṅkaje//53
viṣṇuḥ kṣīrodaśāyī ca	id.
vaikuṇṭhe yaś caturbhujaḥ//58	id. /
vilīnā vāmapārśve ca	vilīno vāmapārśve ca
kṛṣṇasya paramātmanaḥ/	id. //54
rudrādyā bhairavādyāś ca	
yāvantaś ca śivānugāḥ//59	
śivādhāre śive līnā	
jñānānande sanātane/	
jñānādhidevaḥ kṛṣṇasya	
mahādevasya cātmanaḥ//60	
tasya jñāne vilīnaś ca	yasya jñāne śivo līno
babhūvātha kṣaṇaṃ hareh/	jñānādhīśaḥ sanātanaḥ/
durgāyāṃ viṣṇumāyāyāṃ	id.
vilīnāḥ sarvaśaktayaḥ//61	id. //55
sā ca kṛṣṇasya buddhau ca	id.
buddhyadhiṣṭhātṛdevatā/	id. /
nārāyaṇāṃśaḥ skandaś ca	id.
līno vakṣasi tasya ca//62	id. //56

[1] This term is often applied to the androgynous form of Śiva. See Ingalls, *An Anthology of Sanskrit Court Poetry*, pp. 70, 150.

śrīkṛṣṇāṃśaś ca tadbāhau	id.
devādhīśo gaṇeśvaraḥ/	id. /
padmāṃśabhūtā padmāyāṃ	padmāṃśāś caiva padmāyāṃ
sā rādhāyāṃ ca suvrate//63	id. //57
gopyaś cāpi ca tasyāṃ ca	id.
sarvā vai devayoṣitaḥ/	sarvāś ca devayoṣitaḥ/
kṛṣṇaprāṇādhidevī sā	id.
tasya prāṇeṣu sā sthitā//64	tasya prāṇeṣu saṃsthitā//58
sāvitrī ca sarasvatyāṃ	id.
vedaśāstrāṇi yāni ca/	vedāḥ śāstrāṇī yāni ca/
sthitā[2] vāṇī ca jihvāyāṃ	id.
tasyaiva paramātmanaḥ//65	id. //59
golokasthasya gopāś ca	golokasya ca gopāś ca
vilīnās tasya lomasu/	id. /
tatprāṇeṣu ca sarveṣāṃ	id.
prāṇā vātā hutāśanaḥ//66	prāṇavātāhutāśanāḥ//60
jatarāgnau vilīnaś ca	jatarāgnau vilīnāś ca
jalaṃ tadrasanāgrataḥ/	id. /
vaiṣṇavāś caraṇāmbhoje	id.
paramānandasaṃyutāḥ//67	id. //61
sārātsāratarā bhakti-	id.
rasapīyūṣapāyinaḥ/	id. /
virāṭ kṣudraś ca mahati	virāḍaṃśāś ca mahati
līnaḥ kṛṣṇe mahān virāṭ//68	līnāḥ kṛṣṇe mahāvirāṭ//62
yasyaiva lomakūpeṣu	id.
viśvāni nikhilāni ca/	id. /
yasya cakṣunimeṣeṇa	yasya cakṣuṣa unmeṣe
mahāṃś ca pralayo bhavet//69	prākṛtaḥ pralayo bhavet//63
cakṣurunmīlane sṛṣṭir	id.
yasyaiva paramātmanaḥ/	yasyaiva punar eva saḥ/
yāvan nimeṣe sṛṣṭis syāt	yāvat kālo nimeṣeṇa
tāvad unmīlane vyayaḥ//70	tāvad unmīlanena ca//64
brahmaṇaś ca śatābdena	brahmaṇaś ca śatābde ca
sṛṣṭis tatra layaḥ punaḥ/	sṛṣṭeḥ sūtralayaḥ punaḥ/
brahmasṛṣṭilayānāṃ ca	id.
saṃkhyā nāsty eva suvrate//71	id. //65
yathā bhūrajasāṃ caiva	id.
saṃkhyāṇaṃ ca niśāmaya/	saṃkhyānaṃ naiva vidyate/
cakṣurnimeṣe pralayo	id.
yasya sarvāntarātmanaḥ//72	id. //66
unmīlane punaḥ sṛṣṭir	id.
bhaved eveśvarecchayā/	id. /

[2] Veṅk has misprinted an extra *sthitā*.

	sa kṛṣṇaḥ pralaye tasyāṃ *prakṛtau līna eva hi*//67
	ekaiva ca parā śaktir *nirguṇaḥ paramaḥ pumān*/ *sad evedam agra āsīd* *iti vedavido viduḥ*//68
	mūlaprakṛtir avyaktā *'py avyākṛtapadābhidhā*/ *cidabhinnatvam āpannā* *pralaye saiva tiṣṭhati*//69
tadguṇotkīrtanaṃ vaktuṃ brahmāṇḍeṣu ca kaḥ kṣamaḥ //73	id. id. /70

APPENDIX B

VERBAL SIMILARITIES BETWEEN *BRAHMA KHAṆḌA* 3 AND *PRAKṚTI KHAṆḌA* 2.54–90 IN THE DESCRIPTION OF DEITIES

As indicated in our chapter on Prakṛti's cosmogonic role,[1] PKh 2.54–90 is evidently based on BKh 3–4. Therefore, in the following columns, verses from the BKh are in their proper order, and the corresponding PKh verses placed in parallel. The PKh verses are thus often not in order. Italics indicate identical wording.

As for the nature of the similarities and identities of the two texts, it should be pointed out that certain epithets and descriptions of the deities are quite standard, and thus the use of the same phrases in some instances would not necessarily prove the dependence of one text upon the other. However, it seems here that there are too many such identities, as well as over-all similarity of the passages involved, for there not to be some more direct connection. It is of course possible, as already mentioned, that the PKh borrowed from an earlier version of BKh 3–4, or itself has been somewhat modified.

In any case, it is clear that the PKh in general is the borrower, and not the other way around. Most obviously, BKh 3–4 has no reference to Rādhā, and is therefore probably the older text. This is also suggested by certain details in the two texts. In the description of Durgā, in the BKh she is called "hundred-armed," in the PKh, "thousand-armed." It seems doubtful that the author of the PKh would have been willing to diminish, rather than expand, the greatness of Durgā, as symbolized by the number of her arms. Further, the list of Durgā's

[1] See pp. 156–158 above.

several weapons appearing in the BKh is summarized in the PKh by the one word *nānā*. To be sure, one could argue that *nānā* had been expanded and made more specific by the BKh. But throughout our Purāṇa, the interest in weaponry, as in the GKh, belongs to a layer older than that of the final recast, which is more concerned with specifically theological problems. It would thus be more likely for the list of weapons to have been abbreviated than expanded. In the description of Śiva, the BKh says he is naked; the PKh also says Śiva is naked, but elsewhere states that he is dressed in a tiger skin. This latter statement must surely be an addition to the original. One final feature may be noted. In the description of Sarasvatī, the PKh begins apparently by following the BKh, but then the last part of the BKh's description is taken over for Brahmā's wife, Sāvitrī.

DESCRIPTION OF ŚIVA

BKh 3	PKh 2
śuddhasphaṭikasaṃkāśaḥ	*śuddhasphaṭikasaṃkāśaḥ* 85a
pañcavaktro digambaraḥ// 18	*pañcavaktreṇa* 88a; *digambaraḥ*
	87a
	vyāghracarmadharo haraḥ//85
taptakāñcanavarṇābha-	*taptakāñcanavarṇābha-*
jaṭābhāradharo varaḥ/	*jaṭābhāradharaḥ* paraḥ/86
īṣaddhāsyaprasannāsyas	(Cf. description of Durgā, 69c)
trinetraś candraśekharaḥ// 19	*sasmitaś candraśekharaḥ//* 86
triśūlapaṭṭīśadharo	*triśūlapaṭṭīśadharo* 85c
	bibhrad dakṣiṇahastena
japamālākraḥ paraḥ/ 20	*ratnamālāṃ susaṃskṛtām//* 87
mṛtyor mṛtyur īśvaraś ca	saṃstūya mṛtyor mṛtyuṃ taṃ
	[kṛṣṇaṃ]
mṛtyur mṛtyuñjayaḥ śivaḥ/ 21	jāto *mṛtyuñjayā*bhidaḥ/
ratnasiṃhāsane vare/27	*ratnasiṃhāsane* ramye
nārāyaṇaṃ ca sambhāṣya	
sa uvāsa tadājñayā//27	samuvāsa hareḥ puraḥ//90

DESCRIPTION OF BRAHMĀ

āvirbabhūva tatpaścāt	nissasāra pumān mune//80
kṛṣṇasya *nābhi*paṅkajāt/	padmanābho *nābhi*padmān 80c
mahā*tapasvī* vṛddhaś ca	*tapasvī* jñānināṃ varaḥ/81
*kamaṇḍalu*karo varaḥ//30	*kamaṇḍalu*dharaḥ śrīmāns 81a
śuklakeśaś *caturmukhaḥ*/31	*caturmukhas* taṃ [kṛṣṇaṃ]
	tuṣṭāva 81c

ratnasiṃhāsane varam/	*ratnasiṃhāsane* ramye 83a
nārāyaṇeśau sambhāṣya	
sa uvāsa tadājñayā//38	uvāsa svāminā sārddhaṃ 83c [The subject of this verse is Brahmā's wife. Cf. the NārP parallel verses in Appendix C, in which Brahmā is the subject. NārP I.83. 22cd reads:
	niṣasādāsane ramye vibhos [kṛṣṇasya] tasyājñayā mune//]

Description of Sarasvatī

ekā devī	āvirbabhūva kanyaikā
śuklavarṇā	*śuklavarṇā* manoharā//54
vīṇāpustakadhāriṇī//54	*vīṇāpustakadhāriṇī*/55
vahniśuddhāṃśukādhānā	*vahniśuddhāṃśukādhānā*[2]
ratnabhūṣaṇabhūṣitā//55	*ratnabhūṣaṇabhūṣitā*//82
sasmitā *sudatī* śyāmā	*sudatī*
sundarīṇāṃ ca *sundarī*/56	*sundarī*
śreṣṭhā śrutīnāṃ śāstrāṇām 56c	*śreṣṭhā* 82a

Description of Durgā

sarv*ādhiṣṭhātṛdevī sā*	buddhy*adhiṣṭhātṛdevī sā* 67c
mūlaprakṛtir īśvarī//70	*mūlaprakṛtir īśvarī*/68b
taptakāñcanavarṇābhā	*taptakāñcanavarṇābhā*
sūryakoṭisamaprabhā/71	*sūryakoṭisamaprabhā*/69
īṣaddhāsyaprasannāsyā 71c	*īṣaddhāsyaprasannāsyā*[3] 69c
nidrā tṛṣṇā *kṣut pipāsā*	*kṣut pipāsā* dayā śraddhā
dayā śraddhā kṣamādikāḥ//72	nidrā tandrā kṣamā dhṛtiḥ/78
bhayaṅkarī śatabhujā durgā 73c	sahasrabhujasaṃyutā//69
ātmanaḥ śaktirūpā sā 74a	yayā ca śaktimān ātmā 76a
nārāyaṇāstraṃ brahmāstraṃ	nānāśastrāstranikaraṃ
raudraṃ pāśupataṃ tathā/	
pārjanyaṃ vāruṇaṃ vāhnaṃ	
gāndharvaṃ *bibhratī* satī//76	*bibhratī* sā trilocanā/70

[2] This and the remaining lines of the description are applied to Sāvitrī.
[3] The Veṅk reading is somewhat different. This is the Vaṅg text in this one line.

sarvaśaktisvarūpā ca	*sarvaśaktisvarūpā* yā 75c
mayā ca *śaktimaj jagat*//77	yayā vai *śaktimaj jagat*/76
ity evam uktvā sā durgā	
ratnāsiṃhāsane vare/85	*ratnasiṃhāsana*ṃ tasyai
uvāsa natvā śrīkṛṣṇaṃ 85c	pradadau rādhikeśvaraḥ//79

APPENDIX C

ON THE ORIGIN OF RĀDHĀ'S OR PRAKṚTI'S FIVE FORMS, AS SEEN IN THE PARALLEL TEXTS OF *NĀRADĪYA PURĀṆA* I.83.5–32 AND *PRAKṚTI KHAṆḌA* 2.29; 2.54–90

For the discussion of these text parallels, see pp. 158–162 above. Parentheses indicate the verse or line is out of order at that point. Italics indicate identical wording, in some cases to a variant reading in a footnote.

NārP I.83.5 ff.	PKh 2.29; 2:54 ff.
nārada uvāca brahmaṃs tvayā samākhyātā vidhayas tantracoditāḥ/ tatrāpi kṛṣṇamantrāṇāṃ vaibhavaṃ hy uditaṃ mahat//5 yā tatra rādhikā devī sarvādyā samudāhṛtā/ tasyā aṃśāvatārāṇāṃ caritaṃ mantrapūrvakam//6 tantroktaṃ vada sarvajña tvām ahaṃ śaraṇaṃ gataḥ/7 tac chrutvā vacanaṃ tasya nāradasya mahātmanaḥ//8 sanatkumāraḥ provāca smṛtvā rādhāpadāmbujam/ śṛṇu nārada vakṣyāmi rādhāṃśānāṃ samudbhavam//9	

śaktīnāṃ paramāścaryaṃ
mantrasādhanapūrvakam/

yā tu rādhā mayā proktā
kṛṣṇārddhāṅgasamudbhavā
//10
golokavāsinī sā tu
nityā kṛṣṇasahāyinī/
tejomaṇḍalamadhyasthā
dṛśyādṛśyasvarūpiṇī//11
(tataḥ kālāntare brahman
kṛṣṇasya paramātmanaḥ//29
vaktrāt
sarasvatī jātā

vīṇāpustakadhāriṇī/30)

(rādhikāyāś ca vāmāṅgān
mahālakṣmīr babhūva ha/13)
kadā cit tu tayā sārddhaṃ
sthitasya munisattama/

kṛṣṇasya vāmabhāgāt tu
jāto nārāyaṇaḥ svayam//12

rādhikāyāś ca vāmāṅgān
mahālakṣmīr babhūva ha/
(tām ādideśa bhagavān 30c
[tiṣṭha] caturbhujasamāśrayā/
31)

tataḥ kṛṣṇo mahālakṣmīṃ
dattvā nārāyaṇāya ca//13
vaikuṇṭhe sthāpayām āsa
śaśvat pālanakarmaṇi/

svecchāmayaḥ [kṛṣṇa] svecchayā
ca
dvidhārūpo babhūva ha/
strīrūpā vāmabhāgāṃśād
dakṣiṇāṃśaḥ pumān smṛtaḥ//
29

etasminn antare
devī-
jihvāgrāt sahasā tataḥ/
āvirbabhūva kanyaikā
śuklavarṇā manoharā//54
pītavastraparidhānā
vīṇāpustakadhāriṇī
ratnabhūṣaṇabhūṣāḍhyā
sarvaśāstrādhidevatā//55
atha kālāntare sā ca
dvidhārūpā babhūva ha/
vāmārddhāṅgā ca kamalā
dakṣiṇārddhā ca rādhikā//56
estasminn antare kṛṣṇo
dvidhārūpo babhūva ha/
dakṣiṇārddhas syād dvibhujo
vāmārddhaś ca
caturbhujaḥ//
57

(Cf. 56 cd)

uvāca vāṇīṃ śrīkṛṣṇas
tvam asya bhava kāminī/

atraiva māninī rādhā
naiva bhadraṃ bhaviṣyati//
58

evaṃ laksmīṃ sampradadau
tuṣṭo nārāyanāya vai
saṃjagāma ca vaikuṇṭhaṃ
tābhyām sārddhaṃ jagat-
patiḥ//59

	anapatye ca te dve ca yato rādhāṃśasambhave/ nārāyaṇāṅgād abhavan pārṣadāś ca caturbhujāḥ//60
	tejasā vayasā rūpa- guṇābhyāṃ ca samā hareḥ/ babhūvuḥ kamalāṅgāc ca dāsīkoṭyaś ca tatsamāḥ//61
atha golokanāthasya *lomnāṃ vivarato mune*//14 jāt*āś cāsaṃkhyagopālās* tejasā vayasā *samāḥ*/	*atha golokanāthasya* *lomnāṃ vivarato mune*/ āsann[1] *asaṃkhyagopāś* ca vayasā tejasā *samāḥ*//62
	rūpeṇa suguṇenaiva veṣād vā vikrameṇa ca/
prāṇatulyapriyāḥ sarve *babhūvuḥ pārṣadā vibhoḥ*//15	*prāṇatulyaḥ*[2] *priyāḥ sarve* *babhūvuḥ pārṣadā vibhoḥ*// 63
rādhāṅgalomakūpebhyo *babhūvur gopakanyakāḥ*/ *rādhātulyaḥ sarvataś* ca *rādhādāsyaḥ priyaṃvadāḥ*// 16	*rādhāṅgalomakūpebhyo* *babhūvur gopakanyakāḥ*/ *rādhātulyāś* ca *sarvās* tā nānyatulyāḥ[3] *priyaṃvadāḥ*// 64
	ratnabhūṣaṇabhūṣāḍhyāḥ śaśvat susthirayouvanāḥ/ anapatyāś ca tāḥ sarvāḥ puṃsaḥ śāpena santatam//65
etasminn antare vipra *sahasā kṛṣṇadehataḥ* *āvirbabhūva sā durgā* *viṣṇumāyā sanātanī*//17	*etasminn antare vipra* *sahasā kṛṣṇadehataḥ*/ *āvirbabhūva sā durgā* *viṣṇumāyā sanātanī*//66
	devī nārāyaṇīśānā sarvaśaktisvarūpiṇī/ buddhyadhiṣṭhātṛdevī sā kṛṣṇasya paramātmanaḥ//67
devīnāṃ bījarūpā ca *mūlaprakṛtir īśvarī*/ *paripūrṇatamā tejaḥ* *svarūpā triguṇātmikā*//18	*devīnāṃ bījarūpā ca* *mūlaprakṛtir īśvarī* *paripūrṇatamā tejaḥ* *svarūpā triguṇātmikā*//68 taptakāñcanavarṇābhā

[1] Vaṅg: bhūt*āś cāsamkhya*
[2] Vaṅg: *prāṇatulyapriyāḥ*.
[3] Vaṅg: *rādhā*tulya*priyaṃvadāḥ*
Ānand (the main text agrees with Veṅk, but an alternate reading is given): *rādhādāsyaḥ priyaṃvadāḥ*.

	sūryakoṭisamaprabhā/
	īṣaddhāsaprasannāsya
*sahasrabhujasaṃyu*ktā	*sahasrabhujasaṃyu*tā//69
nānāśastrā	*nānāśaṣtrā*stranikaraṃ
trilocanā	bibhratī sā *trilocanā*
	vahniśuddhāṃśukādhānā
	ratnabhūṣaṇabhūṣitā//70
	yasyāś cāṃśāṃśakalayā
	babhūvuḥ sarvayoṣitaḥ/
	sarvaviśvasthitā lokā
	mohitā māyayā yayā//71
	sarvaiśvaryapradātrī ca
	kāmināṃ gṛhamedhinām/
	kṛṣṇabhaktipradātrī ca
	vaiṣṇavānām ca vaiṣṇavī//72
	mumukṣūṇāṃ mokṣadātrī
	sukhināṃ sukhadāyinī/
	svargeṣu svargalakṣmīḥ sā
	gṛhalakṣmīr gṛheṣv asau//73
	tapasviṣu tapas yā ca
	śrīrūpā sā nṛpeṣu ca/
	yā cāgnau dāhikārūpā
	prabhārūpā ca bhāskare//74
	śobhāsvarūpā candre ca
	padmeṣu ca suśobhanā/
	sarvaśaktisvarūpā yā
	śrīkṛṣṇe paramātmani//75
	yayā ca śaktimān ātmā
	yayā vai śaktimaj jagat/
	yayā vinā jagat sarvaṃ
	jīvan mṛtam iva sthitam//76
yā tu *saṃsāravṛkṣasya*	*yā* ca *saṃsāravṛkṣasya*
bījarūpā sanātanī//19	*bījarūpā sanātanī*/
	sthitirūpā buddhirūpā
	phalarūpā ca nārada//77
	kṣut pipāsā dayā śraddhā
	nidrā tandrā kṣamā dhṛtiḥ/
	śāntir lajjā tuṣṭipuṣṭi
	bhrāntikāntyādirūpiṇī//78
	sā ca saṃstūya sarveṣaṃ
	tatpuraḥ samupasthitā/
ratnasiṃhāsanaṃ tasyai	*ratnasiṃhāsanaṃ tasyai*
pradadau rādhikeśvaraḥ/	*pradadau rādhikeśvaraḥ*//79

etasminn antare tatra
sastrīkas tu *caturmukhaḥ*//20
jñāninām pravaraḥ śrīmān
pumān oṃkāram uccaran/
kamaṇḍaludharo jātas
tapasvī nābhito hareḥ//21
sa tu saṃstūya sarveśaṃ
sāvitryā bhāryayā saha/

niṣasād*āsane ramye*
vibhos tasyājñayā mune//22

atha kṛṣṇo mahābhāga
dvidhārūpo babhūva ha/
vāmārddhāṅgo mahādevo
*dakṣ*ārddho *gopikāpatiḥ*//23

pañcavaktras trinetro 'sau
vāmārddhāṅgo munīśvaraḥ/

stutvā kṛṣṇaṃ samājñapto

etasminn antare tatra
sastrīkaś ca *caturmukhaḥ*/
padmanābho nābhipadmān
nissasāra pumān mune//80
*kamaṇḍaludhara*ḥ śrīmāṃs
tapasvī jñāninām varaḥ/
caturmukhas taṃ tuṣṭāva
prajvalan brahmatejasā//81
sudatī sundarī sreṣṭhā
śatacandrasamaprabhā/
vahniśuddhāṃśukādhānā
ratnabhūṣaṇabhūṣitā//82
ratnasiṃh*āsane ramye*
stutā[4] vai sarvakāraṇam/
uvāsa svāminā sārddhaṃ
kṛṣṇasya purato mudā//83
etasminn antare kṛṣṇo
dvidhārūpo babhūva saḥ/
vāmārddhāṅgo mahādevo
dakṣiṇo gopikāpatiḥ//84
śuddhasphaṭikasaṃkāśaḥ
śatakoṭiraviprabhaḥ/
triśūlapaṭṭiśadharo
vyāghracarmadharo haraḥ//85
taptakāñcanavarṇābha-
jaṭābhāradharaḥ paraḥ/
bhasmabhūṣaṇagātraś ca
sasmitaś candraśekharaḥ//86
digambaro nīlakaṇṭhaḥ
sarpabhūṣaṇabhūṣitaḥ/
bibhrad dakṣiṇahastena
ratnamālāṃ susaṃskṛtām//87
prajapan pañcavaktreṇa
brahmajyotiḥ sanātanam/
satyasvarūpaṃ śrīkṛṣṇaṃ
paramātmānam īśvaram//88
kāraṇaṃ kāraṇānāṃ ca
sarvamaṅgalamaṅgalam/
janmamṛtyujarāvyādhi-
śokabhītiharaṃ param//89
saṃstūya mṛtyor mṛtyuṃ taṃ
jāto mṛtyuñjayābhidhaḥ/
ratnasimhāsane ramye

[4] Vaṅg: samstūya.

niṣasāda *hareḥ puraḥ*//24
atha kṛṣṇaś caturvaktraṃ
prāha sṛṣṭiṃ kuru prabho/
satyaloke sthito nityaṃ
gaccha māṃ smara sarvadā//
25
evam uktas tu hariṇā
praṇamya jagadīśvaram/
jagāma bhāryayā sākaṃ
sa tu sṛṣṭiṃ karoti vai//26
pitāsmākaṃ muniśreṣṭha
mānasīṃ kalpadaihikīm/
tataḥ paścāt pañcavaktraṃ
kṛṣṇaḥ prāha mahāmate//27
durgāṃ gṛhāṇa viśveśa
śivaloke tapaś cara/
yāvat sṛṣṭis tadante tu
lokān saṃhāra sarvataḥ//28
so 'pi kṛṣṇaṃ namaskṛtya
śivalokaṃ jagāma ha/
tataḥ kālāntare brahman
kṛṣṇasya paramātmanaḥ//29
vaktrāt
sarasvatī jātā
vīṇāpustakadhāriṇī
tām ādideśa bhagavān
vaikuṇṭhaṃ gaccha mānade//
30
lakṣmīsamīpe tiṣṭha tvaṃ
caturbhujasamāśrayā/
sāpi kṛṣṇaṃ namaskṛtya
gatā nārāyaṇāntikam//31
evaṃ pañcavidhā jātā
sā rādhā sṛṣṭikāraṇam/
āsāṃ pūrṇasvarūpāṇāṃ
mantradhyānārcanādikam//32
vadāmi śṛṇu vipendra

samuvāsa *hareḥ puraḥ*//90

(etasminn antare
devī
jihvāgrāt sahasā tataḥ/54
āvirbabhūva kanyaike 54c
vīṇāpustakadhāriṇī/55
uvāca vāṇīṃ śrīkṛṣṇas

tvam asya bhava kāminī/58)

GLOSSARY

ādhāra: support, container; applied in the BVP to the feminine principle of the universe, in contrast to the *ādheya* (that which is to be supported), applied to the masculine principle.

ādheya: that which is to be supported; see *ādhāra.*

advaita: non-dualism; the Vedāntic school of Śaṃkara according to which the inner Self of man and the Absolute are ultimately identical.

ahaitukī: unmotivated, without external purpose, as in devotion to God without regard for personal gain or happiness.

ahaṃkara: egoism; the second of the twenty-three material evolutes of *prakṛti* (q.v.) or nature.

aikya: oneness; union or unity of the soul with God; in the BVP *aikya* is contrasted to *dāsya,* or servitude to God, in which the soul remains distinct from God in order to perform his (her) service; cf. *līnatā.*

aiśvarya: lordship, sovereignty, supremacy; one of the six non-natural (*aprākṛta*) qualities of God; see *ṣaḍguṇas.*

ambikā: mother, one of many similar epithets applied to Rādhā in the BVP; also a name of Durgā.

aṃśa: part, portion; applied especially to the various manifestations, incarnations, and emmanations of God; in the BVP, all female beings, divine or human, are thought of as greater or lesser *aṃśas* of Rādhā, all male beings as *aṃśas* of Kṛṣṇa.

aṃśāvatāra: partial incarnation of the Lord, in contrast to *pūrṇāvatāra* (q.v.) or complete incarnation.

aṃśin: whole, that which contains the parts; applied to God in contrast to his (her) *aṃśas* (q.v.).

anaśana: fasting, an act of merit; such acts in the BVP are considered inferior to devotion or service to God.

aṇḍa: egg, refers to the cosmic or golden egg (*hiraṇyagarbha,* q.v.).

anirvacanīya: indescribable, indefinable; an epithet of God.

anugraha: favor, grace (of God); similar to *prasāda;* cf. *kṛpā.*

aprākṛta: non-natural, not derived from material nature (*prakṛti,* q.v.).

arcā: worship of an image of a god or God.

arcana: praising, honoring, worshipping God.

artha: wealth.

asat: non-being; non-existent.

atisādhya: easily subdued or conquered; applied to God in relation to his (her) devotees.

Ātman: Self; the true Self of man in contrast to his empirical, individual soul (*jīva*) and identified with the Absolute; in the BVP, commonly used as an epithet of Kṛṣṇa.

ātmanivedana: surrender of one's self (to the Lord); one of the "nine acts" or stages of devotion; at times (though not in the BVP) thought to be the culminating phase of the nine stages (see *navadhā bhaktilakṣaṇa*).

ātmasamarpaṇa: another name for *ātmanivedana.*

āvaraṇi: obscuration; the power of the Goddess to delude all beings, in contrast to her power to give them enlightening knowledge (*vivecikā,* q.v.).

avatāra: incarnation, descent of God to earth, usually in times of trouble.

aviveka: lack of discrimination (cf. *āvaraṇi*).

bala: force, strength; one of the six non-natural (*aprākṛta*) qualities of God; see *ṣaḍguṇas.*

Bhagavat (or *bhagavān*): The Blessed One, the Lord.

Bhāgavata: a devotee of Bhagavat.

Bhagavatī: the Blessed One, the Goddess.

bhakta: a devotee in general.

bhakti: devotion, worship; one of the three traditional ways to salvation, along with *jñāna* and *karma.*

bhaktir navalakṣaṇā: see *navadhā bhaktilakṣaṇa.*

bhāva: inner emotion.

bhāvabhakti: devotion realized through inner emotion rather than by external means; a type of devotion higher than *sadhanabhakti* (q.v.) and lower than *premabhakti* (q.v.).

bhedābheda: non-difference in difference; the philosophical-theological view that God is not different from man and the world, and yet neither is God identical with them.

brahmacārin: a student of sacred knowledge leading a continent life; the first of the four stages of life.

Brahman: the Absolute, Supreme Reality; it is neuter in gender, suggestive of a non-personal Ultimate, but in the BVP often identified with the masculine Kṛṣṇa and even with the feminine Rādhā (or Durgā).

Brahmāṇḍa: the egg of Brahmā, the world-egg, the universe.

Brahmanirvāṇa: dissolution, extinction, or mergence into Brahman; in the BVP it is considered to be an inferior state of salvation to service (*dāsya,* q.v.) to God.

brahmarandhra: the aperture at the crown of the head where the vital wind or energy of a person is said to escape at death.

buddhi: intellect, seat of discrimination; in the BVP, Durgā is called the presiding deity of *buddhi.*

cakra: wheel, disc; in Tāntric theory, there are said to be six wheels or centers along the spine leading up to the top of the head, and by piercing these centers, a person may force his vital energy to ascend the *cakras* in order, finally to unite with the Supreme.

cakrapūjā: the special ritual worship of the left-handed Tantrics involving celebration of and participation in the five "forbidden elements" or *makāras* (q.v.) such as meat, drink, and sexual intercourse.

caraṇāmṛtapāna: drinking the water used to bathe the feet of an image of God; sometimes included as one of the "nine acts" of devotion (see *navadhā bhaktilakṣāṇa*).

caraṇodakapāna: another name for *caraṇāmṛtapāna.*

dāna: charity, an act of merit; cf. *anaśana.*

dāsa: servant (of God); another name for *kiṃkara, pārṣada.*

dāsya: service (to God); considered by the BVP to be the supreme aim of man and the highest form of salvation; though it is included as one of the "nine acts" of devotion (see *navadhā bhaktilakṣaṇa*), it also serves to indicate the "nine acts" as a whole; further, outside the BVP, *dāsya* is seen as one of five attitudes a person may adopt towards the Lord, the others being *śanta* (awe at the Lord's supremacy), *sākhya* (friendship), *vātsalya* (parental affection), and *mādhurya* (erotic love).

dayānidhi: ocean of mercy; an epithet of God.

devapūjā: ritual worship of a god or gods.

devaṣaṭka: the "six deities," usually Gaṇeśa, Sūrya, Vahni, Viṣṇu, Śiva, and Durgā; these six are to be given special worship before giving any offerings to other deities, according to the BVP; the notion of the "six deities" seems closely related to the more usual idea of the "five deities" involved in the *pañcāyatanapūjā* (q.v.).

Devī: the Goddess; also used as a name for Durgā.

dharma: duty, law, righteousness, cosmic order.

dharmaśāstra: treatise or instructions on *dharma.*

dhātrī: wet-nurse, mother; an epithet of Rādhā in the BVP.

dhyāna: meditation; in the BVP it is often closely related to remembrance (*smaraṇa*) of God and sometimes included as one of the "nine acts" of devotion (see *navadhā bhaktilakṣaṇa*).

ḍimbha: egg, another name for *aṇḍa, hiraṇyagarbha* (q.v.).

dvāpara yuga: the third of the four ages constituting one cosmic cycle; in every cycle, each age is inferior in virtue to the preceding one, so the *dvāpara yuga* (during which Kṛṣṇa incarnated himself on earth) is the worst except for the last or present *kali yuga.*

ekādaśī: ritual fasting on the eleventh day of a fortnight, a rite strongly recommended for Vaiṣṇavas.

Gāṇapas: devotees of Gaṇeśa.

garbha: womb, seed; cf. *hiraṇyagarbha.*

Goloka: the World of Cows, Kṛṣṇa's heaven, the highest of all worlds; Kṛṣṇa's devotees aspire to become servants in Goloka.

gopī: cowmaid; Kṛṣṇa, in his divine sport, dallies with the *gopis*, the chief of whom is Rādhā.

guṇa: quality, attribute, virtue; often, *guṇa* refers specifically to the three qualities (*triguṇas*) of material nature, *sattva* (goodness), *rajas* (activity), and *tamas* (darkness, inertia); prior to creation, these *guṇas* are thought to be in equilibrium within nature (*prakṛti,* q.v.), until the "approach" of spirit (*puruṣa,* q.v.) upsets the balance and then material evolution commences; in this view, spirit is regarded as untouched or beyond the *guṇas* of matter; *guṇa* may also refer to the six attributes of the Lord, such as splendor and strength, that are said not to be associated with or derived from nature (*aprākṛta*); see also *nirguṇa, saguṇa, triguṇā.*

guṇaśravaṇa: listening to the virtues (of God); a specific form of listening or hearing (*śravaṇa*) in general, considered as one of the "nine acts" of devotion (see *navadhā bhaktilakṣaṇa*).

guṇāvatāra: an incarnation of a quality; in the Caitanya school, Brahmā, Viṣṇu, and Śiva are considered as *avatāras* of Kṛṣṇa; Brahmā, the creator, is traditionally associated with the *guṇa* of *rajas,* Viṣṇu with *sattva,* and Śiva with *tamas;* Kṛṣṇa in himself is *nirguṇa* or beyond these attributes.

haribhakti: devotion to Hari or Viṣṇu.

haridāsya: service to Hari or Viṣṇu (see *dāsya*).

hiraṇyagarbha: the golden egg or germ out of which the world arises; it is an ancient mythological notion that has been variously interpreted throughout the ages; in the BVP, it is regarded as the offspring of Rādhā and Kṛṣṇa.

icchā: wish, desire; commonly associated with creative desire.

icchāśakti: power of desire, representing the creative energy of the Lord and often personified as his consort.

Iḍā: one of the energy channels in the body, on the left side.

indriya: an organ of sense.

Īśa: Lord, ruler.

iṣṭadevatā: a chosen deity; a man may choose, or rather may be called by, a particular god to render him special service and devotion; the worship of one's *iṣṭadevatā,* however, does not exclude the general reverencing of other deities; cf. *pañcāyatanapūjā.*

Īśvara: Lord, ruler.

Īśvarī: the heavenly Queen, the Goddess.

itihāsa: historical account; an epic.

jagadyoni: womb of the world; an epithet of *prakṛti* (q.v.).

janaka: father; in the BVP it is applied to Kṛṣṇa, with Rādhā as mother.

jananī: mother, one of many similar epithets applied to Rādhā in the BVP.

japa: recitation; often, recitation of *mantras* (q.v.) to the Lord; sometimes included in the "nine acts" of devotion (see *navadhā bhaktilakṣaṇa*).

jīva: the empirical or individual soul, in contrast to the true Self (Ātman) that is identified with Brahman.

jīvanmukta: one who is released from all worldly bonds while still living.

jīvanmukti: the state of release while still living.

jñāna: knowledge of Supreme Reality, mystical knowledge; one of the three traditional ways to salvation along with *bhakti* and *karma;* also, one of the six non-natural (*aprākṛta*) qualities of God (see *ṣaḍguṇas*).

jñānin: one who possesses knowledge of Supreme Reality.

kaivalya: emancipation, isolation, absolute unity.

kalā: fraction; similar to *aṃśa* (q.v.), but often indicating a somewhat lesser or smaller fraction than *aṃśa.*

kalāṃśāṃśa: part of a part of a fraction; see *aṃśa* and *kalā.*

kalāvatāra: minor partial incarnation of the Lord; a somewhat lesser incarnation than an *aṃśāvatāra* (q.v.).

kali yuga: the last and most degenerate of the four ages constituting a cosmic cycle, when *dharma* has practically disappeared, but when the means to salvation are actually made easier than in the preceding age, to compensate for man's dwindling moral capabilities.

kāma: desire, sexual longing, often associated with creation by copulation; cf. *icchā* and *sisṛkṣā.*

kāmādhāra: the abode or support of desire; in the BVP an epithet of Kṛṣṇa.

kāraṇa: cause, in contrast to effect (*kārya*); in the BVP, Kṛṣṇa is called both cause (of the world) and effect.

karma: action in general; the cosmic law of retribution by which everyone must experience the consequences of his acts whether good or bad, and by which, therefore, a person is bound to the wheel of life (*saṃsāra*) and prevented from attaining liberation; also, specifically, ritual action and acts of merit, which if done in the proper spirit constitute one the three traditional ways to salvation, along with *bhakti* and *jñāna.*

karmārpaṇa: the surrender of all one's actions (to the Lord), renouncing the fruits of action; sometimes included as one of the "nine acts" of devotion, as a substitute for *nivedana, ātmanivedana, ātmasamarpaṇa* (see *navadhā bhaktilakṣaṇa*).

kartā: agent, doer.

kārya: effect, cf. *kāraṇa.*

kavaca: an amulet; a sacred syllable forming part of a *mantra* (q.v.) used as an amulet.

kiṃkara: a servant (of God); another name for *dāsa, pārṣada.*

kīrtana: singing in praise (of the Lord); one of the "nine acts" of devotion (see *navadhā bhaktilakṣaṇa*).

kṛpā: compassion, mercy (of the Lord).

kṛpāmaya: consisting of mercy; an epithet of Kṛṣṇa.

kṛpāmayī: consisting of mercy; and epithet of Prakṛti or Durgā.

kṛṣṇabhakti: devotion to Kṛṣṇa.

kṛṣṇajanmāṣṭamī: the celebration of Kṛṣṇa's birthday on the eighth day of the second half of the month of Srāvaṇa.

kṛṣṇamārga: the path to Kṛṣṇa, encompassing devotion and knowledge.

kṛṣṇapadārcana: honoring the feet of Kṛṣṇa.

kṛṣṇapadasevana: serving the feet of Kṛṣṇa.

kṛṣṇapremamayī: full of ecstatic love for Kṛṣṇa; an epithet of Rādhā.

kṛṣṇaprīti: the delight or pleasure of Kṛṣṇa.

kṛṣṇaprītikāma: desirous of pleasing Kṛṣṇa; an attribute of the highest devotees.

kṛṣṇasevana: service to Kṛṣṇa (similar to *dāsya,* q.v.).

kṛṣṇavāmāṅgasambhūtā: arisen from the left side of Kṛṣṇa; an attribute of Rādhā.

kṣudro virāṭ: the small ruler of the universe; according to the BVP, he is the shrunken form of the great ruler arising out of the cosmic egg.

kuṇḍalinī: in Tāntric theory, the serpent power that lies at the base of the spine till aroused by yogic techniques and raised through the six *cakras* to the top of the head and united with the Absolute.

līlā: sport, play; the divine sport of the Lord; one of the main "reasons" for the Lord's incarnations, since the Lord has no ulterior purposes to accomplish; though the Lord's *līlā* is "purposeless," it is in this sport, especially with the *gopīs* or cowmaids, that the Lord experiences his own sweetness and bliss.

līlāvatāra: incarnation of the Lord for sport, such as Kṛṣṇa's incarnation in Vṛndāvana, in contrast to the *guṇāvatāras* (q.v.) and *puruṣāvatāra* (q.v.).

līnatā: mergence (into the Lord); similar to *aikya* (q.v.).

liṅga: the male organ; specifically, the symbol of Śiva, expressing in part his creative powers, in part his formless and unmanifest aspect that produces all form yet is beyond form; it is the counterpart of the female organ, or *yoni* (q.v.), symbol of Pārvatī.

mādhurya: erotic love (for the Lord); in the Caitanya school, one of five attitudes a person may adopt towards the Lord; cf. *dāsya.*

Madhyā: one of the energy channels in the body.

madya: wine, intoxicating drink; one of the five "forbidden elements" or *makāras* (q.v.).

mahat: the great principle, often called *buddhi* or intellect; the first of the twenty-three evolutes from *prakṛti* (q.v.) or nature.

Mahāvirāṭ: the great ruler of the universe, born of the cosmic egg according to the BVP; cf. *kṣudro virāṭ.*

maithuna: sexual intercourse; one of the five "forbidden elements" or *makāras* (q.v.).

makāras: the (five) "m's" or "forbidden elements" used in the *cakrapūjā* of the left-handed Tāntras; the five "m's" are *madya* (wine), *māṃsa* (meat), *matsya* (fish), *mudrā* (parched grain), and *maithuna* (sexual intercourse).

māṃsa: meat; one of the five "forbidden elements" or *makāras* (q.v.).

manas: mind, or heart.

maṇḍala: mystical diagram, a geometric pattern using concentric and overlapping squares, triangles, and circles, often used as an aid in meditation.

Maṇipūra: third of the six *cakras* along the central energy channel.

Manohara: fourth of the six *cakras.*

mantra: a sacred formula or prayer, often composed in part of mystical syllables or sounds.

mantrajapa: the recitation of a *mantra;* sometimes included as one of the "nine acts" of devotion (see *navadhā bhaktilakṣaṇa*).

manvantara: an interval or age of a Manu, comprising about seventy-one *mahāyugas,* one-fourteenth of a day of Brahmā, twelve thousand divine years, or 4,320,000 human years.

mārga: path, way to salvation.

maryādābhakti: devotion in compliance with scriptural injunction, according to the school of Vallabha; it corresponds to the *vaidhibhakti* (q.v.) of the Caitanya school.

mātṛ: mother; one of many similar epithets applied to Rādhā in the BVP.

matsya: fish; one of the five "forbidden elements" or *makāras* (q.v.).

māyā: the magical, mystical, or illusory power of the Lord, by which he creates the world; often personified as his consort, who functions not only in creating the world, but also in deluding all beings by her illusory power; she also serves to remove the veil of ignorance from her devotees.

māyāśakti: energy or power of delusion; nearly synonymous with *māyā.*

māyin: one who possesses *māyā;* an epithet of Kṛṣṇa in the BVP.

moha: delusion, infatuation.

mokṣa: liberation from the bonds of the world or *saṃsāra;* in the BVP, *mokṣa,* or *mukti* (q.v.), is often said to be of two general kinds, the inferior having the form of *nirvāṇa* (extinction or mergence in the Absolute), the superior having the form of *sevā* or *dāsya* (service); at times, *mokṣa* itself (as well as the desire for *mokṣa*) is considered as opposed to or destructive of true *bhakti* by the BVP.

mudrā: certain symbolic positions of the hands and fingers; also parched grain used as one of the five "forbidden elements" or *makāras* (q.v.).

mukhyāvatāras: chief incarnations, of three kinds: *purṇāvatāra* (q.v.), *aṃśāvatāra* (q.v.), and *kalāvatāra* (q.v.).

mukti: another name for *mokṣa* (q.v.); the BVP says there are six specific kinds of *mukti: sārṣṭi* (attaining the power or condition of God), *sālokya* (attaining the same world as God), *sārūpya* (attaining the form of God), *sāmīpya* (attaining the presence of God), *sāmya* (sameness with God), and *līnatā, nirvāṇa,* or *aikya* (mergence, dissolution, or oneness with God); it is especially the last notion, of mergence or oneness, that the BVP disparages, for in unity the master-servant relationship dissolves and thus *dāsya* (service), the highest end of man, becomes impossible.

muktimārga: way to salvation; traditionally, three main ways have been taught, those of *karma,* of *bhakti,* and of *jñāna.*

Mūlādhāra: the first or lowest of the six *cakras* along the central energy channel.

Mūlaprakṛti: fundamental or primordial nature, often personified as a goddess and used as an epithet of Rādhā.

mūlaprakṛtir īśvarī: the Goddess Primordial Nature (identified frequently with Rādhā).

mumukṣu: one who desires *mokṣa.*

nāḍīs: the various energy channels in the body, the most important of which is the central *suṣumnā,* along which the six *cakras* are situated.

naivedyabhojana: eating the remnants of food offered to (an image of) the Lord; sometimes included as one of the "nine acts" of devotion (see *navadhā bhaktilakṣaṇa*).

nāmaguṇakīrtana: singing the name and virtues of God; a specific form of *kīrtana,* one of the "nine acts" of devotion (see *navadhā bhaktilakṣaṇa*).

naramedhaka: human sacrifice.

navadhā bhaktilakṣaṇa: the ninefold marks of *bhakti,* the "nine acts" of devotion; the acts included in the nine differ somewhat in the texts; the BhP gives the following: *śravaṇa* (hearing), *kīrtana* (singing), *smaraṇa* (remembering), *pādasevana* (service to the feet), *arcana* (worshipping), *vandana* (adoration), *dāsya* (service), *sakhya* (friendship), and *ātmanivedana* (self-surrender); both *dāsya* and *sevā* (service) are used in the BVP to indicate the "nine acts" as a whole.

nirādhāra: without support; an epithet of Kṛṣṇa in the BVP, even though Rādhā is often spoken of as his *ādhāra.*

nirākāra: without form; an often-used epithet of Kṛṣṇa, indicating his utter transcendence, yet, paradoxically, Kṛṣṇa ultimately is endowed with form (*sākāra,* q.v.) according to the BVP.

nirañjana: unstained; an epithet of God.

nirguṇa: without attributes; often modifying Brahman, indicating the qualityless Absolute, in contrast to the *saguṇa* (q.v.) Brahman; in the BVP, it sometimes apparently has the meaning of denying only evil qualities or the three defiling qualities of nature; it is applied to both Kṛṣṇa and Rādhā.

nirlipta: unstained; an epithet of God.

nirmālyadhāraṇa: another name for *naivedyabhojana* (q.v.).

nirvāṇa: extinction, final dissolution or mergence; in the BVP, subordinated to *dāsya* (q.v.) as the highest form of salvation.

nirvāṇamukti: liberation in the form of *nirvāṇa.*

niṣkāma: having no desires; an attribute of the true devotee.

nityadehin: possessing an eternal body; one of many similar epithets of Kṛṣṇa in the BVP.

nityavigraha: another name for *nityadehin.*

nivedana: surrender (to God); cf. *ātmanivedana, karmārpaṇa.*

nivṛttimārga: the path of inaction, cessation of worldly activity, in contrast to *pravṛttimārga* (q.v.); in the BVP both *nivṛttimārga* and *pravṛttimārga* are subordinated to *dāsya* (q.v.).

nyāsa: a Tāntric ritual involving the placing of the hands and fingers on various spots of the body, whereby various tutelary deities are assigned to these places.

pādasevā: service to the feet (of God); a specific form of service in general; sometimes included as one of the "nine acts" of devotion (see *navadhā baktilakṣaṇa*).

padasevana (or *pādasevana*): another name for *padasevā.*

Pāñcarātrikas: an early Vaiṣṇava sect, among whom image-worship of God was very important, and whose cosmological ideas seem to have exerted significant influence on the Vaiṣṇava Purāṇic compilers.

pañcatattvas: the five ("forbidden") elements used in the *cakrapūjā* of the left-handed Tāntrics: also known as the five "m's" (*makāras*, q.v.).

pañcāyatanapūjā: the ritual involving worship of the "five gods" (Gaṇeśa, Sūrya, Viṣṇu, Śiva, and Durgā); these deities, the chief gods of the five principal orthodox cults, are often seen simply as five forms of the Supreme Godhead; usually, a devotee chooses one particular form or god as his favorite deity (*iṣṭadevatā,* q.v.), whose symbol is then placed in the center of the other four during worship; cf. *devaṣaṭka.*

parakīyā: a woman belonging to another (i.e., unmarried, or wed to another); Rādhā has sometimes been portrayed in the Vaiṣṇava tradition, especially by the Vaiṣṇava Sahajiyās (q.v.), as *parakīyā* in relation to Kṛṣṇa; adulterine love, with its passionate disregard of human morality and social convention, has been seen as a paradigm for the divine love between the soul and God; in the BVP, however, Rādhā is portrayed as married to Kṛṣṇa (*svakīyā,* q.v.).

para (or *parama*): supreme; an epithet of both Kṛṣṇa and Rādhā; often used with Brahman (q.v.) and Ātman (q.v.).

Paramājñā: highest of the six *cakra*s, located between the eyebrows.

parameśvara: the Supreme Lord.

paripūrṇatama: most fully complete or perfect; used of Kṛṣṇa in himself, in contrast to his lesser *avatāra*s and manifestations through *aṃśa*s (q.v.); also used of the five main forms of Prakṛti, and of Rādhā herself.

pārṣada: servant (of God); another name for *dāsa, kiṃkara.*

phalānusandhānaśūnya: void of seeking the fruits (of action); an explanation of the term *ahaitukī* (q.v.), describing the true nature of devotion.

Piṅgalā: one of the energy channels in the body, on the right side.

pitṛ: father; an epithet of Kṛṣṇa, as father of the world (*jagatpitṛ*); in the plural, the deceased ancestors.

pradakṣina: circumambulation (of a sacred shrine, mountain, *etc.*); regarded as an act of merit; cf. *anaśana.*

pradhāna: chief, foremost; also, a name for the material cause of the universe; cf. *prakṛti.*

prākṛta (or *prākṛtika*): derived from material nature, in contrast to *aprākṛta,* or non-natural.

prakṛteḥ para: beyond material nature (*prakṛti*); an epithet of Kṛṣṇa.

prakṛti: material nature, insentient matter as opposed to spirit (*puruṣa,* q.v.) according to classical Sāṃkhya; in the BVP personified as a goddess, Mother Nature, identified with both Durgā and Rādhā, and representing the supreme feminine principle of the cosmos.

prākṛtika laya: natural dissolution, in which all the elements dissolve back into nature, or in which nature dissolves back into the Supreme.

pralaya: dissolution of the universe at the end of a cosmic cycle, to be followed by an endless series of re-creations and dissolutions.

prāṇa: vital breath.

prāṇāyāma: breath control; part of yogic exercises taken over in Tāntrism.

prapatti: taking refuge (in the Lord), similar to *nivedana;* considered in some circles as a minimum necessary effort on the part of man to obtain God's grace.

prasāda: favor, grace (of God); similar to *anugraha;* cf. *kṛpā.*

prasū: mother; one of many similar epithets applied to Rādhā in the BVP.

pravṛttimārga (or *pravṛttipatha, pravṛttivartman*): path of worldly activity, in contrast to the path of inactivity (*nivṛttimārga,* q.v.).

premabhakti: ecstatic devotion, the outward signs of which are tears, erection of the hair, stammering, *etc.;* the highest kind of devotion (highest of the three phases of *uttamabhakti,* q.v.), according to the Caitanya school; cf. *bhāvabhakti* and *sādhanabhakti.*

prīti: delight, pleasure; the desire of a devotee to give delight to the Lord is regarded as the one acceptable desire of a true Vaiṣṇava.

prīyatā: "delightedness" (in giving pleasure to a beloved, or to God), in contrast to *sukha* or happiness that is based on personal satisfaction.

pūjā: ritual worship, involving the bathing of an image of a god or God, feeding the image, paying homage, *etc.*

pūjana: another name for *pūjā.*

pūjāvidhi: rules or regulations of ritual worship.

puṃs: another name for *puruṣa* (q.v.).

Purāṇa: an ancient happening, account of ancient events; the name of a number (usually reckoned as eighteen) of works recounting ancient events and regarded as *smṛti* (q.v.).

pūrṇa: full, complete; similar to *paripūrṇatama* (q.v.), but often used to indicate a lesser degree of completeness.

pūrṇā śakti: complete energy or power.

pūrṇatama: most complete or perfect; cf. *paripūrṇatama.*

pūrṇāvatāra: complete incarnation, in contrast to *aṃśāvatāra* (q.v.) and *kalāvatāra;* see also *mukhyāvatāras.*

puruṣa: conscious spirit as opposed to insentient matter (*prakṛti,* q.v.) according to classical Sāṃkhya; the Supreme Being; identified with Kṛṣṇa and representing the supreme masculine principle of the universe.

puruṣatva: maleness.

puruṣāvatāra: incarnation of the Lord as the Puruṣa, for the purpose of creation; cf. *guṇāvatāra* and *līlāvatāra.*

puṣṭi: prosperity, comfort; in the school of Vallabha, the name for divine grace.

Rādhāvallabhins: a late Vaiṣṇava sect devoted to Rādhāvallabha (the beloved of Rādhā or Kṛṣṇa), though in their actual worship, Rādhā plays the more important role.

rāga: passion, emotional attachment.

rāgānugabhakti: devotion prompted by attachment; it is higher than devotion prompted by scriptural injunction (*vaidhibhakti,* q.v.); these two kinds of devotion together comprise *sādhanabhakti* (q.v.).

rajas: the active quality; one of the three *guṇas* (q.v.) of nature.

rasa: taste, flavor; in Vaiṣṇava devotional theory, any of the five devotional sentiments or attitudes a person may adopt toward the Lord, such as *dāsya* (q.v.).

Rāsa: name of the circular dance of Kṛṣṇa with the cowmaids.

Rāsamaṇḍala: the circular dancing ground of Kṛṣṇa with the cowmaids; in the BVP, the name of a marvelous love-chamber in the woods of Vṛndāvana where Rādhā and Kṛṣṇa sport; there is also a celestial Rāsamaṇḍala in Goloka, where Rādhā in the beginning of creation arises from Kṛṣṇa's left side.

Rasātala: name of one of the seven underground regions.

Raurava: name of one of the innumerable hells mentioned in the BVP.

retas: seed, semen virile.

ṣaḍgunas: the six (non-natural) qualities of God, to be distinguished from the three qualities of material nature (see *guṇa*); the six qualities are *jñāna* (knowledge), *bala* (strength), *aiśvarya* (sovereignty), *vīrya* (heroism), *śakti* (energy), and *tejas* (splendor).

sādhanabhakti: devotion attained by external means; it contains two stages: *vaidhibhakti* (q.v.) and *rāgānugabhakti* (q.v.); *sādhanabhakti* is the lowest of the three grades of *uttamabhakti* (q.v.) according to the Caitanya school.

saguṇa: endowed with attributes, as opposed to *nirguṇa* (q.v.); in the non-dualistic, *advaita* school, it is applied to Brahman to indicate the lower or quality-endowed aspect of the Absolute, identified with the personal Lord; in the theistic schools, the Absolute is seen as ultimately endowed with (auspicious) qualities.

Sahajiyās: a name covering various medieval Tāntric sects, including a group of Vaiṣṇavas; the Sahajiyās espoused the ideal of illicit (*parakīyā,* q.v.) love as the highest form of divine-human love.

sahasradala: the thousand-petaled lotus at the crown of the head, conjoined with the *brahmarandhra* (q.v.).

sahavāsa: another name for *sālokya* (q.v.), a kind of liberation.

Śaivas: devotees of the god Śiva.

sakāma: possessing desires, as opposed to *niṣkāma* (q.v.).

sākāra: endowed with form or body, as opposed to *nirākāra* (q.v.); in the BVP, commonly applied to Kṛṣṇa in his ultimate aspect, his formless aspect being subordinate.

sakhī: female companion.

Sakhībhavas: a sect according to which the supreme goal of man is to become a companion (*sakhī*) of Rādhā in heaven.

sakhya (or *sākhya*): friendship; in the BhP one of the "nine acts" of devotion (see *navadhā bhaktilakṣaṇa*); also, one of the five devotional attitudes a person may adopt toward the Lord (cf. *dāsya*).

sākṣin: witness; an attribute of the soul to indicate its inactivity, as the soul is sometimes regarded as only the witness of all acts.

Śāktas: devotees of Śakti, the female energy of the universe.

śaktis: energies, powers, especially creative energies; personified as the consorts of various male divinities; in the singular, representing the female energy or feminine principle of the universe and another name for the goddess Prakṛti, or Māyā, identified with both Durgā and Rādhā; also, one of the six non-natural (*aprākṛta*) qualities of God (see *ṣaḍguṇas*).

Śālagrama: a sacred stone of the Vaiṣṇavas used in ritual worship; it is pervaded by Viṣṇu's presence.

sālokya: attaining the same world (as God); one of six forms of *mukti* (q.v.) mentioned in the BVP.

samabhāva: having the same nature (everywhere), omnipresence; an attribute of God; cf. *samatā.*

sāmānyabhakti: general devotion; the lower of the two basic types of *bhakti* according to the Caitanya school (the higher *bhakti* is called *uttamabhakti,* q.v.).

samarpaṇa: surrender; cf. *ātmanivedana, ātmasamarpaṇa, karmārpaṇa.*

samatā: sameness or omnipresence (of God); impartiality (of God's compassion toward all beings).

sāmīpya: closeness (to God); one of the six forms of *mukti* (q.v.) mentioned in the BVP.

samkalpābhāva: absence of intention, similar to *ahaitukī* (q.v.).
samkalparahita: another term for *samkalpābhāva.*
saṃkīrtana: another name for *kīrtana.*
saṃnyāsin: one who has renounced the world, who has entered the fourth and last stage of life.
saṃsāra: the wheel of life and death, the world process.
saṃsevā ṣaḍaṅgā: six-limbed service (of God); a shorter version of the "nine acts" of devotion (*navadhā bhaktilakṣaṇa,* q.v.).
sāmya: sameness (with the Lord); one of the six forms of *mukti* (q.v.) mentioned in the BVP.
śānta: awe (at the Lord's supremacy); one of the five devotional attitudes a person may adopt toward the Lord; cf. *dāsya.*
śarīra: body.
sārṣṭi: attaining the power or condition (of God); one of the six forms of *mukti* (q.v.) mentioned in the BVP.
sārūpya: attaining the same form (as the Lord); one of the six forms of *mukti* (q.v.) mentioned in the BVP.
sarvanivedana: surrender of all (to God); cf. *ātmanivedana, karmārpaṇa.*
śāstra: instruction, book of instruction.
sat: being; existent.
satsaṅga: good company or society; specifically, association with the devotees of Kṛṣṇa.
sattva: the quality of goodness; one of the three *guṇas* (q.v.) of nature.
satya: true, real.
Sauras: devotees of the Sun (Sūrya).
sāyujya: union (with God); similar to *aikya, līnatā* or *nirvāṇa,* one of the six forms of *mukti* (q.v.).
sevā: service; used synonymously with *dāsya* (q.v.) in the BVP.
sevana: another name for *sevā.*
siddha: a yogic adept who has acquired supernatural powers.
sisṛkṣā: desire to create; cf. *icchā, kāma.*
smaraṇa: remembrance (of God); one of the "nine acts" of devotion (see *navadhā bhaktilakṣaṇa*).
smṛti: remembrance; "that which is remembered," sacred oral and written tradition that is usually considered of human origin, in contrast to *śruti* (q.v.); the Purāṇas are included under *smṛti.*
stavana: praise (of God); sometimes included as one of the "nine acts" of devotion (see *navadhā bhaktilakṣaṇa*).
stotra: another name for *stavana.*
strītva: femaleness.
sudurlabha: hard to attain; an epithet of God with regard to those who are not his devotees.

sukha: happiness; cf. *prīyatā.*

Suṣumnā: the main, central energy channel in the body, along which the *cakras* are located.

svadharma: one's own duty, peculiar to caste and stage of life.

Svādhiṣṭhāna: second of the six *cakras* located along the central energy channel.

svakīyā: one's own (wife); in the BVP, Rādhā is portrayed as Kṛṣṇa's wife; the *svakīyā* interpretation of Rādhā views *parakīyā* (q.v.) or adulterine love as merely lustful; the *svakīyā* interpretation was favored by many but not all "orthodox" Vaiṣṇavas.

svarga: heaven.

svarūpa: essence, own or proper form.

tamas: the quality of darkness and inertia; one of the three *guṇas* (q.v.) of nature.

Tantras: a class of esoteric sacred works, generally teaching the supremacy of the female principle of the universe; many specific practices, such as the *kuṇḍalinī* (q.v.) yoga and theory of the six *cakras* (q.v.), are associated with the Tantras; the followers of the Tantras, Tāntras or Tāntrics, are divided into two broad classes, right-handed and left-handed, the latter practicing more extreme forms of a kind of antinomian yoga, as in the *cakrapūjā* (q.v.); Tāntra is often used synonymously with Śākta.

tapas: austerity, asceticism; ascetic "heat."

tapasvin: an ascetic.

tejas: splendor; one of the six non-natural (*aprākṛta*) qualities of God; see *ṣaḍguṇas.*

tīrtha: ford, sacred place on the banks of a river, place of pilgrimage.

tīrthasnāna: bathing at a *tīrtha;* considered as an act of merit; cf. *anaśana.*

triguṇā: endowed with or possessing the three natural *guṇas* (q.v.); an epithet of Prakṛti, who is also paradoxically called *nirguṇā* (q.v.) in the BVP.

triguṇātmikā: having the three *guṇas* (q.v.) for one's essence; an epithet of Prakṛti, similar to *triguṇā.*

triguṇāt para: beyond the three *guṇas* (q.v.); an epithet of Kṛṣṇa.

trimūrti: the three forms of the Godhead, Brahmā the creator, Viṣṇu the preserver, and Śiva the destroyer.

triśakti: the three energies (of Brahmā, Viṣṇu, and Śiva, often personified as the consorts of these gods).

ukti: pronunciation, utterance (of God's name).

upacāra: ingredient of worship, such as water, unguents, flowers; often, sixteen ingredients are used in worship, though sometimes fewer if the devotee is poor.

Upapurāṇa: a "minor" Purāṇa (q.v.); like the Purāṇas, the Upapurāṇas are usually numbered at eighteen, though the actual number is much greater.

upāsanā: serving, worshipping, or meditating.

utkīrtana: another name for *kīrtana.*

uttamabhakti: supreme devotion; according to the Caitanya school, devotion is of two general types, the lower or general (*sāmānya-bhakti*), and the supreme; *uttamabhakti* itself has three grades: *sādhanabhakti* (q.v.), *bhāvabhakti* (q.v.), and *premabhakti* (q.v.).

vaidhībhakti: devotion prompted by scriptural injunction; one of the two forms or stages of *sādhanabhakti* (q.v.), the other, and higher, stage being *rāgānugabhakti* (q.v.).

Vaikuṇṭha: Viṣṇu's heaven; one of the three eternal worlds, along with Goloka (q.v.) and Śivaloka, but both Vaikuṇṭha and Śivaloka are considered as inferior to Goloka by the BVP.

vairāgya: dispassion or indifference (to worldly concerns, pain and pleasure); regarded as a prerequisite for salvation in the ascetic tradition.

Vaiṣṇavas: devotees of the god Viṣṇu, or of one of his incarnations such as Rāma or Kṛṣṇa; the latter devotees usually raise the incarnations to supreme status, either identical with or even superior to Viṣṇu himself.

Vāmācārins: followers of the left; left-handed Tāntras; the more extreme antinomian branch of Tāntrism, famous for their *cakrapūjā* (q.v.).

vānaprastha: forest-dweller; one who has entered the third stage of life, having left the life of a householder.

vandana: reverence, adoration (of God); one of the "nine acts" of devotion (see *navadhā bhaktilakṣaṇa*).

vara: gift, boon.

varṇana: description (of God); sometimes included as one of the "nine acts" of devotion (see *navadhā bhaktilakṣaṇa*).

vātas: wind, breath.

vātsalya: parental affection; one of the five devotional sentiments a person may adopt toward the Lord; cf. *dāsya.*

vidhātrī: mother; one of many similar epithets of Rādhā in the BVP.

vidyā: knowledge, saving knowledge.

vigraha: body, form.

Virāṭ: cosmic ruler; cf. *kṣudro virāṭ,* Mahāvirāṭ.

vīrya: heroism; one of the six non-natural (*aprākṛta*) qualities of God; see *ṣaḍguṇas.*

viṣṇubhakti: devotion to Viṣṇu.

Viśuddha: the fifth of the six *cakras* (q.v.) along the central energy channel of the body.

vivecikā: discriminating knowledge, as opposed to *āvaraṇi* (q.v.) or obscuration; according to the BVP, the Goddess gives *vivecikā* to Vaiṣṇavas, *āvaraṇi* to non-Vaiṣṇavas.

vrata: vow; an act of merit; cf. *anaśana.*

vyūha: form or manifestation; specifically, the manifestation of the Supreme during the cosmogonic process in the four forms of Vāsudeva, Saṃkarṣaṇa, Pradyumna, and Aniruddha.

yajña: sacrifice; an act of merit; cf. *anaśana.*

yati: an ascetic.

yogyāyogya: fit and unfit; God is seen as merciful to both the fit and unfit.

yoni: the female organ; symbol of Pārvatī, consort of Śiva, representative of her creative energy; often the *yoni* symbol is placed in conjunction with Śiva's symbol of the *liṅga* (q.v.) to express the unity of the male and female principles of the universe.

BIBLIOGRAPHY

I. PRIMARY WORKS

(Titles and publishing data within brackets are not found on the title pages of the works concerned. Sanskrit titles beginning with lower case letters have been transliterated from the *devanāgarī* script, as given on title pages.)

[*Aitareya Upaniṣad.*] *aitareyopaniṣat*, in *Ten Principal Upanishads with Śāṅkarabhāṣya.* Delhi: Motilal Banarsidass, 1964. Pp. 12–35 (1st part).

Alberuni. *Alberuni's India, An Account of the Religion, Philosophy, Literature, Geography, Chronology, Astronomy, Customs, Laws and Astrology of India about* A.D. 1030. 2 vols. Translated by Edward C. Sachau. London: Trübner & Co., 1888.

Amarakośa.

1. *Amarakośa with the Commentary of Maheśvara enlarged by Raghunath Shastri Talekar.* Edited with an Index by Chintamani Shastri Thatte. Bombay: Government Central Book Depot, 1886.
2. *Amarakoṣaḥ, A Metrical Dictionary of the Sanskrit Language with Tibetan Version.* Edited by MM. Satis Chandra Vidyābhūṣaṇa. Calcutta: Asiatic Society of Bengal, 1911–1912.

[*Atharva Veda.*] *Atharva Veda Sanhita.* Herausgegeben von R. Roth und W. D. Whitney. Band I. Berlin: Ferd. Dümmler, 1855–1856.

[*Bhagavadgītā.*] *The Bhagavad-Gītā, with the Commentary of Śrī Śankarācārya.* Critically edited by Dinkar Vishnu Gokhale. Poona: Oriental Book Agency, 1950.

Bhāgavata Purāṇa.

1. [*Bhāgavata Purāṇa with Śrīdharasvāmin's Commentary*. Bombay: Gaṇpat Kṛṣṇāji's Press, 1866.]

2. [*Bhāgavata Purāṇa with Bhāgavatamāhātmya and a Summary Called Bhāgavatacūrṇikā*. Bombay: Veṅkaṭeśvara Press, 1949.]

[*Brahmāṇḍa Purāṇa*. Bombay: Veṅkaṭeśvara Press, 1935.]

[*Brahmasūtras*.] *The Vedānta Sūtras of Bārdarāyana with the Commentary by Śaṅkara*. 2 vols. Translated by George Thibaut. New York: Dover Publications, 1962.

Brahmavaivarta Purāṇa.

1. *brahmavaivartapurāṇam*. [Edited by Jīvānanda Vidyāsāgara. Calcutta: Sarasvatī Press, 1888.]
2. *brahmavaivartapurāṇam*. [Calcutta: Vaṅgavāsī Press, 1890.]
3. [*Brahmavaivarta Purāṇa*. Bombay: Veṅkaṭeśvara Press, 1931 (originally published 1909–1910).]
4. *brahmavaivartapurāṇam*. [Poona:] Ānandāśrama [Press], 1935.
5. *Brahma-vaivarta-puráni specimen. Textum e Codice Manuscripto Bibliothecae Berolinensis*. Editit Interpretationem Latinam Adiecit et Commentationem Mythologicam et Criticam Praemisit Adolphus Fridericus Stenzler. Berolini: ex Officina Academica, apud Ferdinandum Dummler, 1829.
6. *Spécimen des Purâṇas, Texte, Transcription, Traduction et Commentaire des principaux passages du Brahmâvaevarta purâṇa*. Par L. Leupol. Paris: Maisonneuve et Cie Libraires-éditeurs, 1868.
7. *The Brahma-Vaivarta Puranam*. Translated by Rajendra Nath Sen. Allahabad: Panini Office, 1920–1922. Sacred Books of the Hindus, vol. XXIV.

[*Bṛhadāraṇyaka Upaniṣad*.] *bṛhadāraṇyakopaniṣat*, in *Ten Principal Upanishads with Śāṇkarabhāṣya*. Delhi: Motilal Banarsidass, 1964. Pp. 1–374 (2nd part).

[*Chāndogya Upaniṣad*.] *chāndogyopaniṣat*, in *Ten Principal Upanishads with Śāṅkarabhāṣya*. Delhi: Motilal Banarsidass, 1964. Pp. 113–334 (1st part).

[*Devībhāgavata Purāṇa with Nīlakaṇṭha Bhaṭṭa's Commentary*. Bombay: Veṅkaṭeśvara Press, 1919.]

[*Gopatha Brāhmaṇa*.] *The Gopatha Bráhmaṇa of the Atharva Veda. In the Original Sanskrit*. Edited by Rájendralála Mitra and Harachandra Vidyábhushaṇa. Calcutta: Asiatic Society of Bengal, 1872. Bibliotheca Indica, New Series, Nos. 215 and 252.

[*Harivaṃśa*.] *The Harivamśa, Being the Khila or Supplement to the Mahābhārata*. For the first time critically edited by Parashuram Lakshman Vaidya. 2 vols. Poona: Bhandarkar Oriental Research Institute, 1969, 1971.

Jayadeva. *Gīta Govinda,* in M. S. Randhawa, *Kangra Paintings of the Gīta Govinda.* New Delhi: National Museum, 1963. Pp. 119–129.

Kālidāsa. *kumārasambhavam mahākaviśrīkālidāsakṛtam śrī-mallināthasūriviracitayā sañjīvanīsamākhyayā vyākhyayānugatam.* [Edited by Madana Mohana Śarman. Calcutta: Sanskrit Press, 1850.]

———. [*Raghuvaṃśa.*] *mahākaviśrīkālidāsaviracitaṃ raghuvaṃśam mallināthakṛtasamjīvinīsametam.* Bombay: Nirṇayasāgara [Press], 1886.

[*Kālika Purāṇa.* Bombay: Veṅkaṭeśvara Press, 1907.]

[*Kūrma Purāṇa.* Bombay: Lakṣmīveṅkaṭeśvara Press, 1926.]

[*Liṅga Purāṇa with the Commentary Śivatoṣiṇī by Gaṇeśa Ballāla Nātu.* Bombay: Lakṣmīveṅkaṭeśvara Press, 1924.]

Madhusūdana Sarasvatī. *advaitasiddhiḥ.* [Kumbakonam:] 1893. Advaitamañjary Series.

[*Mahābhārata.*] *The Mahābhārata.* For the first time critically edited by Vishnu S. Sukthankar (and others). 19 vols. Poona: Bhandarkar Oriental Research Institute, 1933–1959.

[*Maitrāyaṇīya Upaniṣad.*] *The Maitrāyaṇīya Upaniṣad, A Critical Essay, with Text, Translation and Commentary.* By J. A. B. Van Buitenen. The Hague: Mouton & Co., 1962.

[*Manu.*] *The Laws of Manu.* Translated with extracts from seven commentaries by Georg Bühler. New York: Dover, 1969.

[*Mārkaṇḍeya Purāṇa.* Edited by Śrīdharātmajatryambaka Gondhalekaropāhūya. Jagaddhihecchu Press, 1867.]

[Matsya Purāṇa. Bombay: Veṅkaṭeśvara Press, 1923.]

[*Nāradapañcarātra.*] *The Nárada Pancha Rátra, In the Original Sanscrit.* Edited by K. M. Banerjea. Calcutta: Bishop's College Press, 1865. Bibliotheca Indica.

[*Naradīya Purāṇa.* Bombay: Veṅkaṭeśvara Press, 1923.]

Nimbārka. [*Daśaślokī.*] *Dashashlokee, by Shree Nimbârkâchârya with a Commentary Called Laghumanjusha by Shree Giridhar Prapanna.* Edited by P. Dhundirâj Shâstri Nyâyopadhyây & Kâvyatirth. [Benares: Vidya Vilas Press, 1927.] Chowkhambâ Sanskrit Series No. 358.

———. [*Vedāntapārijātasaurabha.*] *Brahma-mîmâmsâbhâshya, A Commentary on Brahma Sutras Called Vedânta Pârijâta Saurabha by Nimbârkâcharya.* Edited by Pandit Vindhyeshvarîprasâda Dvivedin. Benares: Chowkhambâ Sanskrit Book Depôt, 1910. Chowkhambâ Sanskrit Series work 34, no. 152.

Padma Purāṇa.

1. *padmapurāṇam.* [Edited by Viśvanātha Nārāyaṇa Maṇḍalīka. 4 vols. Poona: Ānandāśrama Press, 1893, 1894, 1894, 1894.]
2. [*Padma Purāṇa.* Bombay: Lakṣmīveṅkaṭeśvara Press, 1927.]

Rāmānuja. *Rāmānuja's Vedārthasaṃgraha, Introduction, Critical Edi-*

tion and Annotated Translation. By J. A. B. Van Buitenen. Poona: S. M. Katre, 1956.

[*Ṛg Veda.*] *The Hymns of the Rig-veda.* Reprinted from the editio princeps. By F. Max Müller. London: Trübner and Co., 1873.

Śabdakalpadruma. By Rajah Radhakanta Deva. Calcutta: Baptist Mission Press, 1886.

[*Sāṃkhya Kārikā.*] *The Sāṁkhya-Kārikā.* In Sarvepalli Radhakrishnan and Charles A. Moore, eds., *A Source Book in Indian Philosophy.* Princeton: Princeton University Press, 1957. Pp. 426–445.

[*Śāṇḍilya Sūtras.*] *The Aphorisms of Śáṇḍilya with the Commentary of Swapneśwara.* Edited by J. R. Ballantyne. Calcutta: Baptist Mission Press, 1861. Bibliotheca Indica.

[*Śatapatha Brāhmaṇa.*] *The Satapatha-Brâhmana According to the Text of the Mâdhyandina School.* Translated by Julius Eggeling. 5 vols. Delhi: Motilal Banarsidass, 1963. The Sacred Books of the East, vols. XII, XXVI, XLI, XLIII, XLIV.

[*Śiva Purāṇa.* Bombay: Veṅkaṭeśvara Press, 1925.]

Śvetāśvatara Upaniṣad. In S. Radhakrishnan, ed., *The Principal Upaniṣads.* London: George Allen & Unwin, 1953. Pp. 709–750.

[*Varāha Purāṇa.* Bombay: Veṅkaṭeśvara Press, 1923.]

Viṣṇu Purāṇa.

1. *Vishnupurana with the Commentary of Sridharaswami.* Edited by Pandit Jibananda Vidyasagara. Calcutta: Saraswati Press, 1882.
2. [*Viṣṇu Purāṇa with Ratnagarbha Bhaṭṭa's Commentary.* Bombay: Oriental Press, 1889.]

Viṣṇudharmottara-Purāṇa, Third Khanda. Vol. I. Critically edited with introduction, notes, etc., by Priyabala Shah. Baroda: Oriental Institute, 1958. Gaekwad's Oriental Series, No. CXXX.

II. SECONDARY WORKS

Agrawala, Vasudeva S. "Hiraṇyagarbha," *Purāṇa,* II (1960), 285–306.

———. *Matsya Purāṇa—A Study (An Exposition of the Ancient Purāṇa-vidyā).* Varanasi: All-India Kashiraj Trust, 1963.

———. "The Pāśupata Yoga," *Purāṇa,* I (1960), 233–245.

Avalon, Arthur (pseud.). See Woodroffe, John.

Banerjea, Jitendra Nath. "Cult-Syncretism," CHI, IV, 329–336.

Barnett, L. D. *A Supplementary Catalogue of the Sanskrit, Pali, and Prakrit Books in the Library of the British Museum Acquired during the Years 1906–1928.* London: Oxford University Press, 1928.

Barz, Richard. *Early Developments within the Bhakti Sect of Vallabhācārya According to Sectarian Traditions.* Unpublished thesis for University of Chicago.

Bhandarkar, R. G. *Vaiṣṇavism, Śaivism and Minor Religious Systems.* Varanasi: Indological Book House, 1965.

Bhatt, Govindlal Hargovind. "Vallabha (Śuddhādvaita)," HPEW, I, 347–357.

Bhattacharya, S. "A Study of the Cult of Devotion," *The Adyar Library Bulletin,* XXV (1961), 587–602.

Biardeau, Madeleine. "Some More Considerations about Textual Criticism," *Purāṇa,* X (1968), 115–123.

Bolle, Kees W. "Reflections on a Puranic Passage," *History of Religions,* II (1962), 286–291.

Campbell, Joseph. *The Masks of God: Oriental Mythology.* New York: Viking, 1962.

Carman, John B. "Rāmānuja's Conception of Divine Supremacy and Accessibility," *Anvīkṣikī,* I (1968), 94–130.

Carpenter, J. Estlin. *Theism in Medieval India, Lectures Delivered in Essex Hall, London, October–December 1919.* London: Williams & Norgate, 1921.

Chatterjee, A. K. "Some Aspects of Sarasvatī," in D. C. Sircar, ed., *Foreigners in Ancient India and Lakṣmī and Sarasvatī in Art and Literature.* [Calcutta:] University of Calcutta, 1970. Pp. 148–152.

Chatterji, Suniti Kumar. "Purāṇa Legends and the Prakrit Tradition in New Indo-Aryan," *Bulletin of the School of Oriental Studies (University of London),* VIII (1936), 457–466.

Chaudhuri, Roma. "Nimbārka (Dvaitādvaita)," HPEW, I, 338–346.

———. "The Nimbārka School of Vedānta," CHI, III, 333–346.

Cope, Gilbert. *Symbolism in the Bible and the Church.* London: SCM Press, 1959.

Dange, Sadashiv A. "Prajāpati and His Daughter," *Purāṇa,* V (1963), 39–46.

Dasgupta, Shashibhusan. *Aspects of Indian Religious Thought.* Calcutta: A. Mukherjee & Co., 1957.

———. *Obscure Religious Cults.* Calcutta: Firma K. L. Mukhopadhyay, 1969.

Datta, Bhagavad. *The Story of Creation as Seen by the Seers.* Delhi: Itihasa Prakashana Mandala, 1968.

De, Sushil Kumar. *Early History of the Vaiṣṇava Faith and Movement in Bengal from Sanskrit and Bengali Sources.* Calcutta: General Printers and Publishers, 1942.

———. "Sects and Sectarian Worship in the Mahabharata," *Our Heritage,* I, 1–29.

Deussen, Paul. *The Philosophy of the Upanishads.* Translated by A. S. Geden. New York: Dover, 1966.

Dikshitar, V. R. Ramchandra. "The Purāṇas: A Study," IHQ, VIII (1932), 747–767.

Dimock, Edward C. "Doctrine and Practice among the Vaiṣṇavas of Bengal," Milton Singer, ed., *Krishna: Myths, Rites, and Attitudes.* Chicago: University of Chicago Press, 1968. Pp. 41–63.

———. *The Place of the Hidden Moon, Erotic Mysticism in the Vaiṣṇava-sahajiyā Cult of Bengal.* Chicago: University of Chicago Press, 1966.

Edgerton, Franklin. *The Bhagavad Gītā Translated and Interpreted.* New York: Harper & Row, 1964.

Eggeling, Julius, ed. *Catalogue of the Sanskrit Manuscripts in the Library of the India Office,* part VI. London: Gilbert and Rivington, 1899.

Farquhar, J. N. *An Outline of the Religious Literature of India.* London: Oxford University Press, 1920.

Gail, Adalbert. *Bhakti im Bhāgavatapurāṇa, religionsgeschichtliche Studien zur Idee der Gottesliebe in Kult und Mystik des Viṣṇuismus.* Wiesbaden: Otto Harrassowitz, 1969.

Ghate, V. S. *The Vedānta, A Study of the Brahma-sūtras with the Bhāṣyas of Śaṁkara, Rāmānuja, Nimbārka, Madhva and Vallabha.* Poona: Bhandarkar Oriental Research Institute, 1960.

Gonda, Jan. *Aspects of Early Viṣṇuism.* Utrecht: N. V. A. Oosthoek's Uitgevers Mij, 1954.

———. *Die Religionen Indiens.* Vols. I and II. Stuttgart: W. Kohlhammer Verlag, 1960, 1963.

———. *Viṣṇuism and Śivaism, A Comparison.* London: The Athlone Press, 1970.

Grierson, George A. "Gleanings from the Bhakta-mala," JRAS, 1909, pp. 607–644.

———. "Rādhāvallabhīs," ERE, X, 559–560.

Griffith, Ralph T. H. *The Hymns of the Rigveda. Translated with a Popular Commentary.* 2 vols. Benares: E. J. Lazarus and Co., 1896, 1897.

Growse, F. S. *Mathurá: A district Memoir; With Numerous Illustrations.* North-western Provinces and Oudh Government Press, 1883.

Gupta, Anand Swarup. "The Apocryphal Character of the Extant Brahmavaivarta Purāṇa," *Purāṇa,* III (1961), 92–101.

———. "Conception of Sarasvatī in the Purāṇas," *Purāṇa,* IV (1962), 55–95.

———. "A Problem of Purāṇic Text-reconstruction," *Purāṇa,* XII (1970), 304–321.

———. "Purāṇas and Their Referencing," *Purāṇa,* VII (1965), 321–351.

Hacker, Paul. "Eigentümlichkeiten der Lehre und Terminologie Śaṅkaras: Avidyā, Nāmarupa, Māyā, Īśvara," ZDMG, C, 246–286.

———. *Prahlāda, Werden und Wandlungen einer Idealgestalt.* In *Akademie der Wissenschaften und der Literatur, Abhandlungen der Geistes- und Sozial-wissenschaftlichen Klasse,* 1959, NR. 9, pp. 517–663 and NR. 13, pp. 889–993.

———. "Zur Entwicklung der Avatāralehre," WZKSO, IV (1960), 47–70.

Hamilton, Alexandre, and L. Langlès. *Catalogue des Manuscrits Samskrits de la Bibliothêque Impériale, Avec des notices du contenu de la plupart des ouvrages, etc.* Paris: L'Imprimerie Bibliographique, 1807.

Hazra, Rajendra Chandra. "The Devī-bhāgavata," JORM, XXI (1953), 49–79.

———. "The Mahābhāgavata-Purāṇa, a work of Bengal," IHQ, XXVIII (1952), 3–28.

———. "The Problems Relating to the Śiva-Purāṇa," *Our Heritage,* I (1953), 46–68.

———. "Studies in the Genuine Āgneya-Purāṇa, alias Vahni-Purāṇa," *Our Heritage,* I (1953), 209–245.

———. *Studies in the Purāṇic Records on Hindu Rites and Customs.* University of Dacca (Bulletin No. XX), 1940.

———. *Studies in the Upapurāṇas.* Vol. I. Calcutta: Calcutta Oriental Press, 1958.

Hiriyanna, Mysore. *Outlines of Indian Philosophy.* London: George Allen & Unwin, 1968.

Hopkins, E. Washburn. *Epic Mythology.* Strassburg: Karl J. J. Trübner, 1915.

———. *The Great Epic of India, Its Character and Origin.* New Haven: Yale University Press, 1920.

Ingalls, Daniel H. H., trans. *An Anthology of Sanskrit Court Poetry, Vidyākara's "Subhāṣitaratnakoṣa."* Cambridge: Harvard University Press, 1965.

———. "The *Harivaṃśa* as a *Mahākāvya,*" in *Mélanges D'Indianisme à la Mémoire de Louis Renou.* Paris: Editions E. De Boccard, 1968. Pp. 387–394.

Jacobi, Hermann. "Incarnation (Indian)," ERE, VII, 193–197.

Jaiswal, Suvira. *The Origin and Development of Vaiṣṇavism (Vaiṣṇavism from 200* B.C. *to* A.D. *500).* Delhi: Munshiram Manoharlal, 1967.

Johnston, E. H. *Early Sāmkhya, An Essay on Its Historical Development according to the Texts.* London: Royal Asiatic Society, 1937.

Kakati, Banikanta. *Viṣṇuite Myths and Legends in Folklore Setting.* Gauhati, Assam: Sri Tarini Das, 1952.

Kane, Pandurang Vaman. *History of Dharmaśāstra (Ancient and Medieval Religious and Civil Law).* 5 vols. Poona: Bhandarkar Oriental Research Institute, 1930–1962.

Karmarkar, A. P. *The Vrātya or Dravidian Systems (Comprising Śaivism, Śāktism, Zoolatry, Dendrolatry and Other Minor Systems)*. Lonavla, India: Mira Publishing House, 1950.

Kirfel, Willibald. *Das Purāṇa Pañcalakṣaṇa, Versuch einer Textgeschichte*. Bonn: Kurt Schoeder, 1927.

———. "Kṛṣṇa's Jugendgeschichte in den Purāṇa," in *Beiträge zur Literaturwissenschaft und Geistesgeschichte Indiens, Festgabe Hermann Jacobi zum 75. Geburtstag*. Bonn: Kommissionsverlag Fritz Klopp, 1926. Pp. 298–316.

Langlois, A. Book review of *Brahma-vaivarta-pourani specimen*, ed. by Adolphus Fridericus Stenzler. *Journal des Savans*, Oct. 1832, pp. 612–621.

Lévi, Sylvain. Book review of *The Mahā Bhārata*, for the first time critically edited by Vishnu S. Sukthankar. *Journal Asiatique*, CCXXV (1934), 281–283.

Maitra, Sushil Kumar. "Caitanya (Acintya-bhedābheda)." HPEW, I, 358–368.

Maity, Pradyot Kumar. *Historical Studies in the Cult of the Goddess Manasā (A Socio-cultural Study)*. Calcutta: Punthi Pustak, 1966.

Majumdar, Asoke Kumar. "A Note on the Development of the Rādhā Cult," ABORI, XXXVI (1955), 231–257.

Majumdar, Bimanbehari. *Kṛṣṇa in History and Legend*. Calcutta: University of Calcutta, 1969.

Mehta, S. S. *A Monograph on Mirabai, The Saint of Mewad*. Bombay: Bharvadi, Giragon, n.d.

Misra, Janardan. *The Religious Poetry of Sūrdās*. Königsberg: Universität zu Königsberg, 1934.

Monier-Williams, Monier. *Brāhmanism and Hindūism; or Religious Thought and Life in India, as Based on the Veda and Other Sacred Books of the Hindūs*. New York: Macmillan, 1891.

Otto, Rudolf. *Viṣnu-Nārāyana, Texte zur indiṣen Gottesmystik*. Jena: Eugen Diederichs, 1917.

Pandey, R. "Brahmavaivarta Mẽ Bhakti Ka Svarup," *Hindi Anusilana*, XIV. Typescript copy.

Pandey, S. M. and Norman Zide. "Sūrdās and His Krishna-*bhakti*," in Milton Singer, ed., *Krishna: Myths, Rites, and Attitudes*. Chicago: University of Chicago Press, 1968. Pp. 173–199.

Parekh, Bhai Manilal C. *Sri Vallabhacharya, Life, Teachings and Movement*. Rajkot: Bhai Manilal C. Parekh, 1943.

Pargiter, F. Eden. *Ancient Indian Historical Tradition*. London: Oxford University Press, 1922.

———, trans. *The Mārkaṇḍeya Purāṇa, Translated with Notes*. Calcutta: The Asiatic Society, 1904.

Payne, Ernest A. *The Śāktas, An Introductory and Comparative Study*. London: Oxford University Press, 1933.

Penner, Hans. "Cosmogony as Myth in the Vishnu Purāṇa," *History of Religions,* V (1966), 283–299.

Pinkham, Mildreth Worth. *Woman in the Sacred Scriptures of Hinduism.* New York: Columbia University Press, 1941.

Raghavan, V. "Tamil Versions of the Purāṇas," *Purāṇa,* II (1960), 225–242.

Ramakoti, K. V. "Telugu Versions of the Purāṇas," *Purāṇa,* IV (1962), 384–407.

Rangacharya, V. "Historical Evolution of Śrī-Vaiṣṇavism in South India," CHI, IV, 163–185.

Rawal, Anantray J. "Some Problems Regarding the Brahmavaivarta-purāṇa," *Purāṇa,* XIV (1972), 107–124.

Roy, S. N. "On the Date of the Brahmāṇḍapurāṇa," *Purāṇa,* V (1963), 305–319.

Ruben, Walter. *Krishna, Konkordanz und Kommentar der Motive seines Heldenlebens.* Istanbul: Istanbuler Schriften, 1944.

Rukmani, T. S. *A Critical Study of the Bhāgavata Purāṇa (with Special Reference to Bhakti).* Varanasi: Chowkhamba Sanskrit Series Office, 1970.

Schrader, F. Otto. *Introduction to the Pāñcarātra and the Ahirbudhnya Saṃhitā.* Madras: Adyar Library, 1916.

Sen, Sukumar. *A History of Brajabuli Literature, Being a Study of the Vaisnava Lyric Poetry and Poets of Bengal.* Calcutta: University of Calcutta, 1935.

Sharma, Dasharatha. "Verbal Similarities between the Durgā-Sapta-Śati and the Devī-Bhāgavata-Purāṇa and Other Considerations Bearing on Their Date," *Purāṇa,* V (1963), 90–113.

Shastri, Haraprasada. *A Descriptive Catalogue of Sanskrit Manuscripts in the Collections of the Asiatic Society of Bengal.* Vol. V. Calcutta: Asiatic Society of Bengal, 1928.

Van der Leeuw, G. *Religion in Essence and Manifestation.* 2 vols. Translated by J. E. Turner. Gloucester, Mass.: Peter Smith, 1967.

Vaudeville, Ch. "Evolution of Love-Symbolism in Bhagavatism," JAOS, XXVIII (1962), 31–40.

Venkateswaran, T. K. "Rādhā-Krishna *Bhajanas* of South India: A Phenomenological, Theological, and Philosophical Study," in Milton Singer, ed., *Krishna: Myths, Rites, and Attitudes.* Chicago: University of Chicago Press, 1968.

Von Glasenapp, Helmuth. *Von Buddha zu Gandhi, Aufsätze zur Geschichte der Religionen Indiens.* Wiesbaden: Otto Harrassowitz, 1962.

Walker, Benjamin. *The Hindu World, An Encyclopedic Survey of Hinduism.* 2 vols. New York: Frederick A. Praeger, 1968.

Weber, Albrecht. *The History of Indian Literature.* Translated by

John Mann and Theodor Zachariae. London: Trübner & Co., 1882.

———. *Die Handschriften-Verzeichnisse der Königlichen Bibliothek.* Vol. I. Berlin: Verlag der Nicolai'schen Buchhandlung, 1853.

Wilson, Horace Hayman. "Analysis of the Puráńas," in his *Essays, Analytical, Critical, and Philological on Subjects Connected with Sanskrit Literature.* Collected and edited by Reinhold Rost. London: Trübner & Co., 1864. I (vol. III of Wilson's *Works*), 1–155.

———. *A Sketch of the Religious Sects of the Hindus.* Vol. I of his *Essays and Lectures Chiefly on the Religion of the Hindus* (vol. I of Wilson's *Works*). Collected and edited by Rost. London: Trübner & Co., 1862.

———. *The Vishńu Puráńa: A System of Hindu Mythology and Tradition.* Edited by Fitzedward Hall. 5 vols. (vols. VI–X of Wilson's *Works*). London: Trübner & Co., 1864–1877.

Winternitz, Maurice. *A History of Indian Literature.* [Calcutta:] University of Calcutta, 1927.

———, and Arthur Berriedale Keith. *Catalogue of Sanskrit Manuscripts in the Bodleian Library.* Vol. II. Oxford: Clarendon Press, 1905.

Woodroffe, John. *The Great Liberation (Mahānirvāna Tantra), A Translation from the Sanskrit with Commentary.* By Arthur Avalon, pseud. Madras: Ganesh & Co., 1927.

———. *Principles of Tantra.* By Arthur Avalon, pseud. 2 vols. London: Luzac & Co., 1914.

———. *The Serpent Power, Being the Shat-chakra-nirūpana and Pādukā-panchaka, Two works on Laya Yoga, Translated from the Sanskrit, with Introduction and Commentary.* By Arthur Avalon, pseud. Madras: Ganesh & Co., 1931.

———. *Shakti and Shâkta, Essays and Addresses on the Shâkta Tantrashâstra.* Madras: Ganesh & Co., 1929.

———, ed. *Tantrik Texts.* Edited by Arthur Avalon, pseud. Vols. VIII and XII [The *Tantraraja Tantra* in 2 parts.] London: Luzac & Co., n.d., 1926.

Zimmer, Heinrich. *Myths and Symbols in Indian Art and Civilization.* New York: Harper & Row, 1962.

Index